How to Hire a Nanny

How to Hire a Nanny

Guy Maddalone
The Nation's Household Help Expert

SPHINX® PUBLISHING
AN IMPRINT OF SOURCEBOOKS, INC.®
NAPERVILLE, ILLINOIS
www.SphinxLegal.com

First Edition: 2007

Published by: Sphinx® Publishing, An Imprint of Sourcebooks, Inc.®

Naperville Office
P.O. Box 4410
Naperville, Illinois 60567-4410
630-961-3900
Fax: 630-961-2168
www.sourcebooks.com
www.SphinxLegal.com

Library of Congress Cataloging-in-Publication Data

Maddalone, Guy.
How to hire a nanny : your complete guide to finding, hiring and retaining a nanny and other household help / by Guy Maddalone. -- 1st ed.
    p. cm.
Includes index.
ISBN-13: 978-1-57248-565-5 (pbk. : alk. paper)
ISBN-10: 1-57248-565-5 (pbk. : alk. paper)
1. Nannies--Selection and appointment. 2. Domestics--Selection and appointment. I. Title.

HQ778.63.M33 2007
640'.46--dc22
                                                                    2006024610

Acclaim for *How to Hire and Retain Your Household Help*

"I believe that one of the most important ways to enact societal change is through education. The Domestic Worker Law that I passed in 2003 was aimed in part at educating workers and employers of their rights and responsibilities. The information in Guy's book is crucial to educating people who employ domestic workers and ensuring that they know and understand the relevant laws and regulations."
—*Gale A. Brewer, New York City council member (D-Manhattan)*

"Guy Maddalone has done it again. After many hours of hard work, he has created an important tool for household employers. Families should review the contents of this book before hiring an employee. They will find a wealth of information to help make the working relationship in their home a success."
—*Annie Davis, president, Alliance of Professional Nannies Association, and president, Annie's Nannies, Seattle, WA*

"After nearly a decade in the field of private service, I am thrilled to finally find the missing link in the employment process. Guy Maddalone's book elevates the employment relationships of the staffed homes of the world—from the servile nature of centuries past—into a functional likeness of today's corporate culture. Many, many thanks!"
—*Natalie Asper Carnes, founder, International Association of Household Professionals, Bloomfield Hills, MI*

"I commend Guy in his effort to educate and support our industry by writing and publishing this very valuable handbook. Employers and agencies will appreciate having this resource to turn to whenever questions arise."
—*Pat Cascio, president, International Nanny Association, and president, Morningside Nannies, LP, Houston, TX*

"As an agency owner for more than 13 years, I have added How to Hire a Nanny to my list of essential guidance books for families. There is so little consistent information available today that provides good, sound advice in this arena. Thank you, Guy, for educating and informing household employers on effective household management!"
—*Julie Biondi, founder, Choice Care Nannies & Baby Nurses, Westfield, NJ*

"Often we only see one side of the story—our own. Guy Maddalone pulls from a variety of viewpoints bringing about a well-rounded glimpse of the domestic employment relationship. Often domestic relationships fail because of unreal expectations or a difference in value systems. Guy reveals the experiences from all involved and provides families with invaluable information."
—*Leann Brambach, owner, Home Details, Inc., Seattle, WA*

"Having been a nanny agency owner for the past 13 years, I understand that for most families obtaining and applying for tax and labor law information can be cumbersome and confusing. With this easy-to-follow instructional handbook, Guy Maddalone streamlines an otherwise complicated process for the domestic employer. I applaud his contribution, and I look forward to continuing to recommend the services of GTM knowing my clients will be in very good hands."
—*Daryl Camarillo, president, Stanford Park Nannies, Menlo Park, CA*

"For the past 10 years, Guy has been a leader in helping families, nannies and placement agencies. The winners are the children! His ethical business practices underlie all that he oversees. We in the industry are proud to have GTM as our right-hand resource."
—*Barbara Chandra, co-owner, Boston Nanny Centre, Inc., Boston, MA*

"The household employment industry has needed such a book as this for a long time. And I can't think of a better person to have written it. Guy Maddalone is a visionary in the industry and a man of integrity who is very well respected by partners, clients and competitors alike. Guy has greatly contributed to the professionalism and growth of the industry. Thank you, Guy, for bringing these human resource issues to the attention of all and for always being a business partner that we can trust and count on."
—*Denise Collins, CEO, In-House Staffing at Aunt Ann's, San Francisco, CA*

"Guy Maddalone has an unsurpassed commitment to the in-home employment industry. His many years of experience assisting thousands of families, coupled with his personal experience as the eldest of 13 and father of two [sic], enabled him to have an unparalleled perspective and influence on the professional employment needs of today's American families."
—*Betty Davis, president, In Search of Nanny, Inc., Beverly, MA*

"There is arguably no person in the industry better equipped to write this book. As an agency owner, I have followed Guy Maddalone's success (and referred clients to his company) for nearly a decade. As an author, he has the rare combined insight of being a household employer himself and owning a business, which services clientele nationally. His commitment to trade-related organizations (and the sound influence he infuses to the many boards he serves on) immeasurably benefits the industry as a whole. In a sense, Guy has dragged this industry—sometimes kicking and screaming—to a new level of professionalism and recognition. This book is a must read."
—*Emily Dills, president, The Seattle Nanny Network, Inc., Kirkland, WA*

"Working with GTM as a partner has brought so much satisfaction to a number of our client families. We are continually given positive feedback about the high level of service and cutting-edge knowledge of household payroll and taxes. GTM has a marvelous way of answering tough questions and demystifying the complications of taxes and issues of employer vs. employee responsibilities. It is such a relief to refer anxious parents to our prized experts, the kind people at GTM. I hope that they will be around for a long time."
—*Marsha Epstein, president, American Nanny Company, Boston, MA*

"The legal complexities of human resources can be daunting to a non-professional hiring in-home child or house care. This book by Guy Maddalone should ease the burden considerably, as it ties together in a logical and understandable way of the employment process. It is a much needed resource."
—*Alan Friedman, owner, A Choice Nanny, New York, NY*

"I have worked with Guy Maddalone for many years and found him to be an expert in providing clear, concise, up-to-date and valuable information to household employers and their staff. His new book will be a valuable resource to increase the knowledge and raise the standards for all household employers and our industry."
—*Anne Guerin, president, Staffing Solutions @ Mothers' Aides, Fairfax, VA*

"This book is a valuable resource for every household employer. It covers a wide variety of subjects and makes understanding the complexities of household employment seem easy. I am proud to be a part of this effort and highly recommend this book for anyone considering employing any household employee."
—*Bob King, Esq., Legally Nanny, Irvine CA*

"Guy Maddalone has been an innovator in this profession for many years. His book is the first I have seen that tells potential nanny (and other domestic staff) employers what they need to be told, what they really know but do not want to admit or recognize. Readers would do well to pay careful attention to its advice. That will result in better hires, longer stays and more pleasant relationships for themselves and their children."
—*Bob Mark, president, America's Nannies, Paramus, NJ*

"With the knowledge and reputation of Guy Maddalone and GTM, this book will be a wonderful aid for families and nannies. It will expertly answer almost any question and addresses the concerns of employers and employees. It will be a valuable tool and a welcome addition to my agency."
—*Andrea McDaniel, owner, The Nanny Agency, Inc., Dallas/Fort Worth Metroplex, TX*

"Over the last 30 years that I have been doing human resources, I have found that many household employers are confused about hiring practices. Most employers want to do the right thing, but don't know what to do or how to go about it.

I think it's a must read for not only household employers but also domestic employees. It really takes the confusion out of the process. I particularly like the approach of giving the facts and then complimenting them with real life stories and comments by folks who are actually involved."
—*Jack McGaughnea, president, Northeast HR for Hire, Schenectady, NY*

"Guy Maddalone is using his business expertise to create a new tool for families and agencies to provide guidance and clarity to the often confusing area of household employment. This new handbook will help agencies to continue to educate parents on issues of hiring, employing and hopefully keeping their household employees. This is a new milestone in 'professionalizing' our industry."
—*Judi Merlin, owner, A Friend of the Family, Athens, GA*

"I have known Guy Maddalone professionally for more than a decade and have always admired his dedication and integrity to his business. This book is a must read for anyone hiring a household employee. It is clear, concise and full of invaluable information and applicable tools. It is a well-needed book in this industry."
—*Janet Nodine, owner, Heaven Sent Nannies, Derry, NH*

"Guy Maddalone has been a pioneer in the household human resource industry and has established the nanny industry with professional standards practiced from successful small businesses to Fortune 500 companies. In his book, Guy has defined confusing legal domestic employment tax issues in a simplified manner without sacrificing any details. How to Hire a Nanny is an immensely helpful guide for parents, nannies and nanny placement agencies."
—*Gena James Pitts, owner/director, Child Care Resources, Alpharetta, GA*

"In a comprehensive guide, Guy Maddalone has compiled all the information a household employer needs to properly manage anyone working in the home. He covers the range of domestic help from hiring one nanny to employing a full staff. With practical information and accurate facts, How to Hire a Nanny will be a valuable resource and handy tool for all household employers and employees."
—*Wendy Sachs, president, The Philadelphia Nanny Network, Inc., Philadelphia, PA*

"Most of our clients are extremely busy and are relieved to hear that there is a payroll tax service to help process legally mandated household employee payroll obligations. When we meet with our clients and give them a GTM brochure, a smile and look of relief returns to their face. GTM provides a 'real value' that eliminates a time-consuming activity a parent doesn't have to worry about when hiring and employing a nanny. GTM has been a consistent and exceptionally helpful resource for our clients."
—*Lorna and Courtney Spencer, owners, A Choice Nanny, Columbia, MD*

"I'm delighted that Guy Maddalone and GTM have created a much-needed manual on household employment issues. It will bring focus and understanding of these most important issues to both employers and service staff. As Starkey International has long stood for the importance of education in the household, my sincere congratulations to GTM for positioning itself at the forefront of giving sound and pertinent advice on how to comply with labor laws and how to better manage household service employee(s). Mr. Maddalone's handbook should be an essential resource for all successful household employers."
—*Mary Louise Starkey, CEO, Starkey International, Denver, CO*

"Caring for children is the most important profession there is. A handbook for household employers will be a tremendous help in ensuring adequate compensation for these valuable employees. I applaud Guy Maddalone for seeing and responding to this need."
—*Sue Vigil, owner, A Choice Nanny, Florham and Wyckoff, NJ*

"GTM is the leading provider of household employment HR and payroll services. It's easy to get sloppy in dealing with a nanny and often a spouse is left with the task of managing this person with very little experience— it's bad enough if you're having problems at the office!! Guy's book fills this important gap."
—*Verne Harnish, CEO of Gazelles, Inc and Author of* Mastering the Rockefeller Habits.

"*How to Hire & Retain Your Household Help* is a one-stop shop of very useful and often hard-to-find information related to household employees. Guy Maddalone's handbook provides a wealth of facts for every family in the process of staffing and trying to figure out those thorny areas of immigration, discrimination, termination, taxation etc. This fact-packed book is a must-have for every household with employees."
—*Barbara Kline, President of White House Nannies, Inc. and Author of* White House Nannies, *Bethesda, MD*

To my supportive and loving wife, Diane, who keeps it all together as we strive to achieve an effective work/life balance, and to household employers, who seek to achieve the same by hiring and retaining the best household help possible.

Acknowledgments

... my children, Michael, Elise, and Jeffrey, who provide me great joy as I have watched them give Nanny Ester, Missy, Venus, and now Erin a run for their money.

... my mother, Joyce, for our first entrepreneurial experience in home care, and to Henry, my father, who taught me work commitment, responsibility, and determination.

... my management team and all the GTM experts who give it their all in order to make a difference in our clients lives.

... my good friends Steve, Paul, John, Frank, Mike, Jerry, Bruce, Deborah, and others for all the years of support and encouragement.

... Wayne, Dave, the accountants, attorneys, and advisors who help us stay profitable.

... Bob Mark and no-nonsense seminars that inspired GTM's educational arm.

... Thea, Greg, Dale, Mike, and Amit for helping us with our organization and communication.

. . . PT, Craig, Rusty, Chris, Mike, Steve, Jaime, Paul, and Patty for the monthly peer exchange.

. . . Frank, Brian, Dave, Jamie, Dave, and Todd for believing in my leadership skills and selecting me as your YEO chapter president.

. . . the Growth Guy, Verne Harnish, and my MIT Birthing of Giants classmates, who challenged me to write this book.

. . . all agency, accountant, financial, and legal referral partners who have sent their clients to GTM over the years.

. . . Colleen, Rob, Shelley, Loni, and Gloria at GE for your belief in GTM's work/family benefit program.

. . . my brothers, Todd, and Michael, who strive to make GTM into a company we are all proud to share with others.

. . . household employers, Jim Chaney, Stephanie Oana, Denise Shade, and Zuzka Polishook, who gave their time and shared their stories so others may learn from their experiences.

. . . household employment agency owners and managers Leann Brambach, Pat Cascio, Kim Cino, Denise Collins, Janet Cook, Annie Davies, Sylvia Greenbaum, Cliff Greenhouse, Hilary Lockhart, Judi Merlin, Ilo Milton, Arline Rubel, Mary Starkey, Lin Taylor-Pleiman, and Susan Tokayer, who gave their time and shared advice and experience so others could learn from them.

. . . household employees John Robertson and Bruce Reynolds, both of the International Butlers Guild, as well as Trish Stevens, Liz, and other household employees, who gave their time and shared advice and experience so others could learn from them.

. . . the GTM marketing team who worked diligently to keep this project on track, as well as Debbie Sgroi, who worked tirelessly interviewing and researching information for this book.

. . . employment attorney Robert E King, Esq., of Legally Nanny, who contributed to the federal and California legal aspects detailed within this book.

. . . employment attorneys Heather Diddell, Esq., Ellen Bach, Esq., & Leslie Theile, Esq. of Whiteman, Osterman & Hannah, who contributed to the federal, immigration, and New York legal aspects detailed within this book.

. . . Wendy Sachs, Greg Moran, Wayne Davis, Esq., HR Consultant Jack McGaughnea, and my wife, Diane, for reviewing this book and offering honest and straightforward feedback.

. . . the thousands of household employers who allow GTM to serve their needs daily.

. . . anyone I may have unintentionally omitted.

Contents

Preface

I have been working for twenty years in the household employment industry. All those years of experience in working with thousands of household employers throughout the United States is provided in this handbook to prepare you for employing a nanny or other household help. The most important thing is to simply remember that your nanny is working for you. He or she is doing so to earn a living. It is your nanny's *livelihood*—your nanny's way of living and providing for self and family.

I first became involved in household employment soon after my grandfather became ill. My mother, Joyce, a registered nurse, and I began a home health care and hospital staffing agency. While running this agency, I met many people who juggled caring for their own families while attending to the needs of their ailing parents. Truly, these people were sandwiched between generations, with each demanding extensive care, time, and energy. To help these caregivers further, I knew I needed to add child care to the agency mix. Thus began GTM—which started as a nanny placement agency, then extended to payroll and tax services, and finally evolved to the household employment expert service it is today, including benefits, HR tools, and consulting. GTM Household Employment Experts™ is known throughout the United States as the leader in the industry, building an impeccable reputation and gaining complete client confidence by always providing accurate, timely, and extremely valuable services in a way that consistently yields a 99% client satisfaction rating.

As I am one of thirteen children, family has been and always will be extremely important to me. Naturally, when it came time to raise my own children, I wanted the very best for them. To me, home is where children tend to always feel more secure and comfortable. Part of that security and comfort means they are not forced to adapt to our work schedules. They are not woken up and sped off to the day care center in the morning, or forced to nap at the direction of a day care worker only to be disrupted, bundled up, and brought home in the evening. For Diane and me, there was one choice—employing a nanny to work in our home. Today, with a family of three children parented by two busy professionals, we found that we needed both a nanny and housekeeper.

We prepared for our nanny in many ways, but we have learned much, much more over the years. We entrust that our nanny will follow the standards and procedures we have developed—often with her input—for the daily challenges of our busy household. It really comes down to using common sense and good judgment to handle daily problems or issues. We, as parents, have provided our nanny with control of our children's day. If Grandma drops by unannounced to take the kids out for a treat, my nanny knows that she has the right to say no, or, of course, call Diane or me if necessary. Since we are working and try to keep phone calls to a minimum, our household policies clearly define what is and is not acceptable. Grandma cannot take the kids out for an ice cream at 4 p.m., so close to their dinner time. If a playmate visits for a scheduled play date and unexpectedly brings another friend along to play, that is not okay, and takes advantage of our nanny. Use common sense and good judgment. Ask yourself, "Would you do that without making arrangements first?" and "How does this affect my nanny and what we have agreed that she is expected to do?"

An incident occurred in one of my client's homes that would have put their nanny on the spot if she had not been empowered to say no to unacceptable situations. Before leaving on a weekend trip, my clients gave their son permission to invite a friend over to play. As most would do, the young visitor's parents accompanied their son into the client's home. However, instead of leaving after making sure their son was in good hands, the parents sat right down in the family room and not only engaged the nanny in extensive conversation, but even asked the nanny if they could have a drink. The nanny knew this was not okay, as it distracted her from watching the children, and knew she could address the situation by politely yet firmly asking the parents to come back later to pick up their child. She did not have to call her employers for advice, because she clearly knew where she stood in such situations. My clients did not have their trip interrupted, and their nanny was not overburdened in her workday.

In another incident involving our own nanny, a neighbor asked our nanny to watch her child for an afternoon. When our nanny learned that the neighbor had not spoken to Diane or me about this, she knew that it was her decision to make. We—working as a team—decided that we would not tolerate our nanny being overtaxed and frustrated with any outside, additional responsibility. We also would not want our nanny watching other children while she was caring for our three—not without a prearranged time and date set, or without an agreement made previously with our nanny. Three young children are enough to overload anyone, and we do not want to add to her workload. Because we have discussed our expectations and concerns, our nanny knew that she could say no with our support, or she could say yes, but clearly set the exact time and day she would be available to help.

We can do this because we have set a comprehensive work arrangement and have built a relationship that enables mutual trust and open communication. We always recognize our nanny for her accomplishments and encourage her. We try to help her in any way possible, and often provide examples of alternate ways to handle various day-to-day situations. Diane and I communicate continuously and openly with our household help—not only to set initial standards and boundaries, but also to maintain and build on the employer-employee relationship.

All household employers should strive for open communication. With nannies, you have added a new member to your parenting team, and all of you need to be on the same page when handling the children. At my home, we have a ten-minute huddle when the nanny arrives in the morning and when she is just about to leave in the evening. (We do the same with our housekeeper.) We inform one another of the day's or night's events—for example, Elise was running a fever, Jeffrey is teething, or Michael stayed up late last night watching a movie and is sluggish this morning. Also, we discuss what needs to be done during the day and any activity that is on the

xxii   How to Hire a Nanny

schedule. This provides the nanny with the information she needs to be effective, and in turn, she provides us the information we need to be effective parents and feel secure while at work.

The ten-minute morning huddle also allows us to compliment and support our nanny on her work, particularly with the children. If there is a problem to discuss, we talk about it candidly and make sure we all agree on any decisions made. Open communication means that both the employer and employee are up front with one another, are in agreement, and may move forward as a united team.

We were not always so proficient in working with our help. In fact, like many young families, we employed several nannies before refining our household management skills. It is interesting to note that while the nanny we first hired for our firstborn was terrific at the time, she would not have worked successfully with our middle child. A nanny who works wonderfully for one child or a specific time in a family's life may not work so well with another child. A nanny who is first rate with a newborn may not be the nanny to employ for a five-year-old. It is all part of the learning process, and can be helped by being alert to the employment situation and relationships, as well as your family's needs.

—*Guy Maddalone*

Introduction

Effective household employment contributes to the smooth and sound operation of your most important organization—your home. It also contributes to you achieving an adequate and practical balance between your life and your work—making both your private and professional lives enjoyable, fulfilling, and manageable.

To begin, you opted to sensibly manage your family and home life with your professional life by becoming a household employer. Your nanny or other household employee, such as a housekeeper, gardener, or eldercare provider, is working for *you*. When you first become a household employer, you will probably feel a little overwhelmed by all the unknowns and ambiguities, and the anxiety that comes with inexperience or with doing something very important for the first time. Added to that is a feeling of the huge weight of responsibility that goes along with caring for family and home, and becoming someone's source of employment and a means of that person's sustenance. You may possibly be feeling a bit overprotective of your private life, and perhaps may even be somewhat naïve as to what to expect from your nanny, your family, and yourself.

Your nanny experience can be demystified by defining it as the profession that it is. An American nanny is a professional nanny, just as a nanny in England is a professional nanny. He or she chooses to enter your private life as an employee to tend to the needs of your children. It is his or her career—

a legitimate profession—that just happens to be based in your home and just happens to involve working with your family.

NOTE: *Although many topics in this book are discussed in terms of nannies, most of the laws and ideas cover all types of household employees.*

Household employment is a genuine business. In particular, it is your nanny's business, and it is your business—one recognized by the U.S. government. A big reason why you are reading these pages is that the federal, state, and local governments do recognize household employment as a profession, and as the employer, you have lawful responsibilities. The obligation is on you to know them and to follow them—accurately, legally, completely, and consistently. Treat your household employment as the real business it is. Your children's care, your household's stability, and your nanny's career should not be taken lightly. Why would you skimp on such an integral part of your family life?

Household employers can be anyone—from busy, dual-income, working parents, to large estate owners, to foreign diplomats residing in the United States. This handbook will help you professionally manage your household employee—whether he or she is your nanny, your parent's eldercare provider, your housekeeper, your gardener, your personal assistant, or another staff member—just as you would professionally manage and treat employees at your place of business. As you read through this handbook, you will realize that effective household management relies on clear communication and treating your household employees as professionals.

Today, the household employment industry is working to establish a professional structure around a very informal and often customized situation— a situation frequently viewed differently by employers and employees. Consensus has been painstakingly difficult to achieve—often because employment is in the home, behind closed doors, and not in the open or public eye. It is uncomfortable to access these private homes; it is rife with challenges and thorny areas. However, it must be laid open so industry perspective and accord can be built.

Often, employers view hiring staff for their home and personal lives as an emotional responsibility. Household employees know it is a logical responsibility, as it is their occupation, their profession, and their career. The American attitude toward household employment is changing—and it will continue to change as more and more people consider hiring household help as a way to balance their personal and professional lives. Just by learning about household help and household employment, Americans are recognizing and acknowledging household employment as a real business. This awareness can only grow as the numbers of people choosing to bring employees into their homes increases.

It is clear that many people choose to ignore labor laws and tax requirements. We see it often on television news reports. It is serious stuff, and it is breaking the law. If you choose to disregard labor and tax laws, you jeopardize your personal finances, your professional career, and possibly even your freedom by risking potential jail time.

In the early 1990s, there were several political scandals involving people running for office not properly following the law with respect to household help. The most famous may have been Zoe Baird's short-lived nomination for U.S. attorney general in 1993. Baird had, in the past, knowingly paid two illegal aliens under the table for household child care work. Bringing national attention to legal household management (or mismanagement), Baird's deliberate disregard for U.S. law was dubbed "Nannygate" by the media, and she was forced to step down from consideration as a Clinton administration Cabinet member.

Although Baird's name remains tagged with Nannygate, she is not alone. Some fifteen years after Baird's scandal, these scandals still occur, and it is staggering how often and at what levels. Many no longer make front-page news, but the following detail a few that did.

While serving as California governor, Pete Wilson was accused of failing to pay Social Security taxes for wages paid to an undocumented foreign maid that he and his then-wife employed in the late 1970s. (Although the law did not at that time require the Wilsons to document the maid's eligibility to work in the United States, employment tax laws mandated that taxes be paid on her earnings, as they do today.)

In January 2001, Linda Chavez, Labor Secretary nominee in the first George W. Bush administration, faced problems when it was revealed that she had, in the past, hired an illegal immigrant who lived and worked in her home.

In late 2004, former New York City Police Commissioner Bernard Kerik disclosed that he had not paid taxes for his nanny, an illegal immigrant—derailing his nomination for Homeland Security chief with President George W. Bush's second administration. While Kerik faced allegations of security industry profiteering after 9/11, mafia connections, and violations of conflict-of-interest laws, he chose to remove himself from consideration for a national post by admitting his personal Nannygate. Kerik and Republican Party leaders considered Kerik's Nannygate, or breaking labor laws, the lesser of the above-mentioned issues. It seems they believed America's complacency—the *it's-no-big-deal* attitude—regarding household help would allow Kerik and the Bush Administration to incur the least amount of political and legal damage. That Kerik broke U.S. labor laws by hiring an illegal immigrant and employing her for years did not raise any questions at all.

Others exposed to media attention for failure to comply with household employer's tax responsibilities include: federal judge Kimba Wood; prominent attorney Charles Ruff; Clinton Commerce Secretary Ron Brown; Clinton Surgeon General Joycelyn Elders; Clinton White House Lawyer William H. Kennedy, III; and, Supreme Court Justice Stephen Breyer.

On the plus side, there are thousands of politicians and employers who do comply with the law. For instance, when Arnold Schwarzenegger announced his plan to run for California governor in August 2003, the media investigated how he managed his household help. According to the media reports, no mismanagement was found.

Many more people follow the same path. Practicing insufficient human resource management—out of ignorance, laziness, scrimping on budgets, or disregard for the law—is still common in many household employment situations. Good human resource practices, as you will see in this book, can be quite involved. However, thousands do it properly and are committed to it. GTM Household Employment Experts™ makes it easier with this book, as well as its household HR consulting, employee benefits, and payroll and tax services. (For household employment services, go to **www.gtm.com**.)

Education is vital for the household employment industry. The status of the household employee in America is changing. In fact, it has made great progress during the last decade, and has gained recognition as a genuine and valid profession. However, misperceptions, misunderstandings, and blatant tax-related evasion remain—and household employees still battle for America to accept their professions as legitimate (and long-term) occupations.

This handbook covers everything you will need to know about hiring a nanny or other household help—easy-to-access guidelines, state-by-state contact information, real-life examples, practices, procedures, and information on laws and regulations. With it as your resource, you are well on your way to becoming a successful household employer. You will use it throughout your household employment experience—whether you are reading it through for the first time or referencing specific sections as issues arise.

You Can Be Successful Too!

Everyone struggles at the beginning of their tenure as a household employer, especially as parents who are hiring a nanny to tend to their child's overall care. It is an important time, with many crucial decisions to make. You have this book to learn from and reference as you maneuver through the ins and outs of being a household employer.

This book was created to help you prepare and maintain successful employer-employee relationships. It addresses many lessons learned by household employers from across the United States. In a sense, you will learn from those who have been at this for the last twenty years, and who have mastered—sometimes the hard way—the best ways to handle subjects like hiring, firing, writing work agreements, and managing payroll and taxes. It is all here, including first-hand experiences from employers and employees. They are included for you to gain from these experiences. Plus, you may take some measure of comfort in learning that others have struggled with the same issues that you are encountering.

Once you realize that household employment is still *employment*, a little bit of business experience and personal intuition will help guide you. You most likely are or have been an employee somewhere in the United States, and therefore know many of the requirements, guidelines, and laws that you need to follow and implement. Many first-time household employers worry about keeping abreast of the legal requirements and mandates issued by the federal, state, and local governments. This is sometimes a time-consuming and frustrating aspect of being an employer. However, it is much more time-consuming and frustrating if you do not follow the laws and rules established by the government. In fact, it can cost you greatly both monetarily and in the lifestyle you presently enjoy.

Legislatures and courts throughout the United States are no longer willing to turn a blind eye to issues surrounding household employment. (See "The Latest on Illegal Workers" on p.10.) They are enforcing laws and employer regulations within the home—such as employing documented workers, legally paying payroll taxes, and overtime—at an astounding rate. According to *Time*, state legislatures considered nearly three hundred bills related to immigration policy in the first few months of 2006 alone. (*Time*, Feb. 6, 2006.)

Recently, as reported by the Associated Press, the New York Court of Appeals—New York State's highest court—ruled in two separate decisions that awards of past and future wages to an undocumented worker do not conflict with the U.S. Immigration Reform and Control Act of 1986. In short, the court is saying that if hurt or otherwise rendered unable to work, an employee—even though undocumented to work in the United States—may successfully seek awards from an employer for his or her present and future wages. Last reports of this court case state that the employer's attorney may request the U.S. Supreme Court to hear the case. (For information on the U.S. Immigration Reform and Control Act of 1986 and how to detect legal documentation, see Chapter 2.)

Household employment takes careful thought and preparation. Rules must be set that establish policies, standards, and procedures. By knowing and understanding what the terms of employment are, your nanny and you will avoid the guessing and frustration that otherwise easily occurs. By communicating what your anticipated needs are up front, you ensure that all contingencies are accounted for and any consequence is handled as you would like. As a household employer who wants to maintain a successful working relationship with his or her nanny (or other household employee), you cannot simply get frustrated and ignore the issues. At any moment, any of us can be deluged with unexpected challenges. The careful preparation you take will pay off during these times—and may even help you avoid some challenges altogether. After all, you are hiring a nanny to ensure the smooth and sound operation of your household. You are entrusting to an employee what you hold most precious—your family.

An important consideration faced by all household employers is how they will cope with an employee being in their personal life. While we are talking about a work relationship, business arrangement, and management issues, the reality of the situation is that it is also personal—your home, family, and personal lives. How easily you can cope with an outsider in your home will help you to decide whether to hire a live-in or live-out nanny. Your comfort level will also help you to decide what you wish to designate as off-limit areas to maintain enough personal boundaries so as to keep the working relationship as professional as it needs to be.

Managing your household human resources means learning and abiding by the law, and tailoring policies that work for you and your family. You need to be committed to your employee and to your role as a household employer. Remember, you are hiring household help to help balance your busy personal and professional lives.

Much of the information in this book is kept up-to-date on GTM's website at **www.gtm.com/resourcecenter**.

DISCLAIMER:
The author hopes that you find the information provided herein helpful. However, the information should not be misinterpreted as a replacement for competent legal or accounting advice. **Accordingly, use of this information is at your own risk.** In particular, while the information herein is believed accurate, the applicable laws and regulations are complex and change from state to state. Therefore, the author cannot be held responsible for any errors or omissions in the text, or misunderstandings on the part of the reader. We strongly recommend that you consult an experienced employment law attorney or accountant to address any questions or issues that you may have. Furthermore, any references to outside sources provided herein do not indicate an endorsement of the services or products provided by those sources.

Types of
Household Help

It is not easy to define household employer or household employee, because the terms are used in so many different ways—almost as many ways as there are household help professions. The United States Internal Revenue Service defines a *household employer* as any person who employs housekeepers, maids, gardeners, and others who work in and around an individual's private residence. A nanny is an example of such an employee. That is, a *nanny* is a household employee, stationed within the home, tasked with tending to a child's care.

In the United States, we tend to think of a nanny as a benevolent woman endowed with magical powers or a young woman spending time working as a nanny until something "better" comes along. In fact, a nanny is very different, and those of us with images of Mary Poppins or Nanny McPhee in our heads need to understand the reality of a nanny's job. A nanny is a real person who has, over time, honed his or her talents and expertise in caring for children and in developing his or her chosen career.

New household employers will do well to leave the fictional representations of nannies on the book's page or theater's screen—it will be a smoother ride for all involved.

Outside the United States, nannies do not suffer from a blurred definition. In countries such as England, Ireland, and Germany, nannies and other household employees have long been defined, and thus, treated as professionals. Although employing household help is very much a personal decision, we all need to see nannies, housekeepers, eldercare workers, gardeners, maintenance workers, and other household employees as *real* people performing *real* jobs—professional jobs. The only difference is that these professionals perform their work in your home.

For whatever reason, in the United States, nannies and other household employees have often been viewed as temporary workers, a position taken by people who are deciding on other life matters (such as those who are deciding whether to pursue higher education, what profession they "really" want to do, or where geographically they want to reside). This is changing rapidly, as more and more U.S. households are hiring employees to help the heads of household achieve a manageable life/work balance.

Household Employers

Household employment is no longer only for the wealthy. As the number of U.S. household employers grows, the spectrum of household employers widens to four basic types. Today, household employers are:

1. the wealthy;
2. the comfortable dual-income family with parents who both want to maintain their careers;
3. the dual-income family just getting by with parents who both need to work—even when one parent would prefer to stay home to care for the child; and,
4. the single parent who is dependent on one income.

The following are some important characteristics involved with the different household employer types.

- *The wealthy.* This group often has little difficulty providing a good household workplace for employees, because most often, the wealthy have grown up with household help around them. They are very in tune with this being a work relationship, and often have few problems with an employee being in their home environment. This group may be more concerned with and put more emphasis on confidentiality than others. The wealthy families generally hire nannies, housekeepers, household managers, housemen, and cooks.

- *The established household.* This household has been around help for a while, and may have two to three children. They are working to maintain a successful balance between work and life. Hiring a nanny or other household professional is a way for them to do just that. Many of these families are relatively new to household employment; they likely have employed help for about five years, have learned how to best manage household employees through trial and error, and often find themselves on their third nanny hire before basic employment elements are worked out and agreed upon. These families may ease much of their struggle by following the work procedures offered throughout this book. Established households generally hire nannies or household managers, a housekeeper, and a handyman.
- *The young family.* This household may have one or two children, is balancing work and life, and has accessed household help to permit the parents to continue their careers, while at the same time beginning and growing their family. The young families see household help as a structured, professional situation that allows them control in managing their home life. So new is this group to household help that they will need to establish their home as a workplace, forge a satisfying employee-employer relationship, manage payroll and taxes, and so on. These families may not necessarily have considered employing household help, but have found they need and want in-home care to provide the best possible environment for their children, and to help them maintain a rich quality of life. The young family generally hires a nanny.

Q&A

Q. What is the difference between an au pair and a nanny?

A. An au pair is a foreign national living in the United States as part of the host family, and receives a small stipend in exchange for baby-sitting and help with housework. Legally authorized to live and work (only as an au pair with the host family) in the United States for up to one year in order to experience American life, an au pair may or may not have previous child care experience. An au pair is usually provided with a weekly stipend that is calculated as the federal minimum wage, less an allowance for room and board. Details are included in the 1997 Minimum Wage Law.

In contrast, a nanny works in the household, where he or she may live in or live outside the home, to undertake all tasks related to the care of the children. Duties are generally restricted to child care and the domestic tasks related to child care, such as preparing a child's meals and doing a child's laundry. Although a nanny may or may not have had formal training, she or he often has a good deal of actual experience, and oftentimes has been educated in child development. A nanny's workweek usually ranges from forty to sixty hours, and a nanny typically works unsupervised.

Household Employees

As family needs grew, the demand for different skills expanded, and as a result, various household positions have developed. Other popular household positions in the United States include:

- after-school nanny;
- groundskeeper;
- baby nurse;
- household manager;
- cook;
- housekeeper;
- doula;
- maid;
- driver;
- maintenance worker;
- eldercare provider;
- mother's helper;
- gardener; and,
- personal assistant.

There is a household position for any of the multiple operations that keep a home running. How to go about hiring and maintaining your household help is discussed in future chapters. However, it is critical that prospective household employers begin with a clear definition of what they want in a household employee. First, understand what your objectives are in bringing an employee into your household. Many people have taken that nerve-racking first step. For you, it does not have to be into the unknown. The experiences detailed throughout this book will help you bypass some of the pitfalls and smooth out some of the complexities associated with employing staff.

Deciding What Works for You

Viewing a situation from another person's perspective is always a good barometer for how something will work out. When it comes to employing household help, ask yourself the following questions.

- What do I want to accomplish in the short- and long-term?
- What problem am I trying to solve?
- Who does this benefit?

Most household employers want to balance their personal life with their work life. They want to know that their child, parent, or home is being cared for so that they may focus on their work and careers. By employing staff to tend to concerns at home, they are then able to devote time and energy to their careers. Hiring household staff is your avenue to cultivate a lifestyle of convenience, peace of mind, and freedom.

You may be surprised to discover that more than just the people living in your household are stakeholders in some way or another to your household employment. Other than your spouse, children, and you, a household employee could affect and benefit extended family members, neighbors, friends, and coworkers, among others.

In any household employment, the biggest mistake any one of us can make is not planning on being successful. Many people do not take the time necessary to be a proactive employer/manager. They do not plan for or practice to be a household employer. Without a well-designed ground plan, your nanny, your family, and you may be unprepared for the day-to-day issues that arise. These issues often result in wasted efforts and time, often pulling the employer away from his or her professional duties to attend to a household matter that could likely be handled individually by the nanny or housekeeper if plans had been established.

No matter if you are hiring a nanny to care for your child, an eldercare provider to care for your parent, or a houseman to care for your property, you need to make a real effort to learn about, plan for, and practice being a manager of a household employee. Naturally, you will need to manage your way through some bumps in the road, but once everyone is engaged, you will be positioned to build and maintain a successful employment relationship.

No matter who is working in your home, keep in mind the reality of the situation. You are making difficult decisions that affect your household and your family. Household employment is very much a personal endeavor. You do it to manage your life, provide optimal care for your children or ailing parents, and maintain a smooth and peaceful household. It is not easy, and there is no other hire as important. No matter what the type of household employee, the process is the same—learn, prepare, plan, communicate, gather feedback, and revise (if necessary). By preparing, planning, and practicing as household employer, you are on your way to engaging a critical member of your household team, one that will help you with your goal of achieving life and work balance.

2

Hiring Your Nanny or Other Household Help

Household employment is increasing for Americans who continually strive for a manageable balance between life and work. For many, the solution to managing pressures and obligations in personal and professional worlds is hiring staff to work in the home. Whether an employer hires a household manager to maintain an estate, an eldercare provider to tend to a disabled parent, or a nanny to care for young children, he or she is working to ensure that his or her home is happy, secure, and comfortable. Maintaining committed and contented household help keeps employers and their families content. To achieve a safe, convenient home life, an employer needs to create a happy workplace. A happy employee equals a happy employer, which ultimately yields a happy family.

Employing household help is not just any personnel decision. As a household employer, you are entrusting to your employee what you hold most precious. Whether you are employing a nanny to care for your child, an eldercare provider to care for your parent, or a housekeeper to care for your home, this is one of the most important employment decisions you will ever make. Your loved ones, your property, and your privacy are all dependent upon the household employee's skill and professionalism.

The Citizen and Noncitizen Employee
Household employers should hire only those people who are legally authorized to work in the United States. These people include U.S. citizens, legal

permanent residents, and other aliens authorized to work, such as refugees, asylees, and persons in Temporary Protected Status.

Many household employers in the United States hire noncitizens, largely for financial reasons, and many hire people not legally authorized to work in this country. According to Pew Hispanic Center, a nonpartisan research organization that provides information on the country's diverse Hispanic population and its impact on the nation, by March 2005 there were 11.1 million unauthorized migrants in the United States, based on the last U.S. Bureau of Labor Statistics' Current Population Survey. The survey termed *unauthorized migrants* to be people living in the United States who were not admitted to the United States as permanent residents and who are not in a set of specific authorized temporary statuses that permit longer-term residence and work. This 11.1 million includes all unauthorized migrants, not solely Hispanic or Mexican migrants. According to the Pew Hispanic Center, these unauthorized workers make up a sizable share of workers within specific industries. Topping the list at 21% of unauthorized migrants is those who work in private households.

Employers hiring noncitizens must comply with filings and procedures stipulated under United States immigration law. Compliance is particularly important in light of the United States' Homeland Security programs. All employers in the United States must complete a *Form I-9* for every employee hired. (see p.248.) Completing Form I-9 attempts to ensure that only people legally able to work in the United States are hired. Therefore, employers use Form I-9 to verify the identity and employment eligibility of employees. (For more on Form I-9 and employer payroll and tax responsibilities, please see Chapter 8.)

THE I-9 PROCESS

You have probably filled out several I-9 forms over the course of your employment, and the I-9 form probably looks very familiar to you. You may remember when starting work at a new company or organization that sometime during the first three days of your employment, you submitted to human resources or your new supervisor documents—such as your driver's license, passport, birth certificate, or Social Security card—that verified your identity and your ability to legally work in the United States.

The third page of *Form I-9* (p.248) provides lists of acceptable documents that may be used to verify an employee's eligibility to work in the United States. These lists are there to help you as an employer determine what the U.S. government considers valid documents to establish identification and employment eligibility. However, employers must use some caution when reviewing and accepting an employee's I-9 submission and documentation. The I-9 A, B, and C lists, while helpful, can mislead an employer. For instance, the United States Citizen and Immigration Services (USCIS) web-site (**www.uscis.gov**) states under "Special Instructions" that four of the ten documents included on the hard copy Form I-9 List A can no longer be accepted, including:

1. Certificate of U.S. Citizenship (Form N-560 or N-561);
2. Certificate of Naturalization (Form N-552 or N-570);
3. Unexpired Re-entry Permit (Form I-327); and,
4. Unexpired Refugee Travel Document (Form I-571).

(Focusing on immigration and citizenship services, USCIS was created as a separate bureau by the Homeland Security Act of 2002 and is part of the Department of Homeland Security.)

While employers are not penalized for accepting these documents, you may want to think twice before accepting them, or to be safe, ask the employee for another document.

Form M-274, *Handbook for Employers*, is another tool employers may access to help them ensure the validity of documents being presented with the I-9 form. Form M-274 offers illustrations of various documents and information on such things as which types of green cards or Social Security numbers were issued when. Employers may refer to M-274 when a questionable document is presented to them or when they are uncertain whether a particular form of a document is still valid. Sometimes unauthorized workers modify older documents with newer photos, resulting in situations where a thirty-year-old green card has a picture of a 20-year-old on it. (Source: National Institute of Business Management, "The HR Law Specialist," February 2006.)

Facts & Figures

THE LATEST ON ILLEGAL WORKERS

News reports from across the United States on illegal immigrants working in the United States—from household employees who have been on the job for years to new day laborers—opened 2006. Day laborers are those workers who gather in parking lots and on street corners, waiting for potential employers to collect them for temporary day work or short stints—always paying under the table and not always paying the day laborer what was promised at the job's outset.

In a crackdown lauded by anti-immigration groups and publicized in the media throughout the country, police in East Hampton, NY, took down license plate numbers of the cars at day laborer centers, and sent the plate numbers and identifying information with a letter to the IRS and federal Immigration and Customs Enforcement, stating the cars' owners might be hiring illegal contractors and paying off the books.

ILLEGAL IMMIGRANTS

According to the Pew Hispanic Center's March 2005 Current Population Survey, about 7.2 million unauthorized migrants were employed—accounting for about 4.9% of the civilian labor force—making up a large share of all workers within the following occupational categories:

- 24% in farming;
- 17% in cleaning;
- 14% in construction; and,
- 12% in food preparation.

About 6.3 million illegal immigrants from Mexico live in the United States, reported the Pew Hispanic Center, making up 57% of illegal immigrants; 24% account for those immigrating to the United States from other Latin American countries; and 19% for all others. An average of 485,000 more Mexican immigrants alone arrive each year, stated a Pew Hispanic Center report, noting that an estimated 700,000 undocumented immigrants from around the world continue to enter the United States each year. According to the Urban Institute Immigration Studies Program, almost 65%

of the undocumented population lives in six states: California (27%), Texas (13%), New York (8%), Florida (7%), Illinois (6%), and New Jersey (4%).

In response to these dramatic numbers, *Time* reported that state legislatures are considering close to three hundred bills on immigration policy. As of early February 2006:

- Arizona passed a law banning cities from maintaining public day-laborer centers, where migrants gather to seek employment for the day;
- Idaho rejected a proposed law that would have required counties to pay for transportation of undocumented workers back to their home countries;
- Illinois established an office to study immigrants' contributions and needs, while also passing a new law that allows illegal immigrant children to obtain health insurance;
- Kentucky enacted a law that requires anyone seeking licenses for various professions to show proof of immigration status;
- New Mexico became the ninth state to offer in-state tuition benefits to undocumented immigrant students;
- South Carolina passed a bill requiring Medicaid applicants to present proof of legal residency (if asked);
- Virginia recently passed a bill that would make it the first state to ban illegal immigrants from attending state colleges; and,
- Washington reversed a 2002 measure and restored health care coverage to children, regardless of their immigration status.

According to *Time*, 80% to 85% of new immigrants from Mexico lack legal documentation. This does not seem to be a barrier to U.S. jobs, however. *Time* reported that the median hourly wage of Mexican-born workers in the United States in 2004 was $9, whereas the Mexican hourly wage was $1.86 (21 pesos). However, *Time* stated that increased numbers of migrants competing for work has lowered hourly pay. In the Pew Hispanic Center Current Population Survey, respondents reported a median weekly earning of $300.

With the increased attention on legal hiring practices and legal payroll and tax payments, it is critical that household employers follow the laws and requirements established in their states and municipalities, even if the employee is not authorized to work in the United States. (For more on managing payroll and taxes, see Chapter 8.)

CASE STUDY

JIM CHANEY
HOUSEHOLD EMPLOYER
VICE PRESIDENT, HUMAN RESOURCES
GEORGIA-PACIFIC BUILDING PRODUCTS
ATLANTA, GA
GTM PAYROLL AND TAX SERVICES CLIENT

The trials and tribulations of raising a child were not new to Jim Chaney, father of two older children, and who, just months ago, began a second family with his wife, Carla Chaney, upon the birth of their son, Brandon. The trials and tribulations of human resources (HR) were not new to either Jim or Carla Chaney, as both are HR executives with Georgia-Pacific (GP) in Atlanta, GA. When the Chaneys decided to hire a live-out nanny, they went to an Atlanta agency for help.

"This is not like any other employment," said Jim Chaney, HR vice president for GP's building products division. "It is much more meaningful. I hire people [at GP] with whom I don't spend nearly as much time talking with as I did with our nanny. I had to think, 'Do I really, really want this person in my house alone with my baby?' This is the most important hire you'll ever make. Make sure you do it well."

The Chaneys both work demanding and time-consuming jobs. (Carla Chaney is HR director for GP's consumer products division.) While GP offers a company day care center that Jim Chaney said is "attractive and wonderful" and had a space available, the Chaneys decided to hire a live-out nanny for Brandon's first year of life. They believed that the nanny solution would save their son from disrupted sleep and schedules, protect him from germs and sickness, and ensure that their son had someone to immediately respond to his cries.

The Chaneys required child care from 7:00 a.m. to 6:30 p.m., flexibility to travel with them, and the ability to stay later into the evening when provided with enough notice. "It was hard to find someone to commit to that," Jim Chaney noted. Luckily, the couple found a nanny, who had two school-age children of her own, to fill the job in under five weeks' time.

"You can press right through," Jim Chaney said. *"It was three weeks to contract with the agency and go through the applicants. The agency checked references and did background checks. Then, interviewing took about two weeks. I use agencies all the time [for Georgia-Pacific]. That's what I pay them for. You can do it [all] yourself, but you're going to spend a lot of time. It can be overwhelming."*

Despite a wealth of experience in HR and previous experience hiring household employees for eldercare, Jim Chaney admitted that he was surprised by several household employment issues that arose during the hiring process. Some such issues follow.

- ***Costs.*** *"Quite frankly, it's pretty shocking when first finding out the prices of nanny services,"* he said, adding that there are *"hidden and below-surface"* costs that may present a challenge. *"The margins of whether a person can afford a nanny become somewhat of an issue, but the trade-offs are well worth it."*

- ***Gross vs. net.*** *"You need to understand when negotiating with nannies that they clearly understand what their pay will be,"* he emphasized. *"If a nanny says she needs to be paid $500, you need to be clear if that $500 is $500 less taxes [net]. So, the amount she takes home and the amount stated on her check may not say $500. Or, if she says $500, that $500 will be the full amount she takes home. That was a big thing."*

- ***Auto insurance.*** *According to Jim Chaney, he required his nanny to be a licensed driver with a safe driving record. The nanny uses the Chaneys' car when she is on duty, and the Chaneys ensure that she is covered under their auto insurance.*

- ***Holidays.*** *"Typically, a nanny expects holidays off,"* Jim said, which he admitted was a surprise. *The eldercare workers with whom he worked in the past were ingrained to twenty-four-hour care, holiday or not. Much of this was worked out through the agency and the nanny prior to hire. Following a format offered by the agency, the Chaneys and their nanny pored over a work agreement for more than an hour to clarify expectations.* *"To [the nanny's] credit, she asked for the work agreement,"* Jim Chaney said, *"and we went over it together."*

"It's wonderful having a nanny," he added. "She's got a lot of freedom, and we've built a lot of trust."

One of the biggest challenges facing the new household employer is creating the job description and becoming a manager of an employee while ensuring that all is within budget. The household employer must simultaneously:
- *manage hiring agreements, job requirements, and salary negotiations;*
- *communicate effectively; and,*
- *assess who is the best choice to become the next household employee.*

*To access a handy tool to negotiate and communicate gross to net salary, visit GTM's online salary calculator at **www.gtm.com/ resourcecenter**.*
—Guy

CASE STUDY

LIZ
NANNY
STAMFORD, CT

Liz, a professional nanny for sixteen years, came to Connecticut for work by way of Saudi Arabia, Germany, England, and Scotland.

Born and raised in Ayr, Scotland, Liz said she heeded her mother's advice to be a nanny because of her love of children and because it is a good career choice in the UK. First, she worked for a single father in Scotland, and then moved on to work for military families in Germany and England. Next she served as nanny for the Saudi royal family, and finally she journeyed to the United States—first to New Orleans and then settling in Stamford, CT.

"To be a nanny, you have to be very adaptable," said Liz, who did not want her full name disclosed. "You have to be flexible to family dynamics, the way the family operates. You bring a lot of yourself to the job—your knowledge and experience."

According to Liz, she prefers to work as part of a team with the parents. "You're ultimately responsible for that child and what takes place on a daily basis," she said. "Nannies and families can outgrow each other, and over time, families can take nannies for granted—especially in the United States, where nannies need to be recognized as professionals. In the UK, being a nanny is a career choice."

The disparity between how America and the United Kingdom view household staff propelled Liz to become a political activist. With her knowledge and experience, Liz is working with her congressman and the U.S. Department of Labor (DOL) to gain federal acknowledgment of nannies and other household workers as skilled professionals. To win recognition of the problem and support for a resolution, she has spent much of her own time and money, often burning the midnight oil, to travel to Washington, D.C. for meetings; make important telephone calls every day; and, send faxes to more than one hundred political offices. She said that the DOL has opened the door to defining nannies and household workers as skilled professionals.

One of the problems in the United States, said Liz, is that many people seek household employment while still deciding which profession they really want to pursue. This results in the attitude that being a nanny is not a true profession, but a stepping stone to something else.

"We take our jobs very, very seriously," said Liz. "That child is a very high priority."

According to Liz, a nanny needs the respect and trust of the family to do the job. She recommends that families pay fairly and above board so both the family and nanny are protected, and that they offer benefits. "A happy nanny is a good nanny," said Liz, "so treat her well."

> It is important for household employers to determine how employees view their positions. Perceptions and actuality can often be very different. A realization by the employer about how employees feel within the household organization and how employees feel about their jobs could cause an employer to adopt different management and employment practices.
> —Guy

Employee vs. Independent Contractor

Household employers need to recognize the difference between an employee and an independent contractor. The employer's tax requirements are contingent on whether the professional is working for the employer or is actually working for him- or herself. Under the U.S. *Fair Labor Standards Act* (FLSA), household employers need to determine whether they have control or direction over the worker. In deciding, employers must consider the following.

- Who has the right to control the work being performed? The more control an employer has, the more apt the worker is to be considered an employee.
- Does the worker face an economic risk in doing the job? If so, he or she would more likely be identified as an independent contractor.
- Whose equipment and facilities is the worker using to perform the job? If the worker attends to job requirements on-site at the employer's home or facility, and uses the employer's equipment and tools to do so, then she or he is probably deemed an employee.
- Are specific, specialized skills required for the worker to perform the job? The more specialized, the more probable it is that the worker is an independent contractor.

- Are the worker's contributions integral to the business? Will the business suffer if the worker was not contributing to its operations and success? If so, employee status is likely.
- Is the working relationship permanent? A permanent working relationship is likely an employer-employee relationship.

(For detailed information on FLSA, go to **www.dol.gov**.)

Employers hiring independent contractors are not required to withhold income tax or make employer contributions to the worker's Social Security fund. If an employer pays an independent contractor $600 or more per year (as of 2006), then he or she must report it to the IRS using Form 1099-Misc. Upon hiring the contractor, an employer should request the contractor complete a Form W-9, which provides his or her Social Security number or employer identification number (EIN).

Facts & Figures

BE SURE YOU FOLLOW TAX LAWS: A TOP PRIORITY

If you are one of the families who try to skirt their tax obligations by attempting to define your nanny as an independent contractor, or if you are one of the household employers paying your nanny under the table, you may want to reconsider. The IRS is aggressively pursuing these cases. They add a $500 penalty to tax and interest owed, along with civil penalties of between 20% and 75% of the underpaid tax. Those who pursue the matter in court may face added penalties of up to $25,000.

The vast majority of household workers are employees, not independent contractors. However, some temporary baby-sitters who work for many friends and neighbors on an irregular, sporadic schedule are considered independent contractors. For assistance in determining status, the U.S. Internal Revenue Service (IRS) offers *Form SS-8* (*Determination of Worker Status for Purposes of Federal Employment Taxes and Income Tax Withholding*), which can be downloaded from **www.gtm.com/resourcecenter** or **www.irs.gov** or found in Appendix E. (see p.251.)

The IRS uses twenty factors when determining the status of an employee or independent contractor. Many of the IRS factors follow the FLSA considerations, and both can be used to determine a worker's status. Based on the IRS factors, an employee relationship exists when a worker:

1. must comply with the employer's instructions about when, where, and how to do the job;
2. receives training from or at the direction of the employer;
3. lacks a significant investment in facilities used to perform services;
4. receives payments for business and/or traveling expenses;
5. does not offer services to the general public;
6. receives payment of regular amounts at set intervals;
7. cannot make a profit or suffer a loss from services;
8. can be terminated by the employer;
9. can quit work at any time without incurring liability;
10. has a continuing working relationship with the employer;
11. provides services that are integrated into the business;
12. must provide services personally;
13. hires, supervises, and pays assistants on an employer's behalf or pays assistants for the worker;
14. must work in a sequence set by the employer;
15. must submit regular reports to the employer;
16. relies on the employer to furnish tools and materials;
17. works for only one employer at a time;
18. follows set work hours;
19. works full-time for the employer; and,
20. does work on the employer's premises or on a route or at a location designated by the employer.

(For more information, go to **www.irs.gov**.)

The Hiring Process

There are many concerns to consider when you are involved in hiring an employee, as well as many legalities to abide by to ensure equitable and fair employment opportunities. By taking the hiring process one step at a time, you can proceed with well-planned and well-researched employment offers.

DEVELOPING THE JOB DESCRIPTION

First and foremost, a thorough, comprehensive, and well-developed job description will help any employer immensely in the hiring process. Really think about what the job will entail; cover all aspects of household duties, tasks, responsibilities, work hours, and requirements—and put it into words for everyone to understand. The best job description will clearly set out what the position needs to accomplish; what essential and nonessential tasks and duties are needed; and what skills, abilities, and talents are best used to adequately complete the job. This job description not only helps start the job search, it also helps tremendously in developing the work agreement with the hired employee.

A job description should include the following elements.

- *Title*—The official title of the position for which you are hiring.
- *Summary*—A one- to two-sentence summary that states the primary function of the position.
- *Essential functions*—A listing of the primary responsibilities of the position. These are the functions that are necessary and must be performed on a regular basis.
- *Nonessential functions*—A separate listing of responsibilities that account for only a small part of the job.
- *Knowledge, skills, and abilities*—A listing of topics that an employee should have knowledge of and at what level (i.e., basic, intermediate, or expert). Also, outline specific skills (i.e., reading and writing skills) and abilities (i.e., lifting heavy objects or children, climbing stairs, etc.) the position requires.
- *Supervisory responsibilities*—If managing other employees, list the job titles of those employees.
- *Working conditions*—Guidelines about the working conditions and a description of your home or estate and its layout, provisions for food, any pets in the house, whether or not a vehicle will be provided while working, if work performed will be at any other additional residences, and so on.

- *Minimum qualifications*—A listing of criteria to be met, such as educational background, license requirements, years of experience required, and so on.
- *Success factors*—A list of qualities or personality traits that would make someone successful in this position.

See Appendix D for job description samples for a nanny, eldercare provider, and maintenance worker. Also, see page 256 for a *Work Agreement*.

ADVERTISING A JOB POSITION

With a comprehensive job description prepared, a job advertisement can be written and placed in various media, or provided to an agency. Be as specific as possible in the job ad. List your requirements, such as previous experience, education, a current/valid driver's license, fluency in English (or other languages), and work schedule.

INTERVIEWING

It is good practice to open an interview by reviewing the job requirements (provide a written copy to the applicant) and confirming at the start of the discussion that the applicant can meet them. Prepare a list of questions before the meeting so that you can find out certain information, such as what prior experience the interviewee has, what kind of household he or she has worked in, when he or she is able to start work, and so on. (See Appendix B for sample interview questions.) The prepared list helps to keep the interview on track and helps ensure that all questions are asked and all topics discussed. This is also helpful when multiple candidates are interviewed, allowing the employer to make comparisons and considerations by examining different answers to the same questions.

Employers interview to learn about the candidate, so allow the candidate to do the majority of the talking. You need to hear about the candidate's experiences and how he or she handled various situations. Employers need not dominate the discussion. They can, however, direct it by asking open-ended questions, requiring the candidate to do more than nod his or her head yes or no. This will generate more knowledge about the candidate and force the interviewee to respond more fully. Open-ended questions usually begin with the words *how, why, when, who, what,* and *where.* For instance, when interviewing a candidate for a gardener position, ask, "What is it about gardening that you like?" instead of "Do you like gardening?" The same phrasing can be used when interviewing another candidate. For example, ask a nanny candidate, "Why do you want to work with children?" not "Do you like children?"

Another useful interviewing technique is to begin with softer questions, allowing the interviewer to gain a rapport with the candidate. This can help keep him or her talking openly once more difficult or uncomfortable questions or topics are broached.

When hiring a nanny or other employee who will be working in your home with your family, take the time you need during the interviews to fully cover all the information. You should plan two hours for one nanny interview. Remember, an interview is instrumental in helping you gauge:

- whether this person would be a good addition to your household;
- how his or her temperament would fit or blend in with family members;
- whether he or she has the know-how needed for the job;
- what his or her priorities are in regard to his or her career or employment; and,
- how responsible and reliable he or she will be with your children and other family members.

This is also your opportunity to evaluate your perception of the person and to listen to your instinct. Go with your intuition on whether this person will work well for you.

Many interviewers rate a candidate on his or her job ability, experience, presentation, communication skills, interaction with others, and attitude, as well as how he or she will fit in with the already established household. In addition, use the interview to help determine your household's needs for both today and tomorrow. Think about the future and ask yourself (and maybe even ask your interviewee) if this person you are hiring can do the job now and in six months from now. Many household employers are so focused on getting someone into the position as soon as possible that they barely think about the future of the household and the employee.

All of this should be considered before offering the candidate a position. It is easy to be swept up in an interviewee's excitement or focus on a common interest, and neglect an important consideration. With just a little preparation before the interview and review of an *Application for Employment* (see p.259), an employer helps ensure that he or she gathers all the necessary information from the individual candidates.

Interview Questions: Legal vs. Illegal

United States law—in particular, the EEOC (see Chapter 10)—protects against employment discrimination by prohibiting employers from asking the applicant certain questions. The table on page 28 lists some examples of legal and illegal questions to ask an applicant.

A household employer should be prepared to answer questions, too. This exchange enables the candidate to have a clear understanding of the position and workplace, and lays the groundwork for the work agreement to be developed.

INVESTIGATING BACKGROUNDS AND CHECKING REFERENCES

As with any job application, checking background and references is one of the best ways to learn about a candidate. By speaking with references, employers can learn crucial information about the candidate's abilities, personality, strengths, and weaknesses.

Checking references is particularly important in household employment, according to the owner of a Texas-based nanny agency. "Nannies are people with special talents and personalities that you can't really test for, so this is where references come into play."

A good practice is for an employer to obtain a signed release from the candidate to check employment and personal references. Provide a copy of the reference release to the candidate. (The original should be filed with the applicant's completed job application, and should remain in the employee personnel file if he or she is hired.) Employers need to be cautious not to violate an applicant's right to privacy when performing background checks. Many employers check financial backgrounds to help judge a candidate's responsibility, maturity, and honesty. According to the U.S. *Fair Credit Report Act*, if an employer uses credit reporting as part of the background investigation, then he or she must provide an applicant with a copy and summary of his or her credit report if he or she is rejected for employment.

Facts & Figures

EMPLOYERS: CHECK APPLICANTS' RÉSUMÉS

In a tight job market and in the age of Internet-based "diploma mills," résumé fraud is an increasing concern among employers. On the other hand, with today's Internet-enabled easy and cost-effective access to information, employers can easily verify résumé facts with a few clicks of the mouse.

It is bewildering why candidates continue to misrepresent the facts on résumés, knowing that employers will check and that any misrepresentation, lie, or fraud on an application or résumé is grounds for immediate dismissal—no matter how long an employee has been with an employer or how far up the organizational chart the employee has climbed. The following examples show how seriously résumé fraud is taken.

David J. Edmondson, Radio Shack CEO, resigned under pressure after it was learned that nearly a decade before, he had claimed on his résumé that he held two degrees from a Bible college. The company learned that the school had no record of Edmondson graduating.

Notre Dame football coach George O'Leary was forced to resign just five days after stepping into the coach position after it was revealed that he lied about his academic and athletic achievements.

NASA press liaison George Deutsch resigned after it was found that he falsely claimed he graduated from Texas A&M.

Such is the growing concern of résumé fraud within employers' ranks that the Washington State legislature is debating a bill that would create civil and criminal penalties for lying on résumés or failing to disclose that a degree is from an unaccredited institution. According to news reports, heightened awareness of résumé fraud stems from high-profile examples (such as those mentioned above), enhanced fact-checking capabilities (mostly via the Internet), and the proliferation of "diploma mills" (which offer diplomas from nonaccredited universities based on a person's present knowledge or personal experience).

Another Midwest agency owner said that, although her firm checks references, clients are strongly encouraged to perform their own reference checks. "Sometimes, a mom talking with another mom will provide more information."

Placement agency owners agree that the Zoe Baird Nannygate incident instigated standard background checks on prospective household employees. "In the 1980s, background checks were rarely done," said a Texas-based agency owner. "Since then, the household employment world has changed significantly." She added that she only interviews potential nannies who have legally lived in the United States for at least three years. Why? "It's just too hard to check credentials in some foreign countries," she said, adding that available foreign information is often suspect, because many records are not updated.

Spending an average of two hours with each prospect prior to accepting him or her as a nanny candidate, the Texas-based agency owner cautiously checks backgrounds, only accepts references from the United States, questions the nanny on why he or she wants to be in the profession, and studies a nanny's social interaction. The agency also recommends its clients do the same.

"Now, you can't be too careful," said the agency owner, noting that today, parents' fear extends beyond the U.S. Immigration Service to include kidnapping and child abuse. "You have to become a detective yourself."

> ## Our Advice
>
> *"The key to finding the right nanny for a family is honesty: honesty in job description, honesty in duties and responsibilities, hours, expectations, living arrangements (if a live-in job), etc. Parents that sugarcoat the difficulties of the job are simply going to find themselves hiring the wrong nanny for the job. The net result is that the family will end up in a revolving-door situation. If more families recognize this simple fact, there would be a lot less problems making proper matches."*
> —Bob Mark
>   President
>   America's Nannies
>   Paramus, NJ

When speaking with references, some good questions employers need to ask include the following.

• Would you hire him or her again, and why or why not?
• What do you believe are his or her strengths and weaknesses?

- Why did he or she leave your employment?
- What were the dates of employment?
- Was he or she punctual?
- Were all aspects of the job completed?

Suggested Background Checks and What They Can Tell You

Many first-time household employers are surprised at what can be determined by performing standard checks into an applicant's background. These are necessary—and common—procedures in any employee hire, and household employers should do a thorough job in making these background checks.

- *Driving record*—A Department of Motor Vehicles (DMV) check is very important for any applicant seeking a position that requires driving. A DMV check reveals driving history of the applicant and any alcohol- or drug-related incidents.
- *Social Security*—Checking that the applicant's Social Security number is that person's ensures that the applicant is not fraudulently using another person's number. In addition, a potential employer may verify the applicant's current or prior addresses via the Social Security Administration.
- *Credit history*—Checking an applicant's credit history is becoming more and more common during the application process. Credit history demonstrates an applicant's financial performance and allows a potential employer to judge an applicant's responsibility.

> ## Our Advice
>
> *"We wanted the kids to be on their own schedule, not on our (work schedule)."*
> —Denise Shade
>   Household employer (nanny)
>   Mother of two
>   Key Bank Senior Vice President, Foreign Exchange

> ## Our Advice
>
> *"A good household employee has dignity, nobility, great discretion, and not an ounce of judgment. Judgment is often the death curse for a domestic employment relationship."*
> —Leann Brambach
>   Owner/Operator
>   Home Details, Inc.
>   Seattle, WA
>   GTM partner agency

- *Criminal conviction* (county, state, and federal)—Shows an applicant's criminal activity and prevents negligent hiring.
- *Drug testing*—Presents any drug use by the applicant.
- *Personality testing*—Guides employers in hiring decisions, often allowing the employers to gauge whether an applicant will mesh with others in the workplace.
- *Sex offender/child abuse registry*—Lists any person charged with any crimes involving children.
- *Professional licensing*—When a professional designation is necessary for the job, a check to determine whether the applicant possess the designation or certification helps determine if he or she is qualified to do the job.
- *Higher education verification*—Checks the accuracy of the information submitted by the applicant, and depending on course of study, demonstrates to a degree whether he or she is qualified for the job.
- *Trust line* (for California)—Ensures the applicant has been cleared of background checks and fingerprinting by the FBI and California Department of Justice.
- *Fingerprinting*—Verifies whether the applicant has a criminal history.
- *Character references*—Verifies authenticity from the applicant and allows the employer to determine characteristics of an applicant (i.e., hard worker, caring person, loves children, strongly believes in education).
- *Employment references*—Verifies past employment and dates, as well as the accuracy of the information the applicant submitted.
- *Other screening*:
    - U.S. Department of Commerce Denied Persons List
    - U.S. Department of Commerce Entity List
    - U.S. Department of Treasury Specially Designated Nationals and Blocked Persons List
    - U.S. Department of State Proliferation List
    - U.S. Department of State Debarment List

Facts & Figures

BACKGROUND CHECKS CAN UNVEIL STARTLING INFORMATION IMPORTANT TO ANY EMPLOYER

In late 2003, the media reported a tragic story: a California nanny was arrested for vehicular manslaughter in a hit-and-run accident that killed two children. The woman, who worked as a nanny, drove onto a sidewalk and killed a ten-year-old boy and his seven-year-old sister. Upon investigation, the nanny had neither a current, valid driver's license nor insurance. Plus, Department of Motor Vehicle records showed that the woman's driver's license had been suspended twice for an excessive blood-alcohol level, as well as suspended numerous times for negligent operation and insurance problems. Additionally, the woman had been arrested in the past for public drunkenness.

The woman was hired by the family as a nanny from an advertisement on the Internet, and the family failed to do any background checks. A check of her driving record would have immediately dismissed her from consideration as a nanny or for any other household position.

Maintain Professionalism and Keep to the Business at Hand

Mind your business and stay on track with questioning as it relates to the job and how the applicant will perform the job duties.

In the corporate world, quite a lot of effort, time, and expense is taken to perform background checks on every new hire. The corporate process may include personal and professional reference checking, criminal background checks, drug screening, DMV check, personality testing—even checking someone's credit history for a look into his or her responsibility and fiscal management. All this is done for a corporate job. How much more important is it when you are hiring an employee to come into your home? Your children and loved ones are so much more valuable—and also more vulnerable. Keep them safe by going the extra mile or two with your background checking. Most importantly, follow your instincts.

Listen to your instincts and back that up with your checks. This will be well worth the effort in your overall work to hire an employee that makes everyone in your household feel comfortable and safe—and happy. You are hiring a nanny or eldercare worker to help you *not* worry about what is going on at home. Put in this bit of extra effort now with checking out the person you are bringing into your home and who you are entrusting with your loved ones, your property, and your memories.

Facts & Figures

LEGAL VS. ILLEGAL APPLICANT QUESTIONS

Legal:	Illegal:
Your (applicant's) full name?	Your (applicant's) maiden name?
Have you ever been convicted of a crime? Is there a felony charge pending against you?	Have you ever been arrested?
Are you 18 years or older?	What is your age? What is your date of birth?
How long have you been a resident of this state?	Where were you born?
Are you a U.S. citizen?	In what country are you a citizen?
Name and address of person to be notified in case of emergency?	Name and address of nearest relative in case of emergency?

Source: U.S. Department of Labor

> **Facts & Figures**
>
> **AT-WILL EMPLOYMENT**
> _____
>
> All household employees are employed at will. This employment is at the discretion of the employer and the employee. Employment may terminate with or without notice or cause. Employees are also free to end employment at any time, for any reason, with or without notice. (See page 78 for an example of an at-will statement.)

MAKING AN OFFER

An offer should always be made verbally and in writing. When offering employment to an applicant, take care to avoid any appearance of a promise of long-term employment. Send a job offer letter that states the position, whether it is full-time or part-time, the start date, the schedule, the starting salary, and any available benefits. Remember to state if he or she is an at-will employee. (See Appendix D for an example of an offer letter for household employment.) Ask that the letter be signed, dated, and returned to the employer for the offer to be accepted. It is okay for the employer to request that the letter be signed and completed by a certain date. That way, the employer may contact other candidates until the job is filled.

Stephanie Oana, a lawyer in Oakland, CA, and GTM payroll and tax service client, employs a nanny to care for her two young children. According to Oana, she writes extensive offer letters that include all of the terms of employment. The offer letters, she notes, serve as the work agreement. "The candidates really prefer it, because with it they know what the employer wants," she states.

Oana prefers using the offer letter because in the business world, a countersigned offer letter often acts as the work agreement. Oana includes all pertinent and relevant information in the offer letter, including benefits, vacation, insurance, use of car, use of telephone, hours, when overtime applies, and so on.

Rejecting a Candidate

While not mandated by law, it is common human resource (HR) practice to inform rejected candidates that another person has been hired. Many *Rejection Letters* (p.234) simply state that another candidate deemed more

Q&A

Q. *How do I hire or sponsor someone who is not legally authorized to work in the United States?*

A. *The U.S. Department of Labor Employment & Training Administration (DOLETA) website at **www.dol.gov** provides information on hiring foreign workers, as well as access to the necessary forms. According to DOLETA, hiring foreign workers for employment in the United States normally requires approval from several governmental agencies. A labor certification filed with the Department of Labor via Form ETA 750 (labor certification request) is often the first step. The Department of Labor works with local State Workforce Agencies (SWA) to process Form ETA 750. Then, an employer must petition the U.S. Citizenship and Immigration Services (USCIS) for a visa by submitting Form I-140 (Immigrant Petition for Alien Worker). With a visa number issued by the State Department, the foreign worker gains U.S. entry. Also, an applicant must prove that she or he is admissible to the United States under the Immigration and Nationality Act (INA).*

appropriate for the job has been hired. The letter should be filed with the application and other information regarding that particular candidate. Rejecting candidates is often an awkward and unpleasant task. The benefit of working with an agency is that the agency handles candidate rejection, not the household employer. (see Chapter 3.)

Hiring Laws

Employers must be aware of several federal, state, and local laws when hiring an employee. Key federal laws that all employers must follow are discussed in this section.

According to the U.S. Department of Labor Employment & Training Administration (DOLETA), qualifying criteria for hiring a foreign worker include the following.

- The foreign worker must be hired as a full-time employee.
- The employer must have a bona fide job opening.
- Job requirements cannot be tailored to the foreign worker's qualifications, but must follow what is customarily required for the job within the United States.
- The employer must pay at least the prevailing wage for the job in the location of the anticipated job.

CASE STUDY

Stephanie Oana
Household Employer
Lawyer
Oakland, CA
GTM Payroll and Tax Service Client

After Stephanie Oana watched friends maneuver through their own nanny searches, she and her husband, Joe Osha, elected to use an agency. She said doing so saved her time and helped ensure she was hiring for the role she wanted. With both parents busily juggling demanding schedules, frequent business travel, and unpredictable work hours, they have over several years hired three nannies: one who lived outside their home in New York City, and two live-in nannies in the San Francisco Bay area.

Oana, a lawyer, said she worked with a number of agencies simultaneously each time she searched for a nanny. "You have to be very clear with the agency about what you want," she said. "Agencies are very helpful with identifying and screening applicants, but the matchmaking is up to the employer and the candidate."

"Families need to think clearly and be up-front and fair to the people interviewing," said Oana, "and give a realistic view of the situation." Oana addressed her unpredictable work schedule during the interview process to ensure the nanny would be flexible. "It is a lot easier to balance a schedule with weird hours with a live-in nanny," Oana added. "It can be very hard to balance certain responsibilities if a nanny has her own children or obligations she needs to get home to."

According to Oana, as the job evolves, communication is very important. "I talk every day with my nanny about the kids," she said. "At least every couple of months, we speak about the job and issues."

Oana cited an incident in which a nanny wanted a raise. Because open communication was fostered, Oana and the nanny were able to talk about the circumstances and strike a balance. "It was a very beneficial conversation," noted Oana.

The Oanas sought in-home child care because they believe very young children need a lot of individual attention. "My kids have gotten the kind of attention they would receive from a stay-at-home parent," Oana stated. "I was not interested in being a stay-at-home parent, but I could hire a nanny to provide high-quality, in-home care."

Stephanie Oana's practice of clear communication and presenting a realistic view of the job makes for an effective working relationship—and no surprises for either Oana or her nanny. Plus, as mentioned on p.29, Oana's use of an extensive employment offer letter as a work agreement contributes to an accurate view of the household's situation. In short, she is ensuring the candidate fully understands the job requirements prior to accepting the position. Employers who do this are crossing their t's and dotting their i's before employment begins. As a result, they are preventing problems from arising.
—Guy

Q&A

Q. *How can I legally ask an employee candidate if she or he smokes?*
A. *An employer can ask a candidate whether he or she smokes while working on the job. It is important to keep it in context of the job to be performed.*

ADA

When hiring employees, employers with fifteen or more employees must comply with the *Americans with Disabilities Act* (ADA) and Title VII, which prohibits discrimination. (see Chapter 10.)

EEOC/AA

Federal and state *Equal Employment Opportunity Commission* (EEOC) regulations protect people from discrimination regardless of race, color, gender, age, national origin, religion, disability, sexual orientation, marital status, citizenship status, or veteran status. *Affirmative action* is how an organization or an employer addresses protected classes—such as minorities, women, people with disabilities, and veterans—from problem areas, which may include under-representation in the workforce or some action that may adversely affect that group (or employee). Employers need to be sure that their commitment to the EEOC guidelines and affirmative action is included in hiring, training, compensation, benefits, retention, and promotions.

EMPLOYEE POLYGRAPH PROTECTION ACT

The *Employee Polygraph Protection Act* bars private employers from using any type of lie detector test for either preemployment screening or for testing current employees.

Immigration Hiring Information

Just as it is difficult to define household employment and those positions within the household employment industry, employers new to hiring foreign nationals, immigrants, nonimmigrant aliens, and so on may quickly find themselves confused and uncertain. Just reading the handful of immigrant employee types is enough to intimidate most of us. There are so many different definitions, each with its own specific hiring requirements and legal issues, that it is a courageous household employer who takes on the extra worry and paperwork when he or she hires a non-American.

Yet, since nearly one-quarter of the household industry's employees are noncitizens or non-American workers, immigration is a very real and very important consideration for hiring household help.

WHAT EMPLOYERS NEED TO KNOW ABOUT HIRING FOREIGNERS

While hundreds of pages could be spent on this area alone, this section is a sort of nutshell guide for you to follow when dealing with immigration issues and hiring.

Employment-based immigration is a complex process that involves a number of government agencies—the U.S. Departments of Labor, State, and Homeland Security. The *Immigration and Nationality Act* (INA) regulates the admission of foreign workers into the United States, with the Department of Justice, the Department of State, and the Department of Homeland Security all serving as administrators of its mandates.

An *immigrant* is a foreign-born person who has been sponsored by a qualifying family member or employer, and who has approval to reside permanently in the U.S. as a lawful permanent resident. This person holds a Resident Alien Card, known often as a *green card*. A *nonimmigrant* is an alien who seeks entry into the United States or who has already been admitted for a specific purpose for a temporary period of time. These temporary periods can range from a few days to many years. Nonimmigrants come to the U.S. for many different purposes, including temporary work, longer-term work, study, travel, training, or participation in athletic, cultural, or performance events.

For a nonimmigrant alien to travel to the United States and to apply for admission at a U.S. port of entry, he or she must usually have an entry visa, issued to him or her abroad by a U.S. consulate for the category of activity in which the nonimmigrant wishes to engage. This entry visa allows the individual to travel to a U.S. port of entry and apply for admission, within the dates stated on the entry visa. According to the U.S. Citizenship and Immigration Services (USCIS), possession of a current, valid visa *does not* guarantee admission into the United States. At the port of entry, USCIS will inspect the visa and question the alien to determine whether he or she shall be admitted to the United States and for how long. When admitted, the individual is issued a small white or green card in their passport—a Form I-94 Arrival-Departure Document—endorsed with the visa classification in which he or she was admitted and the duration of the authorized stay.

While an entry visa is necessary to travel to and apply for admission into the United States within the time period authorized by the visa, the entry visa alone does not provide any immigration status or employment authorization. It also does not control the period of time the alien is authorized to remain in the United States. It is the Form I-94, Arrival-Departure Document, that controls the duration of the alien's stay in the U.S. and lists the classification under which the alien is admitted.

Facts & Figures

EXAMPLES OF NONIMMIGRANT VISA TYPES

B-1, B-2	Visitor for business/pleasure
F-1	Student
H-1B	Specialty worker
H-2A	Temporary agricultural worker
H-2B	Temporary nonagricultural worker
J-1	Exchange visitor (may apply to an au pair)
L-1A or B	Intracompany Transferee
TN	Trade NAFTA

NOTE: *By statute, citizens of Canada are exempt from the entry visa requirement. They may enter the U.S. as visitors with no I-94. If they want to enter in a work or other nonimmigrant status, they may process their visa directly at the border and receive an I-94 card listing their status there. They do not need to visit a U.S. consulate. Citizens of Mexico may obtain Border Crossing Cards instead of visitor visas. However, Mexican visitors wishing to stay within the United States for more than 72 hours and within 25 miles of the border zone must obtain a Form I-94. Mexicans seeking entry in other than visitor status must obtain visa stamps at a U.S. consulate in Mexico.*

Some visitors to the U.S. are exempt from the entry visa requirement. Aliens from certain countries with low overstay rates may travel to the United States for business or pleasure trips for up to ninety days without a visa stamp. This *Visa Waiver Program* (VWP) currently applies to aliens from Andorra, Austria, Australia, Belgium, Brunei, Denmark, Finland, France, Germany, Iceland, Ireland, Italy, Japan, Liechtenstein, Luxembourg, Monaco, the Netherlands, New Zealand, Norway, Portugal, San Marino, Singapore, Slovenia, Spain, Sweden, Switzerland, and the United Kingdom.

Once within the United States, many nonimmigrant aliens may extend their nonimmigrant stay under the same classification or change to a different nonimmigrant status. (Aliens traveling on the VWP may neither extend nor change their nonimmigrant status.) However, an alien can change or extend status only if he or she is currently in valid nonimmigrant status. If the alien violates his or her admission terms—such as by overstaying his or her visa before applying for an extension—the application for extension or change will be denied. Form I-797, Notice of Action, provides the alien approval to extend his or her stay, and if applicable, to change status.

As a U.S. employer, you need to be aware of the aliens who are authorized to work within the United States, and if such employment is restricted in any way. There is no such thing as a general *work permit* under U.S. law. Work authorization for aliens is always connected to the visa status that they hold in the U.S. The following three classes of aliens allowed to work in the United States:

1. aliens authorized to work per their immigration status, such as green card holders;
2. aliens permitted to work for a specific employer per their immigration status (this is the case for almost all nonimmigrants that seek to work in the U.S.);
3. aliens who must first apply for and obtain permission from the U.S. Citizen and Immigration Services to accept employment within the United States (this is the case with aliens who are enrolled in U.S. universities and who are authorized to work in certain circumstances as part of their education).

Legal permanent residents of the U.S. (green card holders or immigrants) are legally entitled to work for any employer in the U.S. with no further paperwork, just as a U.S. citizen could. All other nonimmigrant aliens must either hold a visa authorizing them to work (i.e., students with work authorization) or be sponsored by a U.S. employer for one of the visa categories authorizing them to work for that employer.

SPONSORING ALIENS FOR TEMPORARY EMPLOYMENT

There are very few nonimmigrant visa categories that allow nonimmigrants to engage in household employment, and these visa categories are very restrictive. The most common categories are H-2 and J-1.

H-2B—Nonagricultural Temporary Worker

The H-2B category allows a foreigner to work for a period of up to one year in a temporary job. *Temporary* means a job that is seasonal, a one-time need, or peak load employment. The job will expire by its own terms within a year. The job itself must be temporary—it cannot be a permanent job that is temporarily vacant. An employer seeking an H-2B worker must advertise the position in accordance with Department of Labor requirements to provide there are no qualified U.S. workers for the position. The employer then files a petition with the USCIS to have the visa approved for the person the employer wishes to hire. If the alien is overseas, he or she then goes to a U.S. consulate overseas to get an entry visa for that visa category, after which he or she can enter the U.S. and begin work. If the alien is legally in the U.S. at the time of the employer's visa petition, the alien simultaneously files an application for change of status to H-2B status.

The H-2B visa is issued for a year or less. If an alien seeks to continue the same position without interruption, the visa can in theory be extended for up to three years, but the employer must prove each year that the position continues to be temporary. This is a heavy burden. The H-2B visa is often used for seasonal employment, such as landscape workers, summer restaurant help, or summer nannies. The H-2B visa can also be used for child care, where the child care requirement will terminate when the child goes to school. Some families have also sponsored eldercare assistance, seeking to keep their elderly parents at home a little longer before a nursing home is unavoidable.

Only 66,000 H-2B visas can be issued each year to new H-2B workers—33,000 are issued in each half of the government's fiscal year, and employers frequently find themselves unable to bring in workers on a timely basis due to cap issues. *Returning workers*—i.e., seasonal workers who have held H-2B visas within the last three years, but who have returned home at the end of their temporary employment—are not subject to the cap.

J-1—Exchange Visitor

The J-1 visa is for cultural exchange visitors, and covers a variety of different visa types intended to create exchange opportunities for foreigners. The J programs are administered by entities approved by the U.S. Department of

State, and include several different visa types interesting to household employers. There are, for example, two different programs that permit families to bring a foreign au pair to the United States for one to two years to help with child care. There are also summer work-travel programs for foreign college students. Household employers interested in such visas should contact one of the agencies authorized by the Department of State to administer such programs.

SPONSORING FOREIGN WORKERS FOR PERMANENT EMPLOYMENT

Under Sections 203 and 212(a)(5)(A) of the INA, employers may petition the federal government for approval to hire a foreign worker to work permanently within the United States. However, this is very difficult to do. The employer must engage in a defined recruitment process to establish that there are no qualified U.S. workers to take the position. If the employer clears this hurdle, it must next file a *visa petition* with the USCIS, seeking to have the foreign worker approved for a visa in one of the categories for which an immigrant visa can be issued. This can take from nine months to two years, depending on USCIS backlogs at any point in time. The final step is an application by the foreign worker to have the green card actually issued to him or her. At this point, the process founders. There are more applicants for green cards than there are green cards available, and long waiting lists exist, particularly for the visa categories with lower education and experience requirements. Waiting periods for professional and skilled workers currently exceed five years, and waiting periods for unskilled workers are even longer. This is not currently a realistic option for most household employers.

CONSEQUENCES OF HIRING AN UNAUTHORIZED ALIEN

Under the *Immigration Reform and Control Act of 1986*, employers may hire only persons who may legally work in the United States—U.S. citizens, legal permanent residents, asylees, refugees, and other aliens authorized to work in the United States. United States employers who knowingly employ an unauthorized alien in the United States can be ordered to cease and desist, and be fined a civil penalty—which could reach as high as $25,000—for failing to comply with Form I-9. Employers who commit a first offense for a single employee or two often receive only an educational visit and a warning. The U.S. Citizenship and Immigration Services' goal is compliance, not penalization of unknowing employers. Employers who engage in a pattern and practice of employing unauthorized aliens will face full penalties.

Employers of four or more persons must verify the identity and employment eligibility of anyone to be hired through completion of *Form I-9* (*Employment Eligibility Verification*). Each completed I-9 must be kept on file for at least three years, or one year after employment ends, whichever is longer. Employers who fail to properly complete, retain, and present Form I-9 for inspection (as required by federal law) may incur civil penalties of up to $1,100 per employee.

Criminal penalties could include fines up to $3,000 per unauthorized employee and up to six months of imprisonment, as issued by the U.S. Department of Homeland Security.

Employees who knowingly use fraudulent documents, identity documents issued to other people, or other false materials to meet the employment eligibility verification requirements in Form I-9 may face fines and imprisonment for up to five years.

Where You Live Determines the Law

Every household employer is subject to federal law, state law, and local laws. Jurisdiction is generally based on the physical location of the household. Examples from several states and localities follow.

CALIFORNIA FAIR EMPLOYMENT & HOUSING ACT

The *California Fair Employment & Housing Act* (FEHA) requires that any person employing five or more employees not discriminate on the basis of sex, race, age, national origin, or physical disability in employment or housing.

MASSACHUSETTS LABOR LAW

The Massachusetts Department of Labor requires all placement agencies to inform clients about labor laws that apply to them. Each agency has to provide a copy of the Department of Labor's leaflet, which discusses the Massachusetts *Minimum Fair Wage Law* (including information on who is covered, payment of wages, overtime, child labor, service, deductions, meal breaks, minimum daily hours, and so forth), to every family and every employee who applies to the agency.

NEW YORK CITY LOCAL LAW NO. 33:
THE FIRST IN THE NATION

One of the first of its kind in the nation, the City of New York Local Law No. 33 for the Year 2003 mandates that every licensed employment agency under the jurisdiction of the commissioner and engaged in the job placement of household employees must provide to each applicant for household employment, and to his or her prospective employer, a written statement indicating the rights afforded to household and domestic employees under the law, as well as employer obligations under the law ("the law" is that of New York City, New York State, and the United States of America). The statement must include (at least) a general description of mandated employee rights and employer obligations regarding minimum wage, overtime, hours of work, recordkeeping, workers' compensation, Social Security payments, and unemployment and disability insurance coverage.

The New York City Council enacted Local Law No. 33 to protect the rights of the city's hundreds of thousands of domestic workers. Licensed employment agencies must provide to each prospective household employee a written statement, in a form approved by the commissioner, that fully and accurately describes the nature and terms of employment, including the name and address of the person to whom the applicant is to apply for such employment, the name and address of the person authorizing the hiring for such position, wages, hours of work, the kind of services to be performed, and the agency fee. Every employment agency must keep a duplicate copy of the written statement of job conditions on file in its principal place of business for a period of three years.

GTM Household Employment Experts™ testified and provided the council with information on tax laws to be considered in household employment, as well as what is considered reasonable within the industry. Several agencies were involved during the City Council's decision to enact this law, including My Child's Best Friend, A Choice Nanny, Pavillion Agency, Robin Kellner Agency, the Professional Nanny Institute, and Best Domestic.

At present, this is the only such local law in the nation, but it may be replicated in other localities.

CASE STUDY

John Robertson
International Household Trainer, Coach, Consultant
John G. Robertson, Inc.
London, England

A leading trainer and coach for all aspects of the personal service industry—in particular, household services—John Robertson said that after working in the personal service industry and in the corporate world, he much prefers personal service.

Robertson began his career in his early 20s as a household manager/butler in North America, and then spent many years in the Fortune 500 business world. Today, Robertson operates his own international training company for employees and employers in the personal service industry, and teaches at the International Guild of Professional Butlers' International Butler Academy in the Netherlands. Traveling throughout the world, he works one-on-one with household employers and employees, as well as with private associations and service-centered businesses, such as luxury hotels and golf clubs.

In addition, private service employers contract with Robertson to assist them in hiring service employees. Robertson conducts telephone interviews to narrow the field of candidates. One of the first questions he asks candidates is what good service means to them, explaining that by identifying the experience that made someone feel like a million dollars, he can readily equate that episode with what the employee will be doing daily for his or her employer.

"The most important thing to understand in household employment is where you are and what you are doing," he said. "High energy, motivated people do well....Being in service does not mean being servile....The job is not to set the table; it's to support a lifestyle, to provide service....I can teach pigeons to set a table!"

Every household employee must know his or her employer's mission of the home, said Robertson. The key focus of the home may be on the family, the children's education, recreation, charitable fundraising, or political endeavors. Everything the employee does furthers that mission, he said.

"It is a true honor to be allowed to work with someone in his or her home," said Robertson. "There is a tremendous deposition of trust and responsibility—even if the job is dusting baseboards with a toothbrush."

Laughing Robertson said he "was born a butler. I thought it was the neatest job....It is a job for someone who takes control, organizes, and strives for perfection....It must be perfect; that's what we do."

According to Robertson, general awareness of the private service market has grown, particularly within the United States. Stressing that personal service employees must be in the field for the right reasons, Robertson noted that, while the industry offers no job security and no unions, there is a job for everyone—those who want to work weekends, those who do not, etc.—and that if someone loves what he or she does for a living, then the money will follow, and overall employee benefits and perks can be tremendous.

When interviewing, a household employer should try to determine the candidate's attitude toward personal service and the potential effect it may have on the household. Ask yourself, "Is this applicant's outlook appropriate in order to meet the household's service goals?"

—Guy

Hiring Checklist

√ Know and abide by federal, state, and local employment and labor laws.

√ Be thorough and clear in writing job descriptions and work agreements or contracts. To help you keep focused on your positions objectives, reference the job description often—in interviews, in offer letters, and so on.

√ Be professional. Household employees are pursuing their careers in "real jobs."

√ Confirm household employees' employment eligibility status by completing Form I-9.

√ Interview, check references, send offer letters, and provide new hires with an employee handbook.

√ Obtain and file a signed waiver from the job applicant to complete the background checks, and follow the suggested background checks listed on pages 25–26.

√ If working with an agency, contact the agency to determine whether any additional action needs to be done prior to making your hiring decision.

√ Before making your final decision, review the applicant's references and make additional calls to the applicant's prior employers and coworkers.

√ When contacting the applicant to offer the job, have your offer letter prepared, as well as any other pertinent information, such as a contract.

√ Finally, schedule another meeting with the applicant. Review the job description, offer (as written in your prepared letter), contract, and so on. Use this meeting to address any outstanding issues at this point and to finalize the hiring process (i.e., start date, work hours, etc.).

√ Most importantly, when hiring a nanny or other person to work within your home, always hire the best and never compromise.

3

Using an Agency to Hire Household Help

Hiring household employees is not easy. There is much to know and much to do. Retaining a good agency is convenient and efficient. A good agency is a helpful resource in finding an employee. After all, household employers hire staff to make life more convenient, easier, and fun—enabling the employer to direct his or her energies toward enjoying his or her family or home. An agency will take applications, screen candidates, help match candidates with employers, conduct interviews, and offer advice on household employment, job descriptions, work agreements, and employment practices. Ultimately, the household employer saves time and energy by using an agency to sort and match candidates for the specific needs of the home and job description.

First-time household employers may want to work with a licensed agency, leveraging the wealth of knowledge and experience to save time and do it right the first time—and learn along the way. After working with a reputable agency and gaining the knowledge and insight that really only comes with experience, a household employer may feel secure and comfortable when taking on the next household hire. Nanny and household employment agencies are valuable resources. Partner with them. Shadow your agency professionals. Remember, you want to do this right the first time, if possible. It remains up to you to determine if this nanny candidate will work best within your home. While your agency partners will be invested in getting this hire right for you, they will not be living it every day, every hour, every minute—you will.

In the household employment industry today, there are more than six hundred agencies in the United States. The quality of agencies can be as different as night and day. Each offers its own experience level and candidate selection process. A consumer needs to know what to look for when selecting an agency. The following information should help.

Why Use an Agency?

Most household employers seek the knowledge and experience an agency offers them, as well as the saved time and hard work. Plus, many household employers enjoy the security in knowing that an agency is their advocate throughout the entire process and employment of the nanny.

BENEFITS OF AN AGENCY

There are many benefits to using an agency to hire household help. One benefit is saving time. An agency saves you significant time and effort by pre-screening applicants for you. This involves phone screening, face-to-face interviews, and extensive reference checking. The agency also verifies the applicants' references, confirms employment dates, and checks into any gaps in employment. The agency identifies any fake résumés for example, by being thorough when verifying education completed. All in all, this is a very time-consuming process, and most potential employers are unable to take the time out of busy schedules to conduct the in-depth screening needed for hiring a household employee.

A second benefit is that when you are hiring someone to work in your home, experience in finding applicants is a must. An agency is equipped with experienced personnel, focused on finding the right help for you and your family. They will perform a full background check on potential applicants for you. Some will also assist with the hiring process, such as helping you develop the job offer, job description, compensation package, and other considerations. An agency can also offer you resources, such as tax and payroll service, training for the new employee, and ongoing support for the household employee.

While working with you, an agency should be an advocate before, during, and even after your nanny is hired.

How to Find a Reputable Agency

The best way to find a reputable agency is to talk to other people who have already hired a household employee through an agency. Personal recommendations give an honest story and will provide much-needed details. Also, employers may investigate agencies online and in the Yellow Pages. See if the agency is a member of an industry association. For example, a nanny placement agency may be a member of the National Alliance of Professional Nanny Agencies (**www.theapna.org**) or the International Nanny Association (**www.nanny.org**). Also, when contacting an agency, always ask if it is licensed, insured, and bonded.

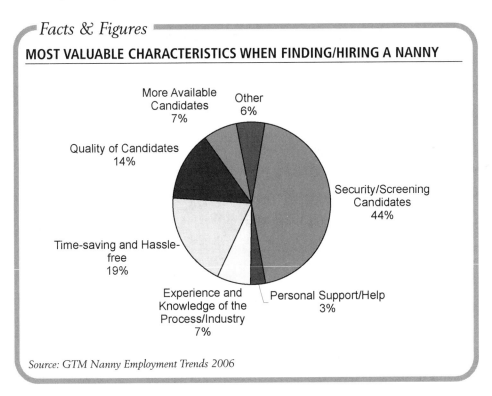

Facts & Figures

MOST VALUABLE CHARACTERISTICS WHEN FINDING/HIRING A NANNY

More Available Candidates 7%

Other 6%

Quality of Candidates 14%

Security/Screening Candidates 44%

Time-saving and Hassle-free 19%

Experience and Knowledge of the Process/Industry 7%

Personal Support/Help 3%

Source: GTM Nanny Employment Trends 2006

What to Ask an Agency

Be as specific as possible about your needs, so the agency can provide the best candidates to you for your position. The following paragraphs provide lists of questions to ask and some things to consider when first starting out with an agency.

The following are specific questions you should ask agencies you are considering:

- How long has the agency been actively placing household employees? What has been the agency's success rate (i.e., how many placements the agency has made, where they were, and generally how long they lasted)?
- Does it have any accreditation or is it licensed by the state?
- Where are applicants recruited from?
- What experience and skills does the agency require from applicants?
- Does the agency provide training for employees (i.e., does the agency hold CPR classes for nannies or time management training for personnel assistants)?
- Does the agency have on-call hours for clients or candidates in case of emergencies?

Other information you will need to know when working with an agency includes:

- the agency's placement practices (i.e., the agency provides the employer with a minimum of three candidates, and the agency will replace a worker if for some reason a placement does not work out during a set probation period);
- the agency's fees and what those fees cover (i.e., whether an agency fee covers a candidate's background checks, or if that is a separate responsibility for the household employer);
- the kind of support the agency provides after a candidate has been hired;
- the extras and their costs;
- if the agency requires payment only when a nanny is placed, or if there are up-front fees that the household employer must pay;
- if there is a payment schedule;

- the agency's guarantee policy and what must occur to ensure that it is in effect (i.e., the employer and employee must fully complete and sign the work agreement and submit it to the agency within three weeks after hire);
- the agency's refund policy;
- if the agency has candidates to fill the position now;
- the standard time frame to fill a position;
- how the agency screens applicants (i.e., whether all applicants are interviewed in person, and if so, how many staff members within the agency interview the applicant);
- who pays for travel expenses when the household employer interviews candidates—the agency, the candidate, or the household employer;
- the number of references required for an applicant (i.e., what questions the agency asks, if the household employer can see the written references, and if the household employer may contact the applicant's references);
- other than background checks, whether the agency conducts other screening, such as personality profile, drug testing, or a medical exam;
- how information about the household is gathered (i.e., whether the agency visits the home or checks references of the family, and if a written application is part of the placement process); and,
- the average candidate's profile (i.e., age, education, salary range).

TOP CONCERNS

A household employer needs to discuss what he or she requires for the nanny to adequately fill the position with an agency. Thinking through these top concerns will help an employer target what candidate qualifications and skills are most important to the household. These top concerns include:

- relevant experience;
- relevant qualifications;
- personality type preferences;
- references;
- salary;

> ## Our Advice
>
> *"Good home care can have a beneficial effect on the children's development and on the family's home life. In-home child care [for instance] should not be perceived as a threat. It should be a welcome joy to a family."*
> —*Ilo Milton*
>   *President*
>   *FamilyWise, Inc.*
>   *Bedford, NY*
>   *GTM Partner Agency*

- benefits (paid vacations, health insurance, car use, holidays, retirement plans, etc.);
- hours/schedule;
- philosophy on service (i.e., a nanny's philosophy on child rearing);
- languages;
- appearance and conduct;
- responsibility;
- communication skills;
- team player;
- reliability; and,
- commitment.

What to Tell an Agency

Honesty is the very best policy. The agency needs a clear and accurate representation of the family, household, job requirements, and so on, to be able to place the best household employee for the position. Employers will need to apply their honesty in *packaging* themselves, their employment practices, the household's culture, and what they need and are seeking in the household employee. When speaking to an agency, employers need to specify details regarding:

- the hiring time frame;
- the work schedule;
- all individuals' needs within the household, including other household help;
- their expectations of the agency;
- their expectations of the household employee;
- compensation and benefits packages; and,
- any and all special requirements, such as extensive travel with the family, holiday needs, and on-call hours.

When first discussing your position, be sure to tell the agency:

- when you are looking to hire the employee;
- how long of a commitment you are looking for from an employee;
- what the job requirements will entail (i.e., strictly child care or any housework included);

- if there is a home office and if the parent/employer works from home (if so, also explain if the parent/employer will be on-site while the employee is working);
- what kind of surveillance you have installed or will install to covertly check on a nanny;
- if travel will be required for this position; and,
- if transportation is required for the position (reimbursement for gas/mileage).

Remember, open communication is the best policy when acquiring agency assistance. Anything but the truth will potentially delay the hire, misconstrue employment objectives, and create uncertainty, misunderstanding, and worse yet, hard feelings, mistrust, and anger.

CASE STUDY

DENISE COLLINS
CEO
IN-HOUSE STAFFING AT AUNT ANN'S AGENCY
DALY CITY, CA
GTM PARTNER AGENCY

In-house Staffing at Aunt Ann's Agency, Inc., in operation for forty-five years, refers an equal number of nannies and other household help to clients in the San Francisco Bay area. According to the agency CEO Denise Collins, clients are highly educated, highly salaried people who often have been raised with staff and are now hiring staff themselves. These employers offer benefit packages to their household help and recognize them as professionals.

"This has been our core clientele, and they take care of their household help very well," said Collins. "In the 1980s, we began to see two-income families looking to hire help, and we experienced huge growth in housekeeping placements and then child care. It is a quality-of-life decision, and along with that came a higher set of expectations that this person would be included in the family. New employers need to put in place all the tools to make the working relationship successful. They have to learn how to hire a person

who will come into their home to work. The accountability of the working relationship is the family's—the employer's—not the agency's."

For these first-time employers, Collins said the agency needs to educate them on everything to do with employing household help. "Even people who handle HR issues at work need to be educated, because of differences in the workweek, payroll, taxes, and laws," she noted. "Plus, they must file different forms."

To help, the agency holds public education sessions on employing child care and eldercare professionals in the home. "It's a buyer beware market," said Collins, who noted that some unethical agencies are a big issue in California. "There's no certification or regulation. It's pretty predatory, and the population most affected are the seniors."

An effective household employer conducts effective human resource management. This begins with deciding whether or not to outsource the recruiting and screening to an agency. The role of an agency is to make it a much easier, more convenient process while presenting the best candidates that match an employer's philosophy and position requirements. A good agency adds value by how well it advises an employer on the position, management techniques, and tools that help the employer be successful.
—Guy

CASE STUDY

Cliff Greenhouse
President
Pavillion Agency
New York, NY
GTM Partner Agency

Continuing a business begun by his father forty years ago, Cliff Greenhouse works in tandem with his brother, Keith, at the Pavillion Agency.

During the growth in dual-income families in the mid-1980s, Greenhouse instituted a nanny placement program that matches well-educated, experienced nannies with affluent families. In addition, he created The Nanny Authority, a sister company based in New Jersey that places high-quality nannies with dual-career families. According to Greenhouse, his agency's success lies in its meticulous and thorough screening and matching services.

The agency not only works to fill clients' requirements, said Greenhouse, but to establish long-term relationships. "The agency guides their clients— we seldom need to give advice or educate them on their role as an employer," *he added. The vast majority of his clients grew up with nannies and house-keepers. "So, basically what I do is identify their needs and find them people that will satisfy their requirements while fitting in to the 'personality' of their home."*

The one issue Greenhouse does see throughout the industry is communication. "Staff not knowing the proper way to communicate, especially when they are unhappy and when employers are not being polite enough," *he said.*

According to Greenhouse, his clients are comforted knowing that the agency has interviewed and spoken with household employees at length before placement. "That's what makes us who we are," he noted. "It works for us, and we are very proud of what we have here."

"We have experience and can handle the needs of very demanding families," Greenhouse added. "Our household help are highly intelligent and accomplished people...but why we are so successful is that we are very professional in an industry that is not very professional. The people I place view this as a career and comparable to any other industry. They are serious, proud of what they do, and extremely professional themselves."

When consulting an agency, a household employer should understand the role the agent can play—from setting an applicant's expectations to developing the job description, defining and communicating the home's culture and what the employer's expectations are long before the employer ever meets the applicant.
—Guy

Using an Agency Checklist

√ Find out as much as possible about the agency, including its placement procedures.

√ Prepare a list of questions for the agency, including practices, fees, post-placement support, and background screening.

√ Ask whether the agency belongs to any industry associations. If so, ask which ones.

√ Ask for and check the agency's references.

√ Go to an agency with a clear idea on the household employee required, and know what responsibilities, experience, and personality traits the household employee should have to best perform within the household.

√ Be sure to ask the agency for a complete list of fees and what is covered. Pay attention to hidden costs, so you are not surprised down the road, when you are already entrenched with the agency in the hiring process.

4

The Work Agreement

Work agreements are essential with household employment, since household positions are so customized to the specific home in question. From the start, the work agreement establishes a clear understanding between the employer and employee regarding the employee's duties and responsibilities, and all that is expected from both the employer and employee. The most effective work agreement is in writing and covers all aspects of working in the household—including the employee's work schedule, required daily duties, compensation, benefits, termination, and confidentiality clause. Lack of a work agreement can contribute to dissatisfaction in the workplace and a high employee turnover rate. Therefore, work agreements can be considered an important step in building a long-lasting relationship in which all parties clearly understand their responsibilities and expectations.

A CRITICAL STEP IN BUILDING A SUCCESSFUL RELATIONSHIP

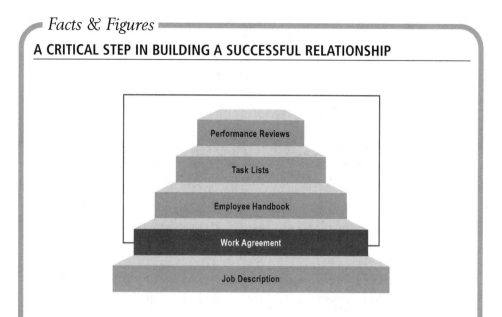

Performance Reviews. A means to communicate employer feedback to employees regarding how well they are meeting the objectives of the household, demonstrated by task list activities and satisfaction of the employee's constituents, such as dependents, other staff, household manager, and homeowner.

Task Lists. The to-do lists to meet the job descriptions objectives. Could be daily, weekly, special projects, seasonal activities, and so on, and if a task has to be done with precision, it may call for a specific procedure.

Employee Handbook. Comprehensive set of policies addressing expectations for employment responsibilities and conduct. Includes use of property, time off, resignation, paydays, performance reviews, and so on.

Work Agreement. Detailed outline of the employment engagement with specific compensation, benefits, terms, and so on. Establishes a clear understanding between the employer and employee regarding the employee's duties and responsibilities, and all that is expected from both the employer and employee.

Job Description. A precisely written description of the responsibilities and requirements that specify employer objectives.

Job Description

A work agreement and job description go hand in hand. Often, they contain the same material, but a household employer needs to develop both, since a job description is written *before* an employee is hired, and a work agreement is written *after* the employee is hired and is developed *with* the employee before his or her first day on the job.

A job description is, essentially, all the work to be done by the nanny, housekeeper, houseman, etc. It is really your first official document regarding your household employee hire. When developing it, in a way, you are detailing how you will accomplish your goal. Before you pick up your pen to write the job description, think about what it is you want to accomplish—what is the goal that has brought you to this need for hiring a household employee?

Before all else, thoroughly think through what the position needs to accomplish, which tasks and duties are required to achieve the position's goals, and what skills, abilities, and talents the employee must have to satisfactorily perform all that is required. Only then can a comprehensive job description be developed. (see "Developing the Job Description" in Chapter 2 on page 19.)

Consider, for example, the following:

- Will the household employee need a car and a valid driver's license? (Will the nanny be required to drive the child to a play date or school? Will the cook need to drive to the grocery store for necessary ingredients? Will the gardener need to drive to a nursery or an equipment store?)
- Will a nanny or household manager be required to take the child to the park or playground on a schedule or from time to time?
- Will a nanny caring for two children be expected to prepare and feed the children breakfast and lunch?
- Will the nanny be required to clean lunch dishes after the children have eaten?
- Will all household employees be expected to answer the telephone and take messages?
- Will all household help be expected to sign for deliveries and packages?

• Will an employee need protective clothing or equipment? (Will the gardener need protective goggles when operating equipment? Will the driver need cover-ups and gloves for car maintenance tasks? Will the eldercare employee need face masks, gowns, and protective gloves?)

There is a lot to think about and much to decide. If you are seeking a nanny, then you will want the nanny to focus fully on caring for the children—not to necessarily perform housekeeping chores. It may be that you need both a nanny and a housekeeper.

Each household's and each household employer's needs vary greatly with each situation. Job descriptions should list all of the necessary qualifications (skills, education, certification, or license), essential job functions, and functions that are desired but not mandatory. Comprehensive job descriptions begin the employment on solid ground. With the job description in hand, the hiring process can begin. (See Appendix D for a sample job description.)

The owner of a northwest placement agency said she can log as much as 150 hours on some accounts when placing a household employee, and she spends hours with clients, meeting in their homes.

"Every job is customized, so you can't have a cookie-cutter job description or profile," she said. "I spend a lot of time getting to know the family and know what they want. I walk them through the whole specifications of the job. This research ensures the right person for the job is placed."

This owner leans heavily on the job description and work agreement. Regarding nannies, the former nanny turned owner, said "Generally, people don't realize how tough of a job it really is—how much work and responsibility it is. It is a real job requiring super-power intuition and the ability to make executive decisions on behalf of someone else, sometimes without guidance or with little feedback."

CASE STUDY

Lin Taylor-Pleiman
Owner/Operator
American Domestic Agency, Inc.
Whiteford and Greenville, DE
GTM Partner Agency

*American Domestic Agency, Inc. offers domestic-related employment place-
ments in Maryland, Delaware, and Pennsylvania. The agency opened in
2002 after the owners spent ten months exhaustively researching household
employment legal issues, contracts, insurance, and other critical matters.*

*Noting the delicacy of the household employment industry, Lin Taylor-
Pleiman said a signed work agreement is proof that "the parties sat down,
talked, and worked out issues so the employee and the employer are fully
aware of each other's expectations."*

*The agency is so adamant about the written agreement that it requires
clients to submit a copy of the agreement within seven days of an employee's start date. If a client fails to do so, the agency will not honor its replacement guarantee if the placement fails.*

*"We've learned it's a must," said Taylor-Pleiman. "It addresses a multi-
tude of areas, even what happens when there's a snow day. Both parties
must know the expectations of the other party in order to have a good relationship, in which the employee can focus on her duties and not worry about
being treated unfairly."*

*Taylor-Pleiman speaks from experience. Her agency was begun after her
daughter left a very dissatisfying experience as a nanny. "There are standard areas that need to be addressed, regardless of position," she noted.
"The importance of communication is paramount. With this work agreement, most of the time problems can be rectified….Most employers want the
employees to be an extension of the family, and for the most part, want a
good, close relationship."*

*Stating that the work agreement is an advantage to both the employer
and employee, Taylor-Pleiman said she believes the work agreement helps*

household employees gain recognition as professionals. "Employees are demanding taxes be paid and that they be legitimized. The work agreement is an instrumental step in that."

> *As a household employer, clear expectations are paramount. This is why the work agreement is so critical to the beginning of the employer-employee relationship, even for a relationship on the best of terms. Work agreements spell out the employment conditions, general tasks, and responsibilities of the employer and employee within that household. With it, both the employer and employee are reducing the likelihood that problems will occur.*
> *—Guy*

Our Advice

"An in-home caregiver's primary responsibility is the care and the nurturing of young children, not folding the laundry or mopping the floor. Employers need to remember the nanny's priorities—first, provide a happy, safe, convenient child care atmosphere; then, if there's time, a nanny can fold the children's clothes."
—Anne Johnson
  Long-term Placement Director
  A New England Nanny
  Clifton Park, NY

Work Agreement

The work agreement is an essential document for both the household employer and employee. A comprehensive work agreement—often written by both the employer and employee—goes a long way in establishing a successful working relationship. Not only will it prevent problems from occurring, it will set the tone of the working relationship with open and clear communications.

WHY THE WORK AGREEMENT IS IMPORTANT

There are many reasons why household employers enter into *work agreements* (p.256) with their new household employee(s). The most popular reason is to help ensure clear and concise communication around terms and conditions of employment. As all relationships seem to have an initial *honeymoon period*, verbal agreements and commitments can sometimes be fuzzy and possibly forgotten, and as a result, cause strain on the employment relationship. The work agreement outlines these commitments in a professional manner, creates the seriousness that the household position and employment require, and help to reduce employment disputes.

WHY ENTER INTO A WORK AGREEMENT

The work agreement helps safeguard the cost of recruiting and obtaining a household employee. Turnover costs could run thousands of dollars, especially considering the cost of advertising; time spent to screen, interview, and reference check; placement agency fee; training costs; and, employer time lost from work or other activities.

A work agreement is legally enforceable. However, an employer may not want to enforce the terms of the agreement, as it would not serve the household to retain an uninterested or disgruntled employee. Yet, an employer may very well want to enforce the *Confidentiality Agreement* (p.266) to protect the family's personal affairs that an employee may have learned during the course of his or her employment. For the nanny or other household employee, a legally enforced work agreement serves to protect his or her compensation, benefits, and severance pay, as well as job description requirements.

Our Advice

"People do treat the work relationship in a relaxed manner, as a friend rather than employer-employee. That's when issues come up."
—Sylvia Greenbaum
    Co-owner
    Boston Nanny Centre, Inc.
    Boston, MA

Our Advice

"I strongly recommend work agreements between household employers and domestic employees. A work agreement outlines your nanny's terms of employment and specifies how you expect her to care for your child. Although not legally required, an agreement is enforceable and greatly reduces potential disputes. Overall, an agreement is an integral part of any working relationship and provides important protections to both the employee and the employer."
—Bob King, Esq.
    Founder and CEO
    Legally Nanny
    Irvine, CA
    GTM Partner

WORK AGREEMENT BENEFITS

A work agreement is a win-win—it helps the employer and nanny clearly establish standards, rules, and procedures for the household and for the nanny job. From listing the hours the nanny is expected to work and what his or her salary is, to explaining what a nanny must do if inclement weather prevents him or her from traveling to work, even to defining if the nanny should be taking meals with the children—it is all specified within the work agreement. No matter is too small, because it all goes to one thing—the smooth operation of your household. This is how you set the stage for success in your employment.

There are many pertinent reasons why you should develop, maintain (i.e., update as needed), and enforce a work agreement.

- A written work agreement helps to ensure the employment of a particualrly desirable employee. It protects an employer's confidential information and helps to ensure the employment of a particularly desirable employee. If a nanny candidate does not want to join you in developing a work agreement, or does not wish to sign one that has been developed, red flags should appear immediately. You need to think: why does this nanny not want to enter into an agreement that details his or her job? The actual existence of a work agreement acts as a tool for you to target the best candidates—and discount those who are disagreeable.
- The work agreement is a cooperative endeavor, ideally to be developed (and revised) together (employer with employee). It details:
  - ✦ the nanny's job, including establishing a term of employment (e.g., the nanny job may be for a one-year term, with a date to review the nanny's performance, the work agreement, and the possible extension of the employment to another year);
  - ✦ your expectations (spell out the nanny's duties—be specific and include important considerations to your household, such as protecting the confidential information contained within the home);
  - ✦ the employee's expectations;
  - ✦ household procedures and instructions the employee will use daily in the job; and,
  - ✦ the employees compensation and benefits.

- Written work agreements must meet the needs of all parties involved. It is even feasible to use a written work agreement to help determine whether an employee may be terminated without *good cause* and possibly on short notice (i.e., at-will employment). Use it as a litmus test, checking if the nanny did the tasks described in the work agreement, in the method described in the work agreement, and in the time frame specified in the work agreement.
- While compensation and benefits should be included in the work agreement, be mindful that the work agreement is an employment contract, and you, as the employer, must abide by it. Therefore, review the compensation and benefits wording to avoid any potential back pay liability.
- When developing a written work agreement, employers have many areas to consider. Be alert to the laws and standards involving employment. Employers must have a working knowledge of federal, state, and local laws, including the following.
    - Employers must abide by federal and state nondiscrimination laws. Many state laws go further than the federal law in barring discrimination based on marital status, arrest records, sexual orientation, and legal behaviors engaged in while off-duty (i.e., smoking).
    - Some states limit an employer's right to terminate an employment contract unless he or she can show good cause.
    - Be certain to consider the *Fair Labor Standards Act* (FLSA), the federal law governing compensation, minimum wage, the hiring of minors, and the *Immigration Reform and Control Act* (IRCA), which requires employers to verify the eligibility of employees to work in the United States. Also, most states enforce some form of minimum wage law for those job categories not covered by the FLSA.

HOW TO CREATE A WORK AGREEMENT

Ideally, consulting with an employment attorney is a best practice in developing a work agreement. However, some placement agencies may offer template agreement or provide samples obtained from its other clients. Employers may extrapolate ideas from template samples, and obtain input from friends or colleagues who have developed their own work agreements for their own household help.

Key Elements of a Work Agreement
The following list of key elements provide an overview of the common components that are included in most work agreements.

- *Recitals*—Employer is an individual and a Household Employer, resident of _____(state), and over the age of 18.
- *Employment*—Employment under this agreement is to begin on _____ and continue unless sooner terminated as provided herein.
- *Compensation* (see Chapter 6)—Subject to the following provisions of this agreement, the Employer agrees to pay the Employee a gross compensation hourly rate of $_____.
- *Benefits* (see Chapter 7)—Employee is entitled to _____ days of paid vacation annually. The vacation must be scheduled thirty days in advance and agreed to by employer. Vacation is based upon normal payment for a forty-hour workweek.
- *Terms and conditions of employment*—Employee may not drink alcohol, use illegal drugs, or smoke while on duty for the employer.
- *Termination of agreement* (see Chapter 11)— Employer may terminate employment by employee for violation of the work agreement's statement (D-1 on the work agreement in Appendix E) that holds an employee may not drink alcohol, use illegal drugs, or smoke while on duty for the employer.
- *Modifications and interpretation*—The job description may change by mutual consent. Therefore, the work agreement must be revised to reflect any changes.
- *Applicable laws*—The provisions of this agreement shall be constructed in accordance with laws of the state of _____.
- *Signature and date line*—Employer and employee should sign and date the original and each revision of the work agreement.
- *Work schedule (optional)*—Additional detail of a daily schedule broken down by day and by hour.

CASE STUDY

SYLVIA GREENBAUM
CO-OWNER
BOSTON NANNY CENTRE, INC.
NEWTON, MA
GTM PARTNER AGENCY

According to Sylvia Greenbaum, co-owner of Boston Nanny Centre, Inc., the lack of clear job requirements is a top reason household positions do not work—particularly when a family wishes a nanny to perform other household work unrelated to child care.

Greenbaum cited an example in which a nanny placed through the agency was charged with caring for twins. A work agreement specified that the nanny tend to the twins, and it did not require her to do any household work. The nanny worked hard caring for the twins, and the family agreed that she was doing an excellent job. Yet, after some time, the family began leaving daily notes asking the nanny to perform household chores and tasks. She became nervous and upset about the daily notes and saw no end in sight to her daily compounding responsibilities, which were not stipulated in the work agreement.

The family, first-time household employers, was upset with the nanny's attitude. Tension quickly and steadily increased. The parents then angrily confronted the nanny, who immediately resigned, believing her employers did not value or appreciate the high-quality care she provided to their children. The family's anger increased when left without a nanny, and the family threatened to withhold payment for the five days the nanny had already worked that week. (The agency reminded the family that as the employer it was legally responsible to pay the nanny for days she had worked.) Both client and nanny felt angry and mistreated.

"Clearly, it would have been better had the family and nanny discussed what household responsibilities were needed and what the nanny felt comfortable doing," said Greenbaum. "If this had been written in the agreement, the nanny and family would not have each felt taken advantage of."

According to Greenbaum, mixing household chores with child care depends on the personalities involved. "Sometimes nannies will do other jobs (around the house) without being asked," she said. "It depends on the relationship. So many factors go into it."

Greenbaum's agency provides each client with a detailed work agreement and strongly encourages clients to complete it. However, many parents are new to parenthood, as well as to the employer role, and they do not yet realize all they wish their nannies to be and do. "They think that it's not totally unreasonable to say, 'Let's see how it is going,' or 'We're sure it'll work out,'" noted Greenbaum. "All nannies who care for children are doing other things, like preparing food, doing the children's laundry, cleaning, and organizing their toys. Yet, when children are in school or napping, some will do some shopping, run errands, and put a load of the employers' laundry in the washer. Some say, 'I'll care for the child but not for the parents,' or some say, 'I like to keep busy.' It is so individual. It's best if all requirements are talked about before the nanny is hired."

Greenbaum said difficulty is inherent in the nanny-employer relationship. "People do treat the work relationship in a relaxed manner," she said. "Sort of as a friend rather than employer-employee, and that's when issues come up."

Greenbaum has great empathy for families, who must learn so many different pieces that go into the employer role during a stress-filled time while trying to meet all of their professional and personal obligations. Plus, added Greenbaum, stress naturally arises when parents first leave their children with another adult.

Often referring parents to GTM for employer information, as well as wage and tax assistance, Greenbaum noted that the hiring process is both complex and lengthy, typically taking a while to find the right person for the right job and the right family. "[Hiring a nanny] is such a personal decision," she said. "People have to feel that it's right. It can be a very long process. Sometimes there's magic, and it all comes together. It could take one day to find the right nanny, but I tell families, if possible, give it at least two months."

Given all of the processes and pieces, Greenbaum is not surprised that a first-time hire does not often go smoothly. "People are busy," she said, "and the nanny process is time-consuming, so all these pieces that need to be included in the work agreement form are pushed to the back burner. It's understandable why some serious problems happen."

Household employers must take the same professional attitude toward job descriptions and work agreements in the household as do corporations. Doing so will greatly help establish the first-time as well as the experienced employer as a professional, and put structure around the position.

—Guy

Work Agreement Checklist

An experienced employment attorney should review your work agreement. As you are preparing the agreement, keep these few tips in mind.

√ Think clearly about what to include in the work agreement, and if using an agency, get its input.

√ Be concise. There is no room for ambiguity in the phrasing of the work agreement.

√ If using a standard work agreement template, customize it to suit the household's specific needs.

√ Leave no stone unturned. Include everything the job will involve.

√ Once written, discuss the work agreement with the employee.

√ Make sure the employee signs and dates the agreement, and receives a copy.

√ Be sure the agreement is in place prior to the employee's start date.

√ The agreement should be signed and dated by both the employer and employee, and it should be witnessed.

√ An agreement should be written so it is understandable by a high school graduate.

√ Font size must be a minimum 10-point size.

√ Agreement should cover all essential facts.

√ Put important passages in boldface.

√ Specify time periods and note reasonable limitations.

√ A confidentiality clause may be included in the work agreement. This clause extends during and after employment with the household.

√ If the employee expresses a concern, the employer should recommend that the employee seek his or her own legal counsel.

√ Provide a signed copy to the employee and file a signed copy in the employee's personnel file.

√ If working with a third party, such as a placement agency or attorney, send a signed copy to the third party for his or her records and for safekeeping.

5

Personnel Practices for the Home

The household employment industry is working to establish a professional structure around a very informal situation. The perception of the household occupation and the role within the home is often different for employers and employees. Many employers view hiring staff for their home as a personal responsibility, whereas household employees see it as employment. Even though the employment is not in an office or a retail setting, it is a worksite where employment laws prevail. Of course, for the employer, it also is a home and a sanctuary. It will take some effort for a household employer to view his or her home as another's workplace.

Clear communications, respectful treatment, openness to discussion, and adaptability should be what everyone in the household works toward to maintain a satisfying workplace.

An employment contract can alter the at-will nature of the employment relationship. As discussed here, the employment contract outlines the relationship, responsibilities, and duties, but is not designed to shift the employment from being at will.

The Employee Handbook

Like any employer, household employers must establish fair personnel practices and policies, and apply them equally to all staff. Providing each employee with an employee handbook that explains the household workplace's rules, practices, and policies is a necessity, and presents clear advantages to the employer.

An employee handbook lets employees know what the rules and practices are within the household. While highly prevalent in the corporate workplace, employee handbooks are noticeably absent in the majority of households today. In tandem with the work agreement, the employee handbook cements the household's employment policies and personnel practices.

All new employees should receive a handbook immediately upon hire or on the employment start date. The employer should have the employee sign an *Employee Handbook Acknowledgment Receipt.* (see p.268.) The employer should file this in the employee's personnel file. The release states that the employee was provided with information on important household HR issues, such as:

- Americans with Disabilities Act;
- antiharassment policies;
- Consolidated Omnibus Budget Reconciliation Act of 1985 (COBRA);
- discipline;
- dress code;
- educational assistance;
- employee assistance;
- employee benefits;
- equal employment opportunity;
- expense reimbursement;
- household philosophy and conduct;
- immigration law compliance;
- in-home surveillance;
- introductory or evaluation period;
- labor laws and how they apply;
- leave of absence;
- medical insurance;
- overtime;
- payroll and taxes;
- performance reviews;
- personnel file;
- references and background checks;

- retirement;
- salary increases, bonuses, and gifts;
- short-term disability;
- Social Security;
- termination, resignation, and exit interview procedures;
- time off;
- timekeeping and work schedules;
- unemployment insurance;
- use of employer property;
- workers' compensation insurance; and,
- workplace safety.

Reference this list when developing your household's employee handbook.

When developing a handbook, address any questions an employee has or any information an employee wants to know about his or her job and the workplace. For more insight into how to develop an employee handbook and create your own customized version, go to **www.gtm.com/resourcecenter**.

INTRODUCTORY ELEMENTS FOR EMPLOYEE HANDBOOK

There are many elements important to an employee handbook. You may want to include items such as a welcome letter to your employee, an at-will statement, and your policies regarding topics like use of technology and how to handle visitors to your home.

You may want to begin your employee handbook with a welcome letter to your employee and an at-will statement. The at-will statement may be included in the welcome letter to the employee, or it may stand alone as a separate written policy. Either way, it may be best for you to include the statement at the front of the employee handbook, thus clearly providing the employee with the at-will condition. A sample at-will employment statement, which is mandatory in fifteen states, is provided in the *Sample Work Agreement Sections*, pages 77–81.

In today's world, there are many technologies used to keep you informed and in touch—and even entertained. However, not all technology should be accessed during the workday. As an employer, you need to set your policy on an employee's access to and use of your computer, the

Internet, text messaging, mobile phone, handheld devices, television, or digitally recorded movies or shows. In addition, you may also need to set a policy for any equipment—your car, exercise machines, landline telephone—that is on the premises and may or may not be available to your employees. Take care in developing your policies, as your employee may need to use your equipment in order to perform his or her work duties.

During the course of the day or work shift, an employee may need to manage guests, visitors, or service professionals that may need or request access to the employer's home or property.

For a policy on dealing with service people, vendors or contractors, you may want to specify the nanny's or other household employee's involvement with repairmen, service professionals, and so on.

Following are sample sections of an employee handbook taken from GTM's Household HR handbook service.

Sample Work Agreement Sections

Welcome letter

Welcome to our home. We wish you every success here.

Please familiarize yourself with this handbook. You are responsible for reading, understanding, and complying with the policies and procedures within it.

The employee handbook is a policy guide and summary of employee benefits and working conditions. It is to be used as a reference tool and guide, and is not intended to be all-inclusive. No employee handbook can anticipate all circumstances or questions. Therefore, we reserve the right to revise, supplement, or withdraw any policy or portion of this handbook as necessary. When amendments to the household employee handbook are made, employees will be notified.

It is our intent to provide the best possible employment for household employees to excel in their positions. Our open door policy allows employees to ask questions and to discuss concerns or suggestions regarding the household and his or her position. By developing and maintaining clear communication, we hope to resolve any difficulties that may arise.

The information provided in the household employee handbook applies to all employees within the household, and is not a contract between the employer and the employee. This is not a work agreement or job description. The work agreement we developed and signed upon your hire details your role within the household. Your work agreement pertains only to you. This employee handbook is an overall guide to the household's employment practices and policies. If at any time the handbook and work agreement specify conflicting policies, the employee should view the work agreement as the superceding document.

The employee handbook does not constitute a contract or contractual commitment of continued employment.

Again, welcome to our household.

Regards,
(Name of Employer), Household Employer

At-will statement

The (Household Employer) household does not offer tenured or guaranteed employment. Employment is at-will and entered into voluntarily. You may resign at any time and for any reason without notice, and you may be terminated at any time—with or without cause—by (Household Employer).

Equal employment opportunity

The (Household Employer) household is committed to a policy of equal employment opportunity, and maintains a policy of nondiscrimination with employees and applicants for employment. Employment within the (Household Employer) household is not influenced in any manner by race, color, religion, sex, age, national origin, physical or mental disability, or any other basis prohibited by law. (Household Employer) household will reasonably accommodate a person with physical or mental disability, as long as the accommodation will not cause the (Household Employer) household undue hardship.

Workers' compensation insurance

The (Household Employer) household carries workers' compensation insurance to cover the cost of work-related and work-incurred injury or illness. Workers' compensation benefits help to pay for an injured or ill employee's medical treatment, as well as to cover a portion of the employee's income that may be lost while he or she is recovering. Workers' compensation benefits are mandated by state law, and benefits depend on the circumstances of each incident.

Social Security

All employees are covered under the federal Social Security Act, which provides for future security in case of retirement, disability, death, survivor benefits to dependents, and Medicare benefits. Employees pay a portion of their earnings into Social Security from each paycheck, and the employer matches the employee's deduction.

Use of employer property

Equipment essential in accomplishing job duties are expensive and may be difficult to replace. Employees who use household equipment, machines, tools, and other property to perform their duties are expected to follow proper usage and care. When using equipment and property, employees are required to follow all operating instructions, safety standards, and guidelines. If any household equipment or property is broken or damaged during an employee's job performance, the employee is expected to report it to the employer as soon as possible. The (Household Employer) household prohibits any household property to be removed from the premises. Unauthorized removal of household property or an employee's possession of household property off work premises will be considered theft, and the employee will be immediately dismissed and criminal charges will be made.

Use of phone, computer, and other equipment

Personal telephone calls and personal use of the household computer, Internet, and other equipment is not permissible unless otherwise directed or approved. The (Household Employer) household understands that employees will need to make personal phone calls (e.g., medical appointments) from time to time. If such phone calls are necessary, employees are required to keep them brief and to a minimum. (Household Employer) also understands that there are some occasions that merit personal use of household computer systems. Household employees using household communications resources do so knowing that the content of all internal and external communications utilizing household resources is the property of the (Household Employer) household and that (Household Employer) reserves the right to monitor and review the use and content of any such communications.

Use of vehicle(s)

The (Household Employer) household may require an employee to use the employer's car in order to complete job tasks. If driving is required, the employee will be permitted to use the employer's car. (Only employees with clean driver's licenses will be allowed use of the employer's car.)

Employees need to be aware that (Household Employer) is taking great expense to allow the household employee(s) to use (Household Employer) household vehicle(s). Repairs may be costly and parts may be difficult to replace. Improper, careless, negligent, destructive, or unsafe use or operation of (Household Employer) vehicle(s), as well as excessive or avoidable traffic and parking violations, may result in disciplinary action, up to and including termination.

Workplace visitors

The household does not allow employees to have visitors on work premises during their working hours without prior permission. On occasion, in specific circumstances and only with prior authorization by the employer, employees may have a family member or friend visit during working hours. During these occasions, employees are responsible for the conduct and safety of their visitors.

If an unauthorized individual is observed on household premises, employees are required to immediately telephone the police and contact the employers at the listed emergency number(s).

Work personnel and contractors

The (Household Employer) household will work directly with service and repair professionals and contractors concerning all household matters. (Household Employer) will arrange an appointment and inform the nanny of the time and date of the scheduled appointment. (Household Employer) requests that while inside the house, the employee:

- require all contractors to sign in and out of a service visit book upon entrance to and departure from the house;
- accompany the service technician, repairman, vendor, or contractor to the area in need of service;
- while at the house, contractors and service technicians should use their own mobile phones; if they do not have a mobile, the employee should accompany the individual to the entrance foyer's telephone, which the technician may use for local calls only;

- when work has been completed, the employee is to accompany the technician back to the entrance; and,
- if a vendor or service bill is left with the employee, the employee will paperclip the bill or service information to the service visit book page the vendor signed. The employee is to inform (Household Employer) that the service was performed and that the invoice or statement is included in the service visit book.

EXPENSE REPORTS AND REIMBURSEMENT FOR WORK-RELATED EXPENSES

An employer should detail—in the employee handbook—the process an employee must follow for reimbursement of work-related expenses or disbursement of spending money for an upcoming event. As part of the process, it is helpful to stipulate that an expense report must be submitted each month, fiscal quarter, or event, and whether the employer requires the original sales receipt or a photocopy of the sales receipt. Also, employers may include guidance on the minimum dollar amount when an original sales receipt or photocopy of the sales receipt is required (i.e., all expenses of $10 or more must be submitted with a receipt or photocopy of a receipt). For example, if a nanny spends $2 on an ice cream bar for a child at the playground, then a receipt (or photocopy of the receipt) is not mandatory. However, if a personal assistant spends $12.50 on office supplies, then a receipt (or photocopy of the receipt) must be attached to the *Expense Report.* (see p.269.)

A list of approved employer-covered expenses should be included within the employee handbook and amended as necessary. To ensure clarity, some employers also include a list of expenses that are not covered. For instance, some employers may cover an employee's mileage, tolls, and parking, but not maintenance costs or gas (which are actually included in the mileage reimbursement rate). Some employers may cover the costs of work-related cell phone calls, but not the cost of the cell phone or its monthly service charge. The handbook and the expense reimbursement form may include a clearly worded sentence recommending that an employee with any questions regarding reimbursement and employer-covered expenses check with the employer regarding coverage approval prior to the event or task.

CASE STUDY

TRISH STEVENS
NANNY
NEW YORK, NY

Trish Stevens said she became a nanny because she wanted to be "Mary Poppins."

"I knew I wanted to take care of children," said Stevens, who has been a nanny for twenty years and has worked in Indiana, Ohio, and New York. "Each job is different....Today, it is more of a profession, with more people thinking of it as a real job. Now, there are personal days and paid holidays. It's more than being a baby-sitter and more like being a teacher."

Stevens, who now cares for three children in New York City, ensures that work agreements are in place with her employers to clearly describe the job requirements. "It's not easy finding (the right) nanny, and it's not easy to find (the right) nanny job," said Stevens.

The agreement helps, but Stevens offers some tips on how household employers should treat their employees, including the following:

- *say thank you;*
- *remember that your nanny is there for the children, not to keep house;*
- *offer the business standard of five paid personal days and five paid sick days each year;*
- *pay for at least half of the employee's health insurance;*
- *if a nanny goes on vacation with the family, remember that it is the employers' vacation—not the nanny's (she or he still must care for the children)—and he or she still needs downtime;*
- *if an employer cannot afford a raise or a bonus, offer some time off, if appropriate;*
- *pay a nanny on the books, with the correct taxes withheld; and,*
- *understand that a household employee does not have the same resources as the employer. If an employer decides to take the next few days off, an offer for the employee to "get away" or use her or his vacation days during that time is not as generous as it may appear to the*

employer. Unexpectedly offering the employee an opportunity to take vacation time in just a matter of days does not allow for economical travel planning and scheduling.

For nannies, Stevens offers these tips:
- speak English, or the language agreed upon by employer and employee;
- support the parent, even if you do not agree;
- be trained in CPR and first aid; and,
- be sure to develop a work agreement with the employer.

A household employee's perspective is interesting to hear and is really no different from the expectations of those who work for large companies. All of these tips may be achieved by taking into account the employer's goals and the employee's needs when developing personnel policies, and by setting the stage for ongoing communication. In this case, an employer would most likely provide an employee handbook stating the termination, personal time off, salary increase, payroll, and employment policies that promote achieving household goals.

—Guy

CASE STUDY

DENISE SHADE
HOUSEHOLD EMPLOYER
SENIOR VICE PRESIDENT
FOREIGN EXCHANGE UNIT, KEY BANK
NEW YORK, NY
GTM PAYROLL AND TAX SERVICE CLIENT

Denise Shade, mother of two and senior vice president of Key Bank's foreign exchange unit, first sought in-home child care so her children could be on their own schedules and not adhere to their parents' work timetables. "Primarily, the kids did not have to mold to our jobs," she said. "They could nap when they wanted and not be woken up by us to be transported some-place else. Plus, as newborns, in-home child care limited their exposure to germs, compared to a setting with many children."

Shade first hired a nanny six years ago when her daughter was born. Although they first intended to hire a nanny who lived outside the home out of concern for their privacy, the Shades hired a live-in nanny because they wanted to hire a particular candidate who needed a live-in situation. They have had live-in nannies ever since.

"It worked out better than we expected," said Shade, who takes great care to respect the nanny's time. "We ensure that the nanny is done with work at 6 p.m. If we need child care at night, we hire a baby-sitter, or, if we need to, we'll hire the nanny for the night as a baby-sitter if she is available."

Respect for the nanny and his or her abilities is the key to Shade's suc-cessful employee relationships—and is the foundation for close connections that continue today. Shade's first nanny was ideal for the care required for a single newborn. When Shade gave birth to her son three years later, anoth-er nanny with multi-tasking skills was hired. Unfortunately, when the Shades moved from Ohio to Connecticut, the second nanny did not relocate, preferring to stay in close proximity to her family.

Shade's current nanny has been with the family since early 2003. In all, the family has had great experiences with nannies, and these have countered one poor experience —the result of the nanny having different expectations, said Shade.

Although already having enjoyed fantastic nanny relationships, Shade said that one was a "difficult experience for everyone in the family. We learned that small issues can quickly disrupt the functioning of the entire family." Along with unrealistic expectations, the nanny was a difficult and unhappy person, Shade said. She explained that the nanny complained about the water bottles purchased just for her because they had screw tops and not pop-up tops; the rug for her room was not soft enough on her feet; and, she disliked the car provided for to her to drive. Because the nanny held an associate's degree in child development, she believed she was the final authority when it came to the children. She also claimed that she was the "number one nanny" the Shades could have.

What really ended the relationship, however, was the nanny's maverick manner. According to Shade, the nanny medicated her daughter three different times without informing either parent—despite the fact that the daughter's father was working from home during her illness. When confronted, the nanny claimed that during her work hours—despite a parent's presence in the home—she had the final say on child care. Also, the nanny caused an incident at her daughter's elementary school by taking her out of school early on a snow day without informing the staff. The nanny had removed their daughter from school when she was picking up their son at the end of his standard half-day. (Her daughter's school, Shade said, locks down when a child is thought missing.)

Along with providing great respect to her nanny, Shade also strictly adheres to fair and honest financial dealings with her nanny. If anything, said Shade, she ensures that all financial circumstances are in the nanny's favor. For instance, Shade rigorously monitors the nanny's time worked. If Shade is late, she pays the nanny for all extra time worked. Also, if during a pay period Shade has come home from work early or taken a vacation day, then she will pay the period's full salary wage.

"We really try not to take advantage of her," said Shade, "and we don't dump extra tasks on her. If the chore is in our contract, she does it. If not, we don't want her to do it."

In exchange for respecting her in-home employee's time and workload, and for her compensating fairly and considerately, Shade said she receives enormous loyalty. "The nanny really makes an effort to be available, because she knows we need her help," she said.

A household employer improves with each new experience. Showing consideration for an employee's feelings helps even the playing field between employee and employer, and is the correct management approach when dealing with employment issues. Employees must understand that an employer needs to be a manager, which includes establishing initial goals, communicating philosophy, and fostering household culture, as well as supervising the household employee. Plus, employees need to know up front how you will measure their performance. Set periodic review meetings to evaluate those goals and the employee's performance, handle lingering communication issues, clarify household policy, and coach the employee to improve his or her skills during his or her employment.
—Guy

Medical Release Forms

For child care and eldercare workers, an employer should prepare a medication release form, allowing the caregiver permission to administer medication for prescribed and over-the-counter medication. Also, employers need to prepare a temporary medical care release form that allows a child to be treated by a physician or health care organization without a parent present. The caregiver can present this medical care release form with the employer's health insurance card to obtain treatment. (See page 270 for a sample *Medical Care Release* form and page 271 for a sample *Medication Permission* form.)

Maintaining an Employee Personnel File

Keeping an employee personnel file ensures that the employer obtains and maintains information required by law, and establishes a documented work history for that particular employee. The file contains all information related to that employee, such as the job description, job application, letter offering employment, *Form W-4* (p.273), the state withholding certificate (if applicable), a signed statement that the employee received an employee handbook, the work agreement, *Attendance Record* (p.274), performance evaluations, benefit forms, compliments and complaints from coworkers, awards, and so on. Keep personnel records confidential and locked in a safe location so no one can access them without the employer's expressed consent.

Some states require employers to allow both past and present employees access to their employment files. Employers usually can ask the employee to look through the file on the worksite, with the employer present, ensuring that nothing is altered or taken. Some states allow employers to copy parts of the file and provide them to the employee, enabling the employer to shield sensitive information from the employee. Employers should include information on employees' access to their personnel records in the employee handbook.

Performance Reviews

Companies of all sizes establish periodic (written) reviews and evaluations of employees. It is a good employment practice to implement, particularly for new employees, because it allows the employer and employee to communicate what the employee has accomplished and areas that may need development. With the reviews, employees are provided an opportunity to improve, and the employer has a documented history of the employee's performance and problems.

While informal employer-employee discussions relating to job performance and goals are encouraged and expected throughout an employee's tenure, it is common practice for an employer to perform a formal written performance review at the end of an employee's introductory period, and then on a scheduled basis. (See page 276 for a sample *Performance Evaluation Form*.) Many employers choose to review employees on a yearly basis. Some prefer to evaluate employees every six months. The work agreement and the employee handbook should detail expected review times.

When reviewing an employee's work performance, employers need to remember to focus on work performance and not on the employee's personality or characteristics. Employers should:

- be as positive as possible, but very clear about situations—speak frankly and straightforwardly;
- offer a review of both strengths and weaknesses;
- cite specific examples of when the employee has exceeded, met, or failed job expectations;
- set reasonable goals for the employee to work toward (and meet) in developing and improving skills;
- schedule a second review to determine the employee's progress if her or his performance is weak (this could be done in three months or six months—whichever is considered a fair amount of time for the employee to improve and demonstrate better performance); and,
- list in the review any disciplinary actions, including termination, if the employee fails to improve his or her performance.

Employees may thoroughly examine all performance reviews and may provide a written opinion to be placed in the personnel file. Some evaluation forms have a designated area for the employee's response. It is common practice for both the employer and employee to both sign the review. This documentation helps protect the employer from any false claim made by a current or former employee.

Performance reviews may or may not be accompanied by a salary increase consideration. Employers should clearly state that salary increases are awarded in light of an employee's significant performance and at the employer's discretion—and certainly are not guaranteed. Salary increases are evaluated by the employee's:

- ability to perform all job tasks and functions;
- attendance and punctuality;
- willingness to work;
- ability to cooperate with other employees and household members; and,
- adherence to all household policies.

CASE STUDY

WILLIAM BRUCE REYNOLDS
OWNER/CONSULTANT
ESTATE CONSULTING AND MANAGEMENT, INC.
COLUMBIA COUNTY, NY

William Bruce Reynolds spends much of his time working with the staffs of private homes, resorts, and restaurants, teaching them how to provide the utmost in customer service. A director of the International Guild of Professional Butlers, a chef trained at the Culinary Institute of America, a Certified Executive Protection Specialist, and an experienced household manager, Reynolds helps others find employment, and uses the wealth of his experiences to train others to succeed in the household and service professions.

Reynolds said he believes the industry is divided into two groups:
1. those people who are trained and highly motivated and
2. those people who are untrained and poorly motivated.

An employer who has spent millions of dollars creating his or her dream property looks to a professional household manager to train and supervise a staff capable of delivering the highest degree of professional service. The position of household manager is quite comprehensive, and requires proper training and education.

The household manager is required to create a multifaceted program specific to the estate that he or she is managing. The plan will include, but not be limited to:
* *safety and security;*
* *property systems;*
* *maintenance;*
* *organization;*
* *operations;*
* *staff management; and,*
* *vendor, trade, and outside laborer management.*

Reynolds reminds those working in the household profession that they do so at the whim of the individual or family. All questions should be answered beforehand, and both parties should know what is expected from the arrangement. The position will last only as long as the requirements set forth in the working agreement are carried out.

"For household help to be treated as professional, they must always conduct themselves as professionals," noted Reynolds.

Hiring a household manager to outsource the management responsibilities of an estate is similar to a growing company's founder hiring a chief operations officer to run the firm's operations. As multimillion-dollar companies have objectives and budgets to manage, so do households. Therefore, a household manager, who is tasked with keeping a close eye on the balance sheet and the estate's expenses, requires higher skill sets than typical household employees. For a maximum return on investment, an effectively run estate—whether a small, 5,000-square-foot estate or a large, 60,000-square-foot estate—benefits from a well-managed program featuring detailed policy and procedure manuals for all aspects of the estate and its operations.
—Guy

Discipline

While household employment is largely at-will employment (see Chapter 4) in most states, an employer will generally take disciplinary actions before dismissing an employee. Such discipline can be implemented in progressively more serious actions, such as a verbal warning followed by a written warning, counseling, probation, suspension, and finally termination. By employing a progressive disciplinary practice, an employer can demonstrate that the employee knew about the problems, and for whatever reason, did not improve the situation. In the employee handbook, detail the disciplinary policy, but state that employees may be fired at will. Ensure, too, that not all employee actions will be spun through the progressive process; a serious infraction of household policy and serious misdeed will result in immediate dismissal. If an employee proves untrustworthy and instills fear that harm will be done to a household member, a coworker, or employer property, by all means, remove the employee from the workplace *immediately*. In the employee handbook, state that the employer will decide which situation warrants what type of disciplinary action. (See the sample offer letter in Appendix D.)

First Days

As an employer, you need to prepare for your nanny's first days on the job. He or she needs to become acquainted with the household, its operations, its environment—even the household's culture. Be ready to spend some time with your new nanny during his or her first several days, perhaps spending the entire day with him or her the first day, and reducing the number of hours on the following day. You want to be there to help the nanny become accustomed to the nuances of the household, the children, and their schedules.

To help, prepare a list of activities and information you need to cover with your new nanny during his or her first few days. Some ideas to make the transition proceed smoothly include the following.

- Introduce your new employee to the members of the household. In particular, take whatever time is necessary for you to encourage your children to become familiar with the new nanny.
- Introduce your new nanny to your neighbors.
- Take your new nanny on a tour of the community, pointing out local drug stores, schools, your doctor's office, playground,

Q&A

Q. As a new parent, I am concerned with leaving my infant with my newly hired nanny. If I install a nannycam in my home, am I required to inform the nanny that she may be monitored?

A. It is fair and proper for a household employer to fully disclose to a job applicant whether he or she will monitor the household. Check your local law for the legal use of these devices in your home and your employee's workplace. Disclose this information during the hiring process to ensure that the applicant is comfortable with this practice.

hospital, and so on. Notify your children's school or day care center if the nanny will be picking the children up from either location, and perhaps visit the school or center to introduce your nanny to the staff.

- Make sure the nanny's name is on the list of authorized persons to pick up the children and that proper documentation is submitted.

- If the nanny will be using your vehicle, spend some time reviewing the vehicle with the new employee. Make sure he or she is comfortable driving the vehicle prior to transporting the children. Practice driving the car with the new hire, quietly observing his or her skills while you cover the typical route the nanny will be taking, such as the route from the home to the elementary school or from the home to the local public library. Also, be certain the nanny can properly install a child safety seat, if applicable. (Local fire departments often provide free training regarding proper child safety seat installation and usage.) Practice with him or her taking the seat in and out of the car, and practice proper restraint of your child.

- Review all household policies and procedures listed in the employee handbook. (Remember, now is a good opportunity to discuss household rules on visitors, as well as phone and computer use.) Be sure the new employee understands these policies, procedures, and rules.

- Address all emergency contact information and post it in a designated area for the nanny.

- Review all safety procedures and appliances for the household. (Alarm system, washer, dryer, and any other household equipment that the employee is expected to use.)

- During the first workweek, review job responsibilities detailed in the job description, and take the time to sit down and discuss with the employee how the first week went.

- Review the work agreement.

- After the first few days, drop by unannounced for a quick visit to see how things are progressing, or telephone at different times during the day to check in.

- Describe your performance review plan. Do periodic performance reviews for the first six months.

- Set aside time at the end of each workday to discuss the day. Remember, you want to have a ten- or fifteen-minute recap of the day's or night's events before handing over responsibility for the children. During these recaps, be sure to encourage the nanny, reinforcing the expectations you have while also boosting his or her self-esteem. Use these recaps to provide alternatives to how the nanny may have handled a situation. These constructive conversations will help in obtaining the household you have been working toward.

- Ask the nanny to keep a daily log, entering important events as well as questions that arise during the first several weeks, and ask the nanny to make note of any supplies needed. At the end of the workday, review the log with him or her, and take the opportunity to establish trust and mutual respect for one another.

To help you prepare for your new nanny, think about the following.

- What results are you seeking?
- What information, tools, and instruction does the nanny need to know to successfully do his or her job?
- What are the priority tasks and what are the secondary tasks?
- What support or assistance do you need to provide to your new nanny to make his or her adjustment to your household as quick and easy as possible?

A welcome practice is for the employer and employee to spend the first days of employment together for training. You can show the new nanny where things are, review household procedures, provide him or her with the established preferences for the household (i.e., keep all bedroom doors closed, or put all notes and messages on a dry-erase board affixed to the refrigerator), demonstrate how to operate household equipment and where he or she can find operations manuals, review work and safety procedures, and so on. It is also an opportunity for both to get to know each other, to treat one another with respect and professionalism, and begin to establish trust. During the first few weeks of employment, you may check in by telephoning and stopping home unexpectedly to ensure that all is well and to be available to answer any questions.

Schedule a meeting for one week after the start date for a discussion on how the job is going, issues that have arisen or may arise, questions that need to be answered, and so forth. This will help ensure that any uncertainty is resolved, and will establish the relationship with open and clear communication. An employer's efforts to be available to employees for reviews and discussions of the job, expectations, work environment, and the like will go a long way to foster a respectful and trusting relationship.

Various training materials are available to household employees. For example, many agencies provide educational materials to parents and caregivers. Parents in a Pinch, a Massachusetts-based agency, offers its clients and nannies a CD-ROM on basic child care training, including health, safety, and developmental topics. These materials are also provided by GTM's online Resource Center at **www.gtm.com/resourcecenter**.

Personnel Practices Checklist

√ Note that while household employment is largely a customized situation, it is often handled as an informal situation. In fact, it is a professional endeavor requiring HR and personnel practices and policies.

√ Write and update job descriptions.

√ Establish household policies and procedures.

√ Develop and maintain an employee handbook detailing all policies, including work schedule, performance reviews, dismissal, severance, references, and so on.

√ Provide an orientation during the first few days of employment with on-the-job training for the household employee.

6

Determining Wages and Scheduling Hours

Wage and hour concerns are complicated; therefore, they create a lot of uncertainty within households that employ help. Through the job description and work agreement, wages and hours should be clearly defined and agreed upon by both employer and employee. To even begin the interviewing process, employers should define a specific work schedule for the employee, as well as a policy for when work is required or performed beyond the specified regular workday. In addition, before beginning employment, wages should be negotiated and agreed upon, and pay schedules should be clearly established. However, there is much more involved with wages and hours in the law. Employers must be aware of their legal requirements on federal, state, and local levels in order to lawfully hire and employ a household employee.

Uncertainty stems from the fact that there are many laws, as well as misinformation and anecdotal recommendations from friends and advisors who are not experts in household employment. In wage and hour issues, the problem exists of not knowing what the requirements are—and there is much to know and manage. This chapter discusses why employers must pay an employee according to the law, and provides information on how to properly plan for and manage wages and hours. With the following information, employers will be more informed—and more comfortable—with wage and hour legal requirements.

Fair Labor Standards Act

The U.S. *Fair Labor Standards Act* (FLSA) establishes minimum wage, overtime pay, recordkeeping, and child labor laws affecting full- and part-time workers. Under FLSA's individual coverage provision, domestic service workers—housekeepers, nannies, cooks, chauffeurs, and so on—are covered if their cash wages from one employer are at least $1,000 per calendar year, or if they work a total of more than eight hours a week for one or more employers.

According to the U.S. Department of Labor (DOL), the FLSA requires employers to pay the more than 80 million covered employees at least the minimum wage (set by the federal government at $5.15 per hour for 2006) and overtime pay of one and one-half times the employee's regular pay rate. (See the table on page 102 for minimum wage rates per state.) Overtime pay must be paid for work over forty hours per week—with some exceptions. (See the box on page 100 on what the FLSA does not require.) Overtime wages (as required by FLSA) are due on the regular payday for the pay period covered. FLSA exempts overtime pay for live-in domestic workers. However, household employers with staff living outside the workplace must comply with the FLSA labor law.

CASE STUDY

Annie Davis
Owner/Operator
Annie's Nannies, Inc.
Seattle, WA
GTM Partner Agency

Annie's Nannies, Inc., a nanny referral agency based in Seattle, places nannies throughout Washington state. Most nannies, who are predominantly viewed as salaried employees, work forty to fifty hours per week, said owner Annie Davis. However, even if they are treated as salaried employees, overtime pay still applies to domestic workers who live outside the workplace.

One nanny who Davis placed cared for a child for four years. At the job's outset, both nanny and employers agreed on hours and salary. After four years, however, the nanny decided to end the relationship because she was working longer hours than previously agreed upon. She submitted one month's notice. The nanny and the child's father argued, and the father asked the nanny not to return to work.

The family blocked the nanny's unemployment insurance claim. The nanny, upset with being out of one month's salary and with being denied unemployment insurance, contacted her attorney.

The nanny took the family to court to obtain unemployment benefits. The family failed to attend the court proceedings, and the judge ruled in favor of the nanny to access unemployment. The judge, reviewing the nanny's hours worked, informed the nanny that she was entitled to overtime pay for the period she worked. The nanny then sued the family for all of the overtime pay she was entitled to during her four years of employment. According to Davis, the case was settled out of court for $15,000, and the nanny likely would have been awarded more money if her suit went through the court process.

It is an expensive lesson to learn. "My guess is most families do not abide by the overtime laws for domestic employees, and in fact, most do not even know domestic employees are covered by law," said Davis. "As an agency, you have to educate families on everything. Families need to know their legal requirements, including tax and payroll requirements."

> Prior to hiring an employee, it is very important for any household employer to understand his or her obligations as an employer, as well as which laws apply to the household. Generally, employers do not look to take advantage of their help, but often feel cheated when matters that adversely affect their financial expectations arise— whether the matter entails tax obligations, misunderstanding gross wages vs. net wages, or assuming overtime rules do not apply to them.
> —Guy

FLSA RECORDKEEPING

According to the law, employers are required to keep records on wages, hours, and other items as specified by DOL recordkeeping regulations. Records to be kept for minimum wage and overtime pay include the following:

- personal information, including the employee's name, home address, occupation, sex, and birth date if under age 19;
- hour and day the workweek begins;
- total hours worked each workday and each workweek;
- total daily or weekly straight time earnings;
- regular hourly pay rate for any week when overtime is worked;
- total overtime pay for the workweek;
- deductions from or additions to wages;
- total wages paid each pay period; and,
- date of payment and pay period covered.

Employers subject to the FLSA's minimum wage requirements must post (and keep posted) in the workplace the federal minimum wage rate. Posters can be easily downloaded at **www.dol.gov** or obtained at state labor departments. For more on FLSA, go to **www.dol.gov** or call the wage hour toll-free information and help line at 866-4USWAGE (866-487-9243).

Facts & Figures

NOT REQUIRED UNDER FLSA

FLSA does not require (but please be advised that some local laws may require):

- vacation, holiday, severance, or sick pay;
- meal or rest periods, holidays off, or vacations;
- premium pay for weekend or holiday work;
- pay raises or fringe benefits;
- discharge notice, reason for discharge, or immediate payment of final wages to terminated employees; or,
- overtime for persons employed as companions to the elderly or infirm.

Source: U.S. Department of Labor, "Handy Reference Guide to the Fair Labor Standards Act."

Facts & Figures

INFORMATION SOURCES WHERE EMPLOYERS FIND APPROPRIATE NANNY SALARY AND BENEFITS

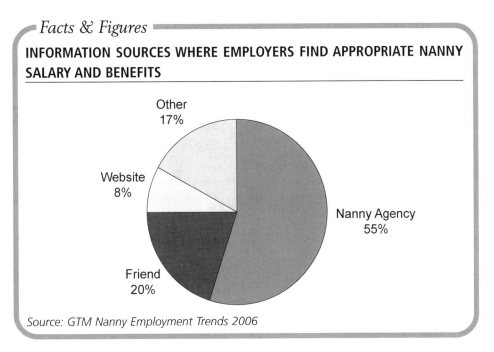

Source: GTM Nanny Employment Trends 2006

In addition, many states set minimum wage and overtime pay laws. Employers need to ensure that they comply with the laws set in their locality. (See page 102 for state minimum wage rates.) State labor departments can provide more information to employers on state and local requirements.

Salaries and Minimum Wage

Salaries vary greatly in the household employment industry—just as household positions and workplaces differ. The household position is often customized to meet the needs of one particular household, and salaries reflect that fact. No standard salaries exist within the household employment industry other than the federal minimum wage requirements. The minimum wage in the United States is $5.15 per hour, unless the state in which the household employee works mandates it to be higher. (The U.S. Congress has been considering raising the minimum wage. To ensure that you know the current minimum wage rate, go to **www.dol.gov**.)

A Philadelphia agency owner said she believes that a nanny's salary and compensation package should reflect her or his background and experience. "The more experienced, educated nanny typically is paid in the higher salary range," she said. "As in any industry, an individual who brings more to the job by way of a broader and deeper experience will be compensated accordingly."

A GTM partner agency owner added that she has little to offer families that want to underpay employees. When it comes to household employee pay, she lives by the maxim "you get what you pay for. Our children are worth more. Salary is not a place to cut corners."

Facts & Figures

MINIMUM WAGE RATES PER STATE IN 2006

State	Rate
Federal	$5.15
Alabama	$5.15
Alaska	$7.15
Arizona	$5.15
Arkansas	$6.25
California	$6.75
San Francisco	$8.50
Colorado	$5.15
Connecticut	$7.65
Delaware	$6.15
District of Columbia	$7.00
Florida	$6.40
Georgia	$7.25
Hawaii	$6.75
Idaho	$5.15
Illinois	$6.50
Indiana	$5.15
Iowa	$5.15
Kansas	$2.65
Kentucky	$5.15
Louisiana	$5.15
Maine	$6.75
Maryland	$6.15
Massachusetts	$6.75

State	Rate
Michigan	$6.95
Minnesota	$5.25
Mississippi	$5.15
Missouri	$5.15
Montana	$5.15
Nebraska	$5.15
Nevada	$5.15
New Hampshire	$5.15
New Jersey	$7.15
New Mexico	$5.15
New York	$7.15
North Carolina	$5.15
North Dakota	$5.15
Ohio	$5.15
Oklahoma	$5.15
Oregon	$7.50
Pennsylvania	$5.15
Rhode Island	$7.10
South Carolina	$5.15
South Dakota	$5.15
Tennessee	$5.15
Texas	$5.15
Utah	$5.15
Vermont	$7.25
Virginia	$5.15
Washington	$7.63
West Virginia	$5.85
Wisconsin	$6.50
Wyoming	$5.15

Many states are currently addressing the issue of minimum wage and have proposed ballot initiatives. Check frequently with the Department of Labor for your state to keep compliant.

Source: www.dol.gov.

Another GTM partner agency located in New York City agreed. "An employer is paying for one-on-one time with his and/or her child, with no downtime. One client who wanted to employ a nanny for forty hours for four workdays flipped out over the suggested salary range of $450 to $550 per week that nannies were being paid. I told her, 'This is not your Mercedes Benz or Toyota Camry. You're trying to cut costs in the wrong place. You must think of it as an investment in your child's well-being.'"

LIVING WAGE

Some organizations are working to raise rates to a higher *livable* wage. One grassroots organization, Association of Community Organizations for Reform Now (ACORN), has been working on legislation and change for higher minimum wages for more than ten years. While the debate concerning living wages rages in various areas, ACORN points to studies showing that by raising the minimum wage, many employers are experiencing more loyal and harder working employees who are not rotating out as much.

Changes on the issue of living wages have been made across the United States. The following are examples of living wages in some areas.

- California localities Port Hueneme and Marin County have experienced recent living wage rates. Port Hueneme requires $9.35 per hour if health benefits are provided by the employer, and $11.85 per hour if health benefits are not provided. For Marin County, the rate now $9.50 per hour if health benefits are provided, and $10.75 per hour if health benefits are not provided. (Port Hueneme Ordinance No. 662, October 2005; Marin County Ordinance No. 3435, November 2005.)
- Brookline, MA, overwhelmingly passed Article 19 in late May 2005 to amend the living wage bylaws from $10.72 per hour to $11.15 per hour. The bylaws cover contracted employees working on town contracts of $25,000 or more.

According to a *New York Times* article published in January 2006, ACORN and its compatriots have conducted hundreds of campaigns throughout the United States to raise living wage rates—particularly since the federal minimum wage rate has held at $5.15 per hour for several years, while the costs of living (specifically housing costs) have risen dramatically in many regions.

While in many states living wage laws apply to those who employ twenty-five or more people, it is an important hiring practice for household employers to keep city and state living wage rates in mind, and helps employers retain the best nannies and household employees.

PENALTIES

Employers not following laws and regulations regulating wage reports could find themselves facing penalties and even jail time. The following table shows some penalties various states impose.

Facts & Figures

EMPLOYER PENALTIES FOR FAILING TO REPORT WAGES

The following are examples of just some of the penalties for failing to report wages in various states.

Alabama

An employer delinquent in paying contributions and/or assessments more than $20, or delinquent in filing contribution or wage reports for any quarter prior to the four quarters of the immediately preceding calendar year, is liable for a penalty rate equal to the maximum rate for the rate year plus the shared cost assessment.

Arizona

Employers not meeting the state's wage report filing requirements are fined 0.1% of the total wages paid to an employee during the quarter. The minimum penalty is $34 and the maximum is $200.

Colorado

Employers that fail to timely file tax reports are fined $50 for each occurrence. Each subsequent quarter in which the employer fails to timely file such report is considered a separate occurrence. Employers that are delinquent in paying taxes by the due date are fined by the Wage and Hour Division. (Penalties may be waived if the employer shows good cause for failing to timely pay taxes or file tax reports.)

Delaware

Employers that fail to file reports within five days after the due date may be fined $15 plus other penalties.

Illinois

Employers face a total penalty for late filing, ranging from $50 to the lesser of $10 for each $10,000, a fraction of the total wages paid during the period, or $5,000. Such penalties may be waived if the employer can prove that the failure to file is the first during the previous twenty quarters and that the amount of total contributions due for the quarter is less than $500. Penalty for willful failure to pay is 60% of the amount unpaid, but not less than $400.

Massachusetts

Employers who file no quarterly reports are assigned the maximum tax rate, plus a 3% penalty. If an employer has submitted some, but not all, of the required quarterly reports, the tax rate is computed based on experience, with a 3% penalty added. If the missing forms are filed within a thirty-day grace period, the rate is recomputed and the penalty dropped. Missing reports submitted after thirty days but before one year result in a recomputed rate based on experience and a reduced penalty of 2% or no penalty, if good cause is shown. If the missing reports are filed after one year but before three years, the rate is recomputed, but the 3% penalty is retained.

New Hampshire

An employer's late-filing fee is equal to 10% of the contributions due, but not less than $5 for each failure. However, upon timely application and payment of $25, the time for filing any report may be extended thirty days.

New Mexico

Quarterly wage and contribution report, Form ES-903A, together with a check or money order, must be mailed on or before the last day of the month following the end of each calendar quarter, except in the case of an employer who relocates from the state or discontinues or transfers its business, in which case the report is due within thirty days. If the required report for any calendar quarter is not filed within ten days after the due date, a penalty of $50 is incurred. If contributions due on such reports are not paid within the ten days, an additional penalty of 5% of the amount due (but not less than $25) is incurred.

Ohio
Failure to file a contribution or wage report on the due date subjects the employer to a forfeiture of .25% of the total remuneration paid by the employer, with a minimum of $30 and a maximum of $500. The interest rate on unpaid contributions is 14%.

Pennsylvania
Delinquent reports are subject to a penalty of from $25 to $250, and delinquent contributions are subject to interest charges.

Puerto Rico
Failure to submit reports within the prescribed time subjects an employer to a penalty of 0.5% of the amount due, up to a maximum of $5, for each month or fraction thereof in which the omission exists. Failure to pay the contributions within sixty days following the date payment was required subjects an employer to a penalty of 5% of the contribution owed.

South Carolina
Employers who fail to file reports or who file incorrect or insufficient reports may be liable for double their contributions. Failure to file a wage or contribution report within fifteen days of demand incurs a penalty equal to 10% of the contribution amount due, but not less than $25 or more than $1,000.

Tennessee
Employers are fined interest at 0.5% per month or any portion of a month from the due date for late payment. Penalty is charged at the rate of $10 per month or any fraction thereof up to a maximum of $50 for late submission of report.

Texas

Employers who fail to file wage reports may incur:

1. $15 for the first fifteen days or less after due date;
2. $30 plus $\frac{1}{20}$ of 1% of wages that the employer failed to report if the report is filed after the fifteenth day but during the first month after the due date;
3. the sum of the amount calculated under #2 above, plus $30 plus 1/10 of 1% of wages not reported, for completed reports filed during the second month after the due date; and,
4. the sum calculated under #3 above, plus $30 plus 1/5 of 1% of wages not reported, for completed reports filed during the third month after the due date. The employer may also be assessed a service charge of $10.

Utah

Failure to timely file subjects an employer to a penalty of 5% of contributions for each fifteen-day period or fraction thereof, but not more than 25% or less than $25. Failure to timely pay the amount due will also result in a penalty equal to 5% of the contribution due. False representations will incur a fine, imprisonment, or both.

Vermont

Employers that fail to timely file any wage or contribution report will incur a penalty of $35 for each report not received by the due date. The penalty may be waived for employers that show reasonable cause for failing to timely file such report.

Virginia

The employer's payroll and tax reports are due quarterly on or before last day of the following month, except for state employers and nonprofit organizations electing reimbursement financing. Employers must pay a $30 penalty for late filing.

CASE STUDY

Judi Merlin
President
Kim Cino
Placement Director
A Friend of the Family
Smyrna, GA
GTM Partner Agency

In its twentieth year of service, A Friend of the Family, which places child care and eldercare workers in Atlanta, GA, sees a trend in the industry: caregivers are raising their salary requirements, even after the 2001 economic downturn experienced throughout Atlanta.

"Some caregivers have not made accommodations regarding the present economic conditions and are not skilled in making cost-of-living adjustments," said Judi Merlin, president of the agency. "The caregiver salary is [generally] in a very good range, but we see cases where the caregiver inflates his or her worth for no other reason than he or she wants to. As an agency, we spend a lot of time educating those clients and caregivers [on how] to meet in the middle."

The agency invests a lot of time educating clients on fair compensation at time of hire and as the relationship progresses. In fact, the agency's staff will check in with recent placements about every four months to ensure fair wages are being paid for the number of hours worked.

According to Kim Cino, the agency's placement director, a key aspect of the agency checking in with clients and household help several times a year is to determine if a new employer-employee contract needs to be drafted to reflect new circumstances and fair compensation. "We feel this will make for happier clients and nannies," she said.

Despite the trend of rising costs to employ in-home caregivers, Cino said many caregivers who have worked with families for a while—and older nannies unsure of their current market worth—are unfairly compensated. She said one reason for this is that the employers, who have worked with a particular nanny for several years, are unaware of the current market rate for child care. A recent incident proves her point.

A nanny took a position caring for a three-year-old child and doing light housekeeping. She worked a 52.5 hour workweek. Three years later, the mother remarried, and a father with two children was added to the household. Still working 52.5 hours per week, the nanny now had a significantly heavier workload. Although provided with a raise during her employment, the nanny was never compensated for the additional responsibilities.

The nanny spoke with her employers about a pay increase to reflect her new duties, but the employers stated they did not believe the nanny should receive a higher salary. At the nanny's second request for fair compensation for the workload, the employer and nanny agreed to keep the nanny's salary the same but to reduce her hours to 45.5 per workweek.

While the nanny was satisfied with the solution, Cino maintains that the nanny remains underpaid, largely because employers working with one employee for many years are not familiar with current compensation practices or other household employment services.

> Ensuring that a household employee is fairly compensated is one of the keys to retaining a household employee. To combat the double threat of an employee feeling underpaid or being pursued by a recruiter, employers must make sure that their employees are paid for all hours worked, including overtime, and that their wages are in line with the market. A good way to assess the market value is to ask agencies and other employers, as well as to participate in annual industry salary surveys.
> —Guy

CASE STUDY

Lin Taylor-Pleiman
President/Manager
American Domestic Agency, Inc.
Whiteford, MD
GTM Partner Agency

As an owner/operator of American Domestic Agency, Inc., Lin Taylor-Pleiman places many household employees who come to her agency because she requires clients to submit a signed work agreement covering all aspects of work hours and wages. One nanny came to the agency after working without a work agreement. She had been caring for three children, one with significant behavioral and emotional problems. The nanny accepted a request to travel with the family on vacation, but when she asked her employer about payment for the vacation work, the employer angrily told her that the trip was on hold. "The family, it turns out, thought room, board, and air were compensation enough," said Taylor-Pleiman.

From that point on, the relationship deteriorated. According to Taylor-Pleiman, the nanny received nastily worded notes daily, and endured constant complaints and nitpicking. The family hired its former nanny to care for the children during the trip and did not pay the current nanny for the days they were away. After six months, the nanny left the position without having a chance to say good-bye to the children, with whom she had established a good relationship.

Household employers must remember that their vacation time is not their household help's vacation also. The employee traveling with the family and performing work responsibilities should be paid accordingly. Many times, employers view family vacations as a perk for the employee, when the employee views it as a continuation of his or her employment responsibilities, which is, of course, exactly what it is.
—Guy

CASE STUDY

SUSAN TOKAYER
OWNER/OPERATOR
FAMILY HELPERS
DOBBS FERRY, NY
GTM PARTNER AGENCY

Susan Tokayer, owner of a household employment referral agency in Dobbs Ferry, NY, said she has seldom seen nannies use sick time. Despite this, Tokayer experienced one incident regarding a nanny's sick time.

A nanny was out sick nine times during the four months that she was employed. The family thought this was excessive. A completed work agreement listed sick days "as needed," so a concrete number of paid sick days was not specified. Therefore, neither the nanny nor the family clearly understood what sick time compensation would be provided.

According to Tokayer, this occurrence demonstrates the need to be explicit in all areas of the work agreement. "Sometimes clients don't get detailed enough, even though we supply a work agreement," she said. "People don't see down the line that it could be a problem. Instead of writing 'sick time as needed,' put 'four days' down on the work agreement. Then, depending on circumstances, be open to compensation after those four days are used." Tokayer said household employees generally have three to six paid sick days (or sick/personal days) to use during an employment year.

According to Tokayer, household employers, particularly those new to household employment, want to start off the relationship congenially—so they behave delicately. "People say the work agreement seems too hard line, too firm," she said. "This relationship is unique. It's a work relationship, but it's an intimate, friendly relationship. Families don't want to come across as too intense or too formal. But if the work agreement isn't completed thoroughly, something could be misconstrued, or there could be a problem down the line."

Tokayer said her clientele is educated, affluent, and knowledgeable about the household employment industry. However, outside of help with a newborn or child, clients most likely have not had household help before.

Tokayer still has advice for all potential household employers—know your-self. "Be honest," she said. "Know who you are, what your family needs, and present that honestly. Then, pay well…. No matter how hard the job is, if the nanny is well compensated, she will stay forever."

Although not required by law, an employee benefit of sick or personal paid time is standard in the corporate workplace and should be considered in the house. Many household employers shy away from hiring temporary help when a household employee is off work, and it is often detrimental if a household employer misses work him- or herself to cover for his or her household help. This is why household employers must and do take great pains to stress the importance of reliability to their household help.

Household employers should consider implementing a sick and personal day policy that distinguishes between sick and personal days, and a plan that accrues available hours each pay period, up to a maximum allotted amount over a one-year period. It is then important to also consider allowing employees to borrow (or not borrow) against time yet to be accrued. A common policy that is not recommended is one that allots time-off hours to those employees who did not miss a workday the previous month. For example, perfect attendance in March translates to an extra day off to be used later. This is not a good policy because as it places the motivation for the attendance on the wrong criteria. If an employee is contagiously ill, no one wants him or her on the worksite, exposing others to the illness. Ultimately, a good policy benefits all, and a well-documented policy safeguards against most eventualities. Employers need to establish a policy that protects everyone within the household and covers all circumstances.

—Guy

Q&A

Q. If I employ a household worker who is an immigrant—not a U.S. citizen—must I pay U.S. minimum wage?

A. Yes. Minimum wage, as well as federal and state labor laws, generally apply to domestic and household employees working in the United States or a U.S. possession or territory, regardless of employee citizenship or immigration status.

See page 98 for more information on FLSA. You should also ensure that the worker is eligible to legally work in the United States.

Time-Off Payments

Time-off payments for sick, personal, or vacation days should be agreed upon by the employer and employee prior to hiring, and should be written in the household employment work agreement and employment handbook. Be certain to specify if time off may be taken in full- and half-day amounts, and when a doctor's note regarding sick time will be required.

Employers are typically mandated to provide time off for voting, jury duty, and military and National Guard training or active service.

Debts Owed by Employee to Employer

Information about whether an employee may borrow money against future wages from the employer should be provided to the employee and included in the employee handbook. If such activity is permissible, then the employer should detail what needs to occur to necessitate an employer loan to the employee, what process an employee needs to follow to request an employer loan, and what steps will be taken to obtain payment of the loan. When considering granting a loan, the employer should take into account the length of time that is considered reasonable for the employee to repay the loan.

Employers should obtain a signed *promissory note* from the employee for any significant amount of money loaned (such as $25 or more). This note should include:

- date of loan;
- loan amount;
- payment method (i.e., loan payments taken directly from paychecks);
- payment schedule; and,
- the employee's and the employer's signatures.

The promissory note should be filed in the employee's personnel file, and a photocopy of the note should be provided to the employee.

Garnishment

The federal wage garnishment law limits the amount that may be legally *garnished* (withdrawn for payment to another, per legal direction, such as an ex-spouse for child care payments) from an individual's income, and protects an employee whose pay is garnished from being fired on account of owing a single debt. For the most part, these amounts cannot be more than 25% of an employee's gross wages. Specific guidelines will be listed on formal garnishment orders.

Overtime

According to the U.S. Labor Department, the federal Fair Labor Standards Act (FLSA) requires employers to pay overtime pay of one and one-half times the regular pay rate. Overtime pay must be paid for work over forty hours per week—with some exceptions (see page 100), this includes live-in employees.

In most circumstances, FLSA requires employers to pay covered employees who live outside the workplace at least the minimum wage, as well as overtime pay at one and one-half times the regular pay rate for hours worked beyond forty in a week. Live-in employees are not subject to overtime regulations; however, state and local laws for overtime vary, and may supersede the federal FLSA. In addition, domestic service workers employed to provide baby-sitting services on a casual basis, or to provide companionship services for those who cannot care for themselves because of age or infirmity, are exempt from the FLSA's minimum wage and overtime requirements, whether or not they reside in the household where they are employed. Finally, it is important to note that some states impose their own requirements, which may differ from federal law.

CALIFORNIA WAGE ORDER 15

Under the California IWC Wage Order 15, household employees who qualify as personal attendants, such as most nannies or eldercare providers, are exempt from the state's overtime requirements, but not the FLSA's minimum wage requirements. However, other household employees who do not qualify as personal attendants, such as most butlers, cooks, gardeners, maids, and so on, are subject to the state's overtime requirements, as well as the FLSA's minimum wage requirements.

To be clear and help avoid overtime issues, an employer and employee should discuss overtime while developing the work agreement. Specify what the overtime rate is and when it will occur, as well as whether overtime will be paid on holidays (and if so, which holidays).

For help with overtime calculations, go to GTM's overtime calculator at **www.gtm.com/resourcecenter**.

Compensation During Travel and Off-Site Events

Before an employer hires an employee, the employee's compensation must be detailed fully, including vacation, mileage reimbursement, paid auto insurance, and so on. It is important to spell out what compensation a household employee will be paid when he or she travels with the family, or when he or she attends an off-site event as part of the workday.

Employees using their own cars for work tasks and work-related events should be reimbursed for mileage. The federal mileage reimbursement rate for 2006 is 44.5 cents per mile. It is useful to include a copy of an *Expense Report*, which includes a section on mileage in the employee handbook. (see p.269.)

While many employers defer to established federal rates, once again, employers need to be certain of what is required by their local laws. Some requirements are quite extensive. For instance, in New York State, the Department of Labor has set standard allowances for meals and lodging.

New York State Meal and Lodging Allowance

According to New York State law, an employee's meal and lodging may be considered part of the minimum wage, but not be valued at more than what is shown in the chart on page 117.

	(All on a per day basis)	
	1/1/06	1/1/07
Meals	$2.30	$2.45
Lodging	$2.90	$3.05
Apartment	$5.40	$5.70

For more, go to **www.labor.state.ny.us/formsdocs/wp/LS210.PDF**.

Breaking Down The Paycheck

Employers should always pay employees by check, so both parties have a record of the payment. Checks need to be *net*—total wages after all taxes and benefit option payments are withheld. Even if an employer directly deposits paychecks per employees' request, a payment record or voucher should be supplied to the employee and kept on file for the employer to access if needed. (See page 244 of Appendix D for a sample *Paycheck and Payroll Earnings Statement*.)

Taxes

Every employer is responsible for several federal, state, and local taxes. A household employer is responsible for the timely payment or deposit of employment taxes withheld from an employee, his or her matching share of Social Security and Medicare (the Social Security and Medicare taxes are combined into what is known as FICA—the Federal Insurance Contribution Act), and all Federal Unemployment Tax Act (FUTA) taxes. (See Chapter 8 for more information on payroll and taxes.)

Facts & Figures

RECOMMENDED PAY STUB INFORMATION

An employer should include the following information on an employee's pay stub:

- employer name and address;
- employee name;
- pay period start and end dates;
- check date;

- check number;
- current payroll information;
- gross earnings;
- total deductions:
    - federal;
    - Old Age Survivors Disability Insurance (OASDI) (i.e., Social Security);
    - Medicare;
    - state withholding; and,
    - local tax withholding;
- net pay;
- year-to-date payroll information;
- sick/vacation time accruals;
- withholding allowances (according to withholding status); and,
- health reimbursement account.

CASE STUDY

LEANN BRAMBACH
OWNER/OPERATOR
HOME DETAILS, INC.
SEATTLE, WA
GTM PARTNER AGENCY

Leann Brambach owns Home Details, Inc. (HDI), an agency that places household employees in positions throughout Seattle. Citing an example of one HDI nanny placement, Brambach said, "Both nannies and clients need to be educated from the get-go about their tax obligations and gross vs. net."

Brambach placed a woman in a position as a part-time nanny and household assistant for $13 per hour. The employee asked her employer to raise her salary to $15 per hour after learning that the job was more work than anticipated and after comparing salaries with other nannies. The employer agreed and asked Brambach to update the work agreement. In updating the work agreement, another issue became apparent—both the *nanny and the employer thought that the other was paying income tax on the nanny's salary. In the end, the employment failed. The employer was willing to pay $15 per hour gross, which equaled approximately $12 per hour net. The nanny resigned, believing that she was misled.*

"This was one big misunderstanding that left both parties feeling frustrated, and trust was broken," said Brambach.

Household employers can opt to not withhold federal and state income taxes from their employee's pay, placing the burden on the employee to make estimated tax payments throughout the year. The rule is that both parties must agree that the employer will withhold these taxes; otherwise, the employee is responsible.

When an employee submits a completed W-4 form to the employer and the employer accepts it, the responsibility of withholding is then placed upon the employer. Withholding is commonly done through payroll deduction. Because this practice is so widespread, an employer who is unwilling to accept the responsibility must clearly spell out in the work agreement his or her stance, as well as notify the employee in person. If it is not, great friction can easily build to a breaking point in the employer-employee relationship— especially since employees frequently misunderstand the calculation and payment of their own income taxes.

—Guy

CASE STUDY

DENISE SHADE
HOUSEHOLD EMPLOYER
SENIOR VICE PRESIDENT
KEY BANK'S FOREIGN EXCHANGE UNIT
NEW YORK, NY
GTM PAYROLL AND TAX SERVICE CLIENT

Denise Shade, senior vice president of Key Bank's foreign exchange unit and mother of two, could easily be considered a financial whiz. Yet, despite her obvious executive-level financial affinity, Shade uses GTM's services for nanny taxes and payroll.

"We first did our taxes and payroll on our own," said Shade, "because we really wanted to understand it, but it is incredibly time-consuming on a weekly basis."

Along with the standard time required to attend to payroll and taxes, Shade said that twice issues arose with the IRS, causing payments to be tracked. While Shade was able to submit to the IRS proof of payments, she explained that the time required for this is particularly lengthy. Noting that such issues arise from time to time, she added that GTM's services were helpful in saving her from what could be stressful and painstaking record searches.

There are many considerations. For example, household employers need to only deduct the employee's share of Social Security and Medicare taxes, and not the employer's portion. Doing so would be doubling Social Security and Medicare deductions.

All employers, including household employers, must deal with the complexity of payroll and taxes as well as the compounded legal requirements from federal, state, and local levels. Along with these concerns is the demand that employers are responsible for the timely payment or deposit of employment taxes. There are many things to learn and to consider, such as while deducting payroll taxes, an employer need only deduct the employee's share of Social Security and Medicare taxes, and not the employer's taxes (as Denise Shade noted). In addition, employers are, at times, questioned by the IRS or their state of residence, and need to submit necessary forms and records. All this is annoying and time-consuming. Many household employers save themselves significant time and effort by using a third-party payroll firm to provide tax and payroll services. By relying on a knowledgeable payroll service, household employers and their employees can be assured that they are protected and will be eligible for assistance if needed.
—Guy

Facts & Figures

DEPENDENT CARE ASSISTANCE PROGRAM (DCAP)—A TAX-SAVING TIP FOR HOUSEHOLD EMPLOYERS

A major concern for families today is how to provide dependent care for family members while family providers are at work. Companies may deduct expenses from an employee's salary to assist the employee with his or her dependent care obligations. The dependent care tax credit also helps families with lower household incomes.

Household employers can access Dependent Care Assistance Program (DCAP) information at their company's human resources department. The DCAP may allow up to $5,000 in pretaxed earnings per year to be set aside for child care or eldercare. This is especially important if the family has undergone a change of life experience (i.e., the birth of a new baby) that might affect its eligibility for the program. There are specific DCAP open enrollment periods during which to apply.

A household employer can learn more through his or her company's HR department.

Facts & Figures

BENEFITS OF PAYING AN EMPLOYEE CORRECTLY

There are numerous benefits to correctly paying an employee for both the employer and the employee, including the following.

Employer Benefits

- It is the law. Federal and state law mandate that each time a taxpayer signs his or her federal 1040 U.S. Individual Income Tax Return, he or she is answering the household tax question. Anything reported that is less than actual amounts is tax evasion.
- Employers have peace of mind that they are practicing good human resources and are legally operating a business.
- An employer saves money, as steep fines (plus interest) and even jail time is paid by employers not paying above board.
- By paying payroll taxes, employers in most states are protecting themselves by paying into the workers' compensation insurance fund, which will help them cover expenses in the event that an employee is injured while working.

- Employers may be eligible for federal assistance programs, such as the Earned Income Credit Program, Child Care Tax Credit, and the Dependent Care Assistance Program (DCAP).
- Employees who know they are legally on the books feel more secure in their employment relationship, and the employer benefits by having a happy and secure employee.

Employee Benefits

- It is the law.
- Employees have a legal employment history to refer to when applying for future jobs, mortgages, loans, credit, and so on.
- Employees are covered by Social Security, Medicare, unemployment, and workers' compensation insurance (if applicable) benefits via payroll taxes.
- Employees may qualify for an Earned Income Credit, which enables them to, in some instances, claim more money from the government than their payroll taxes if their payroll taxes were calculated without the credit. An advantage is an even distribution of money in employees' paychecks throughout the year rather than having to wait for this payout amount until the end of the tax year.
- Employees are eligible for Social Security credits for retirement, disability, and death.

Family Medical Leave Act

The *Family Medical Leave Act* (FMLA) generally requires employers of fifty or more people to provide up to twelve weeks of unpaid, job-protected leave to eligible employees for the birth or adoption of a child, or for the serious illness of a child or parent. While FMLA does not apply to the majority of household employers due to the stipulation of fifty or more employees, family medical leave—or a variation of it—is a valid consideration for employers to offer their domestic help.

Some states have family and medical leave acts, but like the federal law, most apply to employers with at least several employees, generally not to a one-employee business. However, it is best to check on individual state and locality medical leave requirements.

Planning and Scheduling Wages and Hours Checklist

√ Abide by all laws—local, state, and federal.

√ Check your state's minimum wage laws, as some state and local minimum wage laws supersede the federal minimum wage ($5.15 per hour).

√ Check special living wage ordinances and requirements in your locality to ensure you meet those wage rates and are not faced with a penalty.

√ Check to be sure you file your wage reports accurately and on time to avoid penalty.

√ Clearly communicate during preemployment discussions whether wages are gross or net.

√ Clearly identify whether the employer or employee will pay income tax from wages.

7

Employee Benefits to Help Retain the Best

While providing employee benefits is largely optional and seldom required by law, employee benefits greatly help the household employer attract and retain high-level employees. To get and keep the most talented employees, employers must treat employees like professionals. Therefore, offering employee benefits is an important consideration for all household employers. By providing an attractive employee benefits package, the employer is helping to maintain a satisfied workforce. Satisfied employees equal a happy workplace, which in turn equals a happy family and life for the employer.

Health insurance and other employee benefits covered in this chapter are instrumental in recruiting and retaining talented employees. It is prudent for an employer to take the time needed to secure a valuable employee benefits package by reviewing with his or her employee what benefits he or she requires.

Medical Insurance Coverage

Health insurance is often the first benefit requested by any employee and one that is increasingly popular for household employers to provide. While health care is a benefit provided by most employers in the United States, the household employment industry has been slow to provide household help with medical benefits and health care coverage (although this is increasing). Health care insurance coverage is a priority for many workers, including those in household employment, because of the high cost of coverage and medical fees. The cost can be high for the employer as well—especially since most household employers have only one employee or just a few employees. However, various options are now on the market that make coverage more affordable than ever before.

Today, an employer's choice to provide health care coverage as an employee benefit remains optional, except for employers in the state of Hawaii, which mandates that all employees achieving a specific monthly income must be covered. Hawaii mandates that every employer paying a regular employee monthly wage amounting to at least 86.67 times the minimum hourly wage (p. 102) must provide that employee with coverage by a prepaid group health care plan. Since 2003, Hawaii has mandated that minimum wage be set at $6.25 per hour. Therefore, the employee earning a minimum of $541.69 (86.67 x $6.25) a month is eligible for health care coverage.

Employers may offer employees certain types of health plans. The four most popular plans are the following.

1. *Health Maintenance Organization* (HMO)—a member-based organization that provides health care at affordable costs, and in general, emphasizes preventive care.

2. *Closed Panel HMO*—HMOs that own their own facilities or clinics and employ the medical staff who work in them.

3. *Preferred Provider Organization* (PPO)—much like HMOs in their operation, PPOs formed as a way to control managed care and health care costs. PPOs are groups of medical professionals and hospitals that may be controlled independently or by insurance companies. Unlike HMOs, in PPOs doctors are not employed by the PPO, and facilities or clinics are not owned by the PPO. Another PPO advantage is that there are no referral requirements. A member can see any doctor he or she chooses at any time. A member may use doctors who are part of the PPO network, but it is not required. However, using a PPO-member doctor, provider, or facility usually offers financial incentives.

4. *Major Medical*—a health insurance policy with high deductibles to cover most serious health problems and conditions, up to a specific limit or reimbursement maximum. Although most major medical poli-

cies contain lifetime limits of $1 million or more, meeting the lifetime limit usually is not an issue. Major medical policies are indemnity-type policies, in which the insurer covers most medical services with a significant cost-sharing element for the employee.

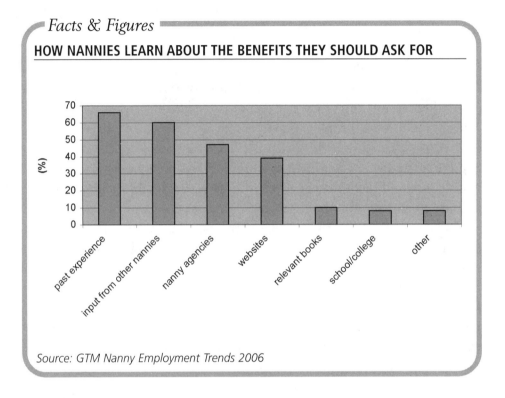

Facts & Figures

HOW NANNIES LEARN ABOUT THE BENEFITS THEY SHOULD ASK FOR

Source: GTM Nanny Employment Trends 2006

HEALTH REIMBURSEMENT ACCOUNT

A *health reimbursement account* (HRA) is a creative option available to the household employer, regardless of budgets, who wants to offer a contribution program for health-related expenses as an employee benefit. Growing in popularity, an HRA is an employer-sponsored plan that reimburses an employee for eligible medical care expenses, as defined by the IRS.

The employer funds a predetermined amount of money for each eligible employee. Monies in the account are not subject to employment taxes. Health Reimbursement Accounts allow employees and employers to take advantage of the lower premiums offered by high-deductible major medical plans and help keep health care costs under control.

The HRA advantage is that monies can roll over each year. Therefore, an employer does not lose a contribution if an employee does not use up the account in any given year. Health Reimbursement Accounts mandate an employee-employer relationship, so independent contractors paid by a Form 1099 are not eligible. For more information on setting up an HRA, go to **www.gtm.com/health_options**.

HEALTH SAVINGS ACCOUNT

A *health savings account* (HSA) is a tax-exempt trust or custodial account established exclusively to pay for qualified medical expenses, and it can be contributed to by an employer or an employee. An HSA is available to anyone with a qualifying high deductible health insurance plan (i.e., at least $1,000 for individual coverage and $2,000 for family coverage). Health Savings Account funds may be used to cover the health insurance deductible and any co-payments for medical services, prescriptions, or products, as well as over-the-counter drugs and long-term care insurance. Health Savings Account funds may also be used toward payment of health insurance premiums during any period of unemployment.

Retirement

Like medical coverage, retirement plans are a standard part of U.S. corporate employee benefit packages. While not legally mandated to offer employees a retirement plan, employers may consider doing so in order to attract and retain the best employees. If a retirement plan is offered, the employer must comply with IRS tax requirements and administrative requirements as set forth in the U.S. *Employee Retirement Income Security Act* (ERISA). Two popular retirement options for household employees are the *Individual Retirement Account* (IRA) and the *Roth IRA*. Both are fairly simple programs to establish as an employee benefit, and therefore, suitable as a household employee benefit.

An IRA is a special savings plan authorized by the federal government to help people accumulate funds for retirement. Traditional IRAs and Roth IRAs allow individual taxpayers to contribute 100% of their earnings up to the IRA's plan-specified maximum dollar amount. Each year, the IRS sets maximum annual contributions for IRAs, with *catch-up* contributions by contributions for people ages 50 and over. For 2006, maximum contributions are $4,000, with an additional catch-up of $1,000 for those ages 50 or older. (See the table below for maximum contributions.)

Traditional IRA contributions may be tax deductible, whereas Roth IRA contributions are not. Roth IRA principal and interest accumulate tax-free. A Roth IRA usually is preferred by those ineligible for the tax deductions associated with the traditional IRA or by those who want their qualified Roth IRA distributions to be tax- and penalty-free, which depends on all conditions being met. Some people prefer a Roth IRA as a means to simply build a retirement egg without the worry of paying taxes at a later date (Roth contributions have already been taxed).

Facts & Figures

MAXIMUM IRA CONTRIBUTIONS*

Year	Maximum contribution	Additional catch-up amount for those over age 50
2006	$4,000	$1,000
2007	$4,000	$1,000
2008	$5,000	$1,000

*Pertains to both traditional and Roth IRAs.

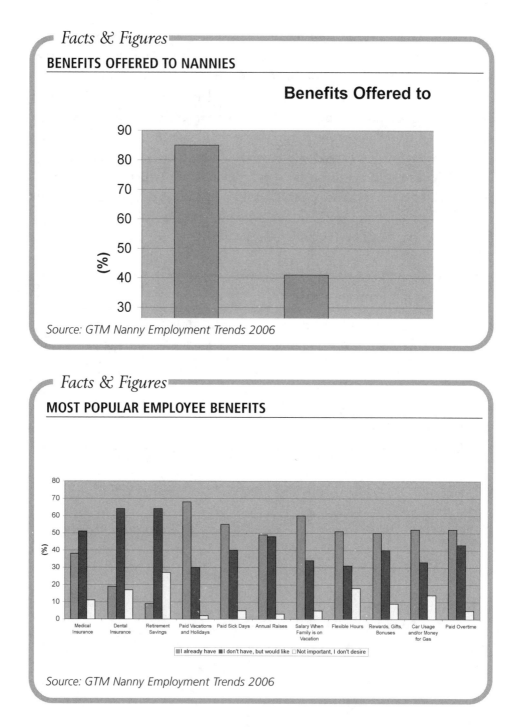

Facts & Figures

BENEFITS OFFERED TO NANNIES

Benefits Offered to

Source: GTM Nanny Employment Trends 2006

Facts & Figures

MOST POPULAR EMPLOYEE BENEFITS

Source: GTM Nanny Employment Trends 2006

Life Insurance

Some employers offer their employees life insurance coverage. The main purpose of life insurance is to provide a death benefit to the employee's dependents or beneficiaries, in order to help replace lost income and protect against the financial losses that could occur from the insured's untimely death.

Generally, there are two types of life insurance: term and permanent (whole). *Term life insurance* pays a death benefit to beneficiaries if the insured dies during the term the policy exists. *Permanent life insurance* generally is designed to provide long-term life insurance coverage for the insured's entire life—up to 100 years old. It has two components:

1. the death benefit and
2. a cash accumulation benefit, which differentiates it from term insurance.

The coverage may vary, but commonly it covers either one full year of an employee's salary (up to a specified limit) or double an employee's salary (up to a specified limit). A policy with a death benefit up to $50,000 is tax deductible to the employer. This helps protect the policy's designated beneficiary in the event of an employee's death. Life insurance coverage is not mandated by law, but it is a desirable employee benefit offered by an employer.

Educational Assistance

Another common employer benefit for employees is educational assistance for education or training pursued outside of working hours. Although optional for an employer to offer, educational assistance is beneficial in providing a satisfying workplace. The employer may tailor the assistance to best suit him or her. Guidelines provided in the employee handbook may include: educational pursuits that will be covered (e.g., classes must be provided by an accredited educational organization and relate to the employee's occupation); the limit available for educational assistance per year; educational expenses that are covered (e.g., tuition only, tuition and books, etc.); and, what requirements the employee must meet to receive assistance (e.g., the employee must achieve a passing grade as defined by the educational organization).

With these guidelines, an employer should include information on the process the employee must follow for assistance. Consider whether the employee needs to:

- provide the employer with a course description and a written request for assistance prior to the class start;
- obtain a signed approval from the employer prior to class start in order to be reimbursed for expenses (see p.277); and,
- achieve a specific grade or higher to obtain reimbursement.

Be precise to ensure that the employee understands what is required. Also, employers may consider paying for professional membership fees, industry conferences, or trade journal subscriptions.

CASE STUDY

MARY STARKEY
FOUNDER, OWNER
STARKEY INTERNATIONAL INSTITUTE FOR HOUSEHOLD MANAGEMENT
DENVER, CO
A GTM PARTNER

Mary Starkey opened the first household service management educational institute in the United States, and has mentored household employment professionals for more than twenty-four years.

"Private service is experiencing an awakening and renaissance into the professional world," said Starkey. "With a new paradigm for private service in hand, certified household management graduates are bringing standards and professionalism to the American household employment industry."

Starkey noted that service management education for employers and staff is taking household service out of a crisis mode of operation into a defined process of identifying service expectations and performing accepted service etiquette practices. Household service management education guides employers to articulate overall household standards and to identify individual needs. Starkey suggested that employers utilize her service management tool, the

Day in the Life. Employers plan and communicate with staff their expected daily activities, slotting them into a time-oriented weekly schedule. Then, the employers carry them out for a week or two. Next, the employers review their weekly plan to determine whether expectations were met and whether the tasks are functional and feasible for the family and the home.

"Private service has become a recognized and well-paid career path," she said. "Now, service professionals must focus on educating themselves and growing our industry in professional standards, state-of-the-art practices, and industry ethics."

Continuing education, training, seminars, and conferences play an important role in corporate employment. This education, as well as Internet learning events that educate employees, are important in promoting professional growth and elevating employee performance—making the educational benefit a win-win proposition for both the employer and employee. It is important for a household employer to decide whether access to education is an important employee benefit, and if so, at what frequency.
—Guy

Flexible Work Hours

Flexible work hours—an often overlooked employee benefit—enable an employee to work different (flexible) hours during the workweek. When an employee can determine elements of a flexible schedule, flexible work hours can be an important employee benefit for staff with significant personal obligations, such as the need to attend to regular medical treatment (e.g., physical therapy, chemotherapy, etc.), or family needs (e.g., children, parents, or other dependents who need assistance at variable hours throughout the week).

Flexible work hours are not an alternative to personal or sick time. A flexible work schedule is most often a long-term arrangement, with the employee working the full workweek but at nonstandard hours. It is generally not to be used for the occasional doctor's appointment or parent-teacher meeting.

Although this may not suit all household schedules, employers willing to consider flexible working arrangements (when requested in advance) are likely to establish a more loyal, stable, and happy household workforce. Recognizing and remembering that employees have a family and a personal and social life outside of work is important to any employer-employee relationship. Many household employers allow for part-time work, time off during the week if the employee worked during the weekend, or time off for the occasional personal commitment or infrequent sick day—with each potential circumstance being discussed in the work agreement, in the employee handbook, and at the start of employment. Clear communication is essential for mutual understanding. Therefore, employers offering permanent flexible work arrangements should carefully plan schedules with the employee, particularly if the household help member is tasked with dependent care.

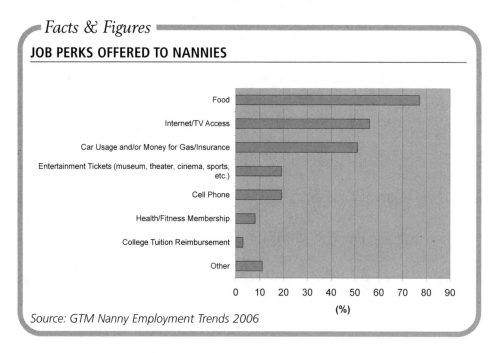

Facts & Figures

JOB PERKS OFFERED TO NANNIES

Source: GTM Nanny Employment Trends 2006

Prepaid Legal Services

Some employers offer employees prepaid legal services as an employee benefit. Prepaid legal services may involve citizenship, divorce, adoption, and so on, and create a unique value to employees who require legal advice and representation. Prepaid legal services may be available through a subscription plan. Employers need to clearly state in work agreements and the employee handbook the premium requirements for prepaid legal services, and if such services are provided at the employer's discretion.

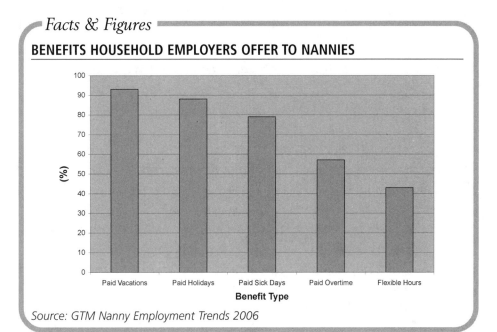

Facts & Figures

BENEFITS HOUSEHOLD EMPLOYERS OFFER TO NANNIES

Source: GTM Nanny Employment Trends 2006

CASE STUDY

ARLINE RUBEL
OWNER AND PRESIDENT
TOWN AND COUNTRY COMPANION AND NURSING SERVICES, INC.
NEW YORK, NY

Arline Rubel, owner and president of the New York City-based Town and Country Companion and Nursing Services, Inc., relies on a lifetime of experience—from orchestrating home care for family members, to teaching mentally challenged adults independent living, to referring employees to work positions in the home. Growing up with a brother with cerebral palsy and then as an adult helping eight ailing family members obtain care in their homes enabled Rubel to hone her skills and expertise in this area.

Many caregivers believe that working in a private home or on a one-on-one basis offers tremendous benefits, noted Rubel. Many enjoy the close relationships that develop, and derive pride and satisfaction from seeing first hand the results of their work. "Many frequently work closely with family and professionals, and develop a team approach to ensure the client receives the best care possible," said Rubel. "The work is challenging and difficult. Those who do it well are to be admired and appreciated."

Rubel and her staff use lengthy and detailed interviews to learn as much as possible about applicants, including work history, personality, level of responsibility previously held, communication skills, motivation ability, and work preferences. "An appropriate, consistent, and checkable work history with written references is the best place to begin," said Rubel. "References communicate important and reassuring information particular to the position."

Employers, advised Rubel, should be candid about their expectations, job duties, and difficulties that may arise on the job. In addition, Rubel said, employers need to discuss with job applicants how emergencies should be handled, who the decision maker is, who to call in certain situations, which professionals need to be involved, household expenses, meals, sick time, personal calls, and visitors.

"A successful and long-term employment relationship is generally a two-way street," she said. Rubel offers a friendly ear to both her client and the caregiver she places—even years after the initial placement—because she believes that most jobs fall apart when issues are ignored or not dealt with constructively. According to Rubel, she encourages each party to find a workable solution. Most issues are solvable, she noted, when both parties use constructive communication.

Professionalism includes open communication throughout employment to ensure employee and employer happiness. Some household employees look for no more employee benefits than just a few extra days off, extra pay on working holidays, and professional treatment. Employee benefits are not necessarily all perks that an employer must purchase for the employee.
—Guy

Use of Employer's Personal Property and Facilities

Use of personal property and facilities normally unavailable to the employee outside of work can be considered a great employee benefit. Many employers allow household employees to use certain household property or facilities not required to perform their jobs. This may include use of the home computer, television, exercise equipment/gym, swimming pool, and so on. The employee handbook needs to clearly list what is available for employee use and to whom this can extend in terms of friends and family of the employee. The employee handbook must also clearly state which parts of the property and facilities are off limits.

Employees should be reminded that the employer owns the property/facility, and that the employer has the right to inspect and monitor usage—including, for example, user history files on the Internet and sent email messages. The employee handbook should outline procedures for reporting needed repairs or any damage or misuse of property and facilities to the employer. (Please see sample policy on p.79.)

Holiday Club Savings Account

An employer may choose to establish what is commonly known as a *holiday club savings account*, which works like other savings plans. Employees may authorize in writing that a specified amount be deducted from their paycheck and deposited into a holiday club savings account. This account usually runs just a few weeks short of a full year and enables the employee to collect his or her savings in the fall (generally mid-October), when he or she may require extra spending money for the holiday season.

Q&A

Q. I would like to be as clear as possible when instructing my household help on what is available to them for use at my home while they are performing their duties. What is the best way to do this?

A. Employers should detail all relevant information in the employee handbooks. This includes not only wages, hours, and job requirements, but also information on auto insurance coverage when a staff member is required to drive to complete a work task and use of an employer's facilities (television, computer, etc.).

Odds are, not every question will be answered, so be sure to meet with the employee to discuss any question or item that arises—particularly during the first week of employment. Once questions are answered, remember to update the employee handbook to clearly specify what has been agreed upon.

Facts & Figures

GIFTS HOUSEHOLD EMPLOYERS GIVE TO NANNIES

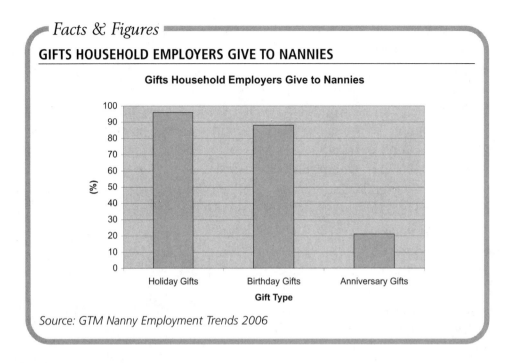

Gifts Household Employers Give to Nannies

Source: GTM Nanny Employment Trends 2006

Facts & Figures

20 IDEAS FOR BENEFITS OR PERKS

1. Sick/personal/vacation time
2. Cell phone use
3. Tuition waivers
4. Education/seminar/conference expense
5. Annual bonuses
6. Sponsorship of employee's family from other countries
7. Purchase of a home
8. Frequent flyer miles
9. Entertainment tickets to ball games/movies/shows
10. Time share/use of a vacation home
11. Gas card
12. Gift certificates
13. Purchase of a computer/PDA
14. Relaxation time
15. Housing allowance
16. Free medical care
17. Retirement funding
18. Education of dependent
19. Life insurance
20. Clothing allowance

Benefits Checklist

√ Investigate health and insurance coverage options thoroughly to see which one best fits an employee's needs and an employer's budget.

√ For the benefit of the family and household help, calculate the amount of personal time to be offered to employees.

√ Set regular review periods for salary changes and salary bonuses, and make sure employees know when these might occur.

√ Be clear on the extra perks the employee receives while working within the household—including use of facilities and property.

√ Consider providing your nanny with mileage reimbursement or a gas card to help with his or her commute or with transporting children.

√ Think about developing a transportation policy. You may, perhaps, provide an auto club membership to your employee who drives as part of his or her job, or periodically provide for the vehicle in use to be maintained with a tune up and oil change.

√ Consider adding special perks to help your nanny. You may establish an employee assistance plan or gift certificate to a spa/health club as a way to help your employee de-stress.

√ Consider providing your nanny with a little scheduled free time each week for him or her to make personal errands and phone calls.

Managing Payroll and Taxes

In the United States today, GTM Household Employment Experts™ estimates that there are more than two million household employees. The United States Internal Revenue Service (IRS) reports that only 239,810 employers of household employees paid taxes using the IRS Schedule H Form in 2003. Even accounting for the percentage of household employees with more than one employer, this amounts to a startling number of household employers in noncompliance with paying payroll taxes.

Many people do not pay payroll taxes because they falsely believe that:
- they will not be caught;
- they know friends or neighbors who are noncompliant;
- their employees do not necessarily want to be paid above board;
- the employees will realize more income;
- it costs the employer more; and,
- it is not a *real* employment situation.

Although household payroll taxes may be confusing to many, this chapter describes an easy-to-follow, step-by-step guide to managing household employment payroll and taxes. (For the latest information on payroll and taxes, visit **www.gtm.com/resourcecenter**.)

Employer Responsibilities

It is your duty to clearly and fully understand what your responsibilities are as a household employer. Ignorance is no excuse or defense for not complying with laws and regulations.

Household employers who choose to pay their nannies off the books are putting themselves and their nannies at risk. By not paying payroll taxes (dubbed the *nanny tax*), the employer is risking hefty fines, penalties, and even jail time, and the employee is losing valuable protections mandated by law, such as unemployment insurance and disability coverage. (See "Paying Off the Books—The Risks" on page 145.)

A household employer must understand the federal, state, and local employment laws that pertain to his or her household. Knowing the risks of noncompliance is part of fully understanding your employment laws. Depending on your location, you may have plenty of requirements to meet. Many laws require the employer to obtain, file, and submit necessary paperwork. For instance, for each person hired, an I-9 Form must be completed. Tax laws also have paperwork requirements, such as reporting wages to the Department of Labor or a state's Wage and Hour Division. While some laws require employers to submit forms to a designated department or division, others require employers to file completed forms and be ready to produce the paperwork when requested by government officials.

Dealing with taxes and payroll is time consuming, nerve-racking, and complicated. GTM calculates that a household employer spends more than sixty hours a year handling payroll and tax administration. It is not easy, and many household employers choose to use the services of a professional payroll service, such as GTM's EasyPay. Many household employers find security in knowing that their household payroll and taxes are taken care of by experienced and qualified professionals.

Facts & Figures

HOUSEHOLD EMPLOYER'S TAX GUIDE

IF you	THEN you need to
A. pay cash wages of $1,500 or more in 2006 to any one household employee	withhold and pay Social Security and Medicare taxes.
Do not count wages you pay to— • your spouse; • your child under age 21; • your parent ; or, • any employee under age 18 at any time in 2006.	• The taxes are 15.3% of cash wages. • Your employee's share is 7.65%. (You can choose to pay it yourself and not withhold it.) • Your share is a matching 7.65%.
B. pay total cash wages of $1,000 or more in any calendar quarter of 2005 or 2006 to household employees	pay federal unemployment tax.
Do not count wages you pay to your— • spouse; • child under age 21; or, • parent.	• The tax is usually 0.8% of cash wages. • Wages more than $7,000 a year per employee are not taxed. • You also may owe state unemployment tax.

NOTE: If neither A nor B above applies, you do not need to pay any federal employment taxes, but you may still need to pay state employment taxes.

Source: IRS Publication 926: Household Employer's Tax Guide for wages paid in 2006.

CASE STUDY

HILARY LOCKHART
PRESIDENT
A+ NANNIES, INC.
MESA, AZ
GTM PARTNER AGENCY

Hilary Lockhart of A+ Nannies said a nanny she placed learned the importance of being paid above board. This nanny was working in a position for nine months and was told by her employer that her services were no longer needed. The employer and nanny agreed at the outset to payment under the table. So, when the nanny was let go, she was five months' pregnant and unable to collect unemployment insurance benefits. She looked for work for six or seven weeks unsuccessfully before her doctor ordered bed rest until she delivered her child.

"The nanny couldn't collect any (unemployment) money at all because there was no record of her ever working," said Lockhart. "So, the nanny—five months' pregnant—is unable to find work being a nanny. No one seems to want to hire a nanny for four months and then give six weeks off for maternity leave."

Now, Lockhart tells clients and nannies to follow the law and pay all taxes. "Number one, I tell them it's against the law to pay under the table," said Lockhart, whose business places an average of four to ten child care workers a month. "I give all my clients a lot of information on taxes and the law. I used to ask clients if they were going to pay cash. I don't ask that any more. I tell (nannies) to get the taxes done right, especially in light of situations like this."

As a former nanny for seven years, Lockhart brings to her business a well-rounded perspective—a nanny, mother, and president of a referral agency. Constantly learning, she said she considers her clients' wishes and requirements against her own litmus test of placing herself as the nanny in that situation—which is why she now strongly advocates proper payroll and tax payments.

Paying household employment taxes involves a lot more than adherence to the law. Unemployment coverage also protects employees in instances when they become involuntarily unemployed. If a former employee files a claim for unemployment insurance coverage, then the state unemployment fund, which the employer had paid into through payroll taxes, pays the employee his or her unemployment insurance payment, which is a percentage of the employee's average weekly wage. The employer is not subject to additional or ongoing payments once the employee leaves the household. However, the household employer may incur higher payroll taxes (i.e., a higher unemployment insurance rate) with future employees.
—Guy

Facts & Figures

PAYING OFF THE BOOKS—THE RISKS

There is no doubt about it; paying off the books is risky business. It puts the employer and employee in peril by not providing the payroll coverage employers and employees are entitled to by law.

Liability to household employer:
- increased exposure to an IRS audit;
- the penalty for failing to file (or attempting to evade or defeat tax payments) is $25,000-$100,000 and potential jail time;
- a false or fraudulent statement or failure to furnish a tax statement could result in a $1,000 fine;
- payment of all back employment taxes, interest, and penalties; and,
- no eligibility for tax breaks, Dependent Care Assistance Program (DCAP), or Child Tax Credit.

Liability to household employee:

- IRS penalties due to failure to file timely income taxes;
- no unemployment insurance benefits;
- no legal employment history or credit history;
- no contributions to Social Security and Medicare, and therefore no eligibility to these benefits; and,
- no workers' compensation or disability coverage.

Facts & Figures

NANNIES' PERCEIVED BENEFITS WHEN THEIR EMPLOYER USES A PAYROLL AND TAX SERVICE

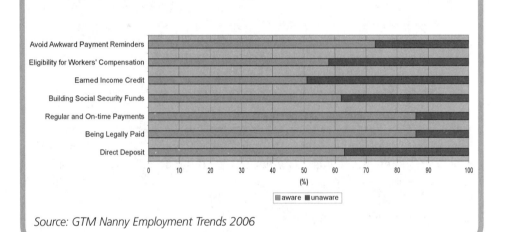

Source: GTM Nanny Employment Trends 2006

Understand the Laws

Ignorance is no excuse for breaking the law. As an employer, it is critical for you to understand the laws and regulations governing household employment, payroll taxes, hiring, and so on.

EMPLOYEE VS. INDEPENDENT CONTRACTOR

As detailed in Chapter 2, the determination of employee vs. independent contractor status is important in household employment. The majority of household employees are just that—employees. Therefore, they need to be accurately paid according to applicable labor and tax laws. More information on employee vs. independent contractor status is available in IRS Publication 926, *Household Employer's Tax Guide* and 15A, *Employee's Supplemental Tax Guide*.

RESEARCHING TAX LAWS

The IRS states that a household employer who pays an employee $1,500 or more (as of 2006) in gross wages during the calendar year must comply with all state and federal laws. (See "Comply with Tax Law" on page 156.) For more information, see IRS Publication 926, *Household Employer's Tax Guide*, at **www.irs.gov** or **www.gtm.com/resourcecenter**.

> ## *Our Advice*
>
> *"I cannot imagine trying to do my own tax payments. To me, doing payroll and tax payments yourself is pennywise and pound-foolish. I am a strong believer in having professionals do the work. These people are professionals, and this is what they're good at."*
> —Stephanie Oana
>   Household Employer (nanny)
>   Lawyer
>   Oakland, CA

FOLLOW PAYROLL REGULATIONS

According to the Fair Labor Standards Act (FLSA), all household employees must be paid at least the federal or state minimum wage, whichever is higher. The federal minimum wage is $5.15 per hour (in 2006), but state minimum wages may be higher. (See page 102 for a state-by-state minimum wage chart.) Under certain conditions, benefits such as room and board can account for a portion of the employee's wage. Overtime pay is required for most live-out employees (according to FLSA) and there may be additional requirements for household employees, including live-ins, depending on the state in which the household resides. (See page 115 for more information on overtime). Paid vacations, holidays, and sick days are not required by law, and are at an employer's discretion.

Q&A

Q: *Can we put our household employee on our company payroll?*
A: *Generally, no. Your company payroll should be reserved for those employees who work for your company. Equally important, you cannot deduct your household employee's wages from your company's expenses. In most cases, you must pay your federal household employment taxes on your own federal income tax return, either annually or quarterly. The only exception to reporting your federal household employment taxes on your personal federal income tax return is if you are a sole proprietor or your home is on a farm operated for profit. In either of these instances, you may opt to include your federal household employment taxes with your federal employment tax deposits or other payments for your business or farm employees. (See IRS Publication 926 for more information.)*

EMPLOYER RESPONSIBILITIES

Household employers are responsible for reporting and paying required payroll taxes. (See Appendix A for a calendar on employer tax responsibilities.) It is definitely not a fun part of household management, but it is a very necessary one. By complying with payroll tax requirements, such as Social Security, Medicare, and unemployment insurance taxes, the employer ensures that the employee is eligible for benefits from these federal or state programs. Household employers are not obligated to withhold federal or state *income* taxes from the employee's gross wages unless the employer and employee mutually agree to it.

Obtain the Necessary Paperwork

It is extremely important that you obtain all the necessary paperwork needed when you hire your household help. This includes several federal and state forms. Some of the documents you will be familiar with, probably having filled them out yourself when starting a job. Others are more unique to to this type of employment or are documents you would probably not be familiar with unless you have been an employer before. From your employee's perspective, these are the forms need to ensure he or she is getting paid and getting paid properly. To properly pay an employee, an employer should obtain the following:

- Form SS-4 *Employer Identification Number* from the IRS
- Form W-4 *Employee's Withholding Allowance Certificate* to provide to newly hired employees
- Form I-9 *Employment Eligibility Verification* to provide to newly hired employees
- Form W-10 *Dependent Care Provider's Identification and Certification* for DCA Dependent Care Assistance (DCA)
- Form W-5 *Earned Income Credit Advance Payment Certificate*, if applicable
- Form 1040 Schedule H *Household Employment Taxes*, an annual form
- Form 1040ES *Estimated Tax for Individuals*, optional
- Registration form for a state unemployment identification number
- Registration form for a state withholding number (if applicable)
- State's new hire report (if necessary)

EMPLOYEE'S SOCIAL SECURITY NUMBER

Save for the SS-4, which is discussed on page 150, before you can complete any of the necessary paperwork, you must ensure that your employee has a Social Security number. Do not assume that the employee has one, especially if he or she is not a U.S. citizen, and verify every employee's number with the Social Security Administration. If an employee does not have a Social Security number and is a legal U.S. citizen, then he or she can apply for one with Form SS-5 (Application for a Social Security Card). If an employee is not a U.S. citizen, an Individual Tax Identification Number (ITIN) can be obtained by using IRS Form W-7 (Application for IRS Individual Tax Payer Identification Number). An ITIN is only used for federal withholding tax purposes.

Facts & Figures

INDIVIDUAL TAXPAYER IDENTIFICATION NUMBER

Regardless of whether a person is legally employed, an IRS Individual Taxpayer Identification Number (ITIN) can be used by those who are ineligible to obtain a Social Security number but who need to pay taxes on wages earned; these people include certain nonresident and resident aliens, and their spouses and dependents. The ITINs are nine-digit numbers beginning with the number nine and formatted like a Social Security number (9XX-XX-XXXX). They are not to be used for non-tax purposes (i.e., proof of identity for a driver's license, residency claim or employment, or to apply for welfare and health benefits). The IRS Form W-7 (Application for IRS Individual Taxpayer Identification Number) is used to obtain an ITIN and may be submitted to the IRS. According to the IRS, people using an ITIN cannot claim the earned income tax credit.

EMPLOYER IDENTIFICATION NUMBER (EIN)

All employers must have an employer identification number (EIN). This is generally the first document you will complete and gives you a specific tax number, much like your personal Social Security number, for dealing with the IRS and other parties. It is provided by the IRS through Form SS-4 *Application for Employer Identification Number*. As SS-4 form may be obtained by telephoning the IRS at 800-829-4933 or visiting **www.irs.gov** and completing it online.

FORM W-4

If an employer and an employee have agreed to withhold income taxes, then employers should provide employees with a Form W-4, *Employee's Withholding Allowance Certificate*, and the employee must complete it. Form W-4 can be downloaded from **www.irs.gov** or **www.gtm.com/ resourcecenter**. The W-4 form documents how much income tax is withheld from an employee's salary. If the W-4 is not submitted, then the employer must withhold the employee's income tax at the highest rate—as a single person with no allowances. (See page 272 for a sample *W-4 Form*.)

Employers who have agreed to withhold income taxes for their employees are required to send a signed W-4 to the IRS when an employee:

- claims an exemption from withholding and the employee's wages are normally more than $200 per week or
- claims 10 or more allowances.

FORM I-9

Employers need to provide employees with an Form I-9 *Employment Eligibility Verification.* All employers in the United States must obtain a completed Form I-9 for every employee hired. Form I-9 attempts to ensure that only people legally authorized to work in the United States are hired. Employers use I-9 to verify the identity and employment eligibility of employees. (See page 248 for a sample of an *I-9 Form.*)

Considering the rapid way in which immigration policies are changing and becoming stricter, it is vital that all employers complete the I-9 and keep it on file with appropriate copies of documentation in the employee's personnel file. In short, this proves your employee is eligible to be employed in the United States.

FORM W-10

Form W-10 *Dependent Care Provider's Identification and Certification* is an optional informational form that any taxpayer can use to obtain information about the dependent care provider (household employees or even day care centers). This is the same information that the taxpayer reports on Form 2441 *Child and Dependent Care Expenses* with the 1040 Personal Tax Return. The IRS states that the taxpayer can use Form W-10 or any of the other methods of due diligence to collect this information, including:

- a copy of the dependent care provider's Social Security card or driver's license that includes his or her Social Security number;
- a recently printed letterhead or printed invoice that shows the provider's name, address, and taxpayer identification number (TIN); if the provider is your employer's company's dependent care plan, a copy of the statement provided by your employer under the plan; or,

- a copy of the household employee's W-4, if the provider is the household employee and he or she gave the employer a properly completed Form W-4 (Employee's Withholding Allowance Certificate).

FORM W-5

Form W-5 (Earned Income Credit Advance Payment Certificate) allows employees to claim *earned income credit* (EIC). Employees can receive this credit with their pay during the year. An employer is encouraged to notify each employee whose combined or total wages for the year are less than $31,030 (2006 filing single or $33,030 filing jointly) that he or she may be eligible for EIC. More information can be found in IRS Publication 596.

SCHEDULE H

Starting in 1995, the Schedule H (Household Employment Taxes) form was added to federal Form 1040 U.S. Individual Income Tax Return for employers who paid more than a total of $1,500 during the calendar year (as of tax year 2006) to household employees, or for employers who paid all employees more than $1,000 in any one quarter during the calendar year. Schedule H enables employers to report wages and taxes withheld for household help to the federal government with their own 1040 form.

According to the IRS, for the tax year 2003, 130,728,360 individual income tax returns were filed. Of these, only 239,810 forms showed an entry for household employment taxes. With the estimated number of households employing household help totaling more than two million, this is a mere fraction of the taxes that should be filed for household employment each year.

FORM 1040-ES

This option of transmitting taxes quarterly versus paying at the end of the year with form Schedule H (Household Employment Taxes) allows a household employer to make estimated tax payments to cover household employment taxes. These vouchers allow you to make payments and pay all of the employment taxes at once or in installments. This form is due on a quarterly basis. (Refer to 1040-ES filing instructions for due dates, and see the table on page 161.)

CASE STUDY

Zuzka Polishook
Household Employer
Pacific Palisades, CA (LA Area)
GTM Payroll and Tax Services Client

Zuzka Polishook hired her first nanny in August 2003, after the birth of her second daughter. With a two-and-a-half-year-old daughter and a second daughter just a few months old, Polishook transitioned her babysitter into a full-time nanny and housekeeper to help care for the two girls, as well as for a large house and two dogs.

Although Polishook knew from experience that the employee was responsible and a hard worker, she still painstakingly drafted an employee contract signed by both the nanny/housekeeper and her. She did this to formalize this existing relationship, but more importantly, to clear any potential problem areas and resolve any unspoken questions. "The nanny knows where she stands with it, and I know where I stand with it," said Polishook. "It's peace of mind for me. No matter how obvious, I wrote it down. It acts as a checklist for both parties."

However, even though she was exceedingly capable of preparing the paperwork and doing the subsequent necessary payroll and tax responsibilities, she quickly was surprised by the amount of paperwork involved in employing a domestic employee. "I am extremely busy," said Polishook. "Time is my most valued currency, and I was clueless where to start. I didn't even know what I needed to know." Thus, Polishook took advice from a friend and contracted with a tax and payroll service to manage the payroll and tax piece of the household employment equation.

"I'm in the know and in control," she said, "but I don't have to figure the details out." By using a payroll service, she was buying peace of mind, and stated, "now, I am able to dedicate the hours I would have spent figuring payroll and taxes to my children."

Polishook advises families considering a payroll and tax service to calculate the value of their time per hour with the number of hours per month spent addressing tax and wage requirements. Once you determine the value of your time against how much time it takes away from spending with your children, using a payroll service may seem like a cost savings.

> *As a household employer going it alone, it can be difficult to devote the time and energy needed to stay abreast of the changing employment regulation and tax laws. Using a payroll and tax service is an inexpensive way to save busy household employers valuable time and money.*
> *—Guy*

STATE UNEMPLOYMENT IDENTIFICATION NUMBER

Household employers are required to obtain a state unemployment identification number with the state where the physical work will be performed. Refer to IRS Publication 926 for a list of State Unemployment Tax Agencies (also available online at **www.irs.gov**). The ID number is needed to pay state unemployment taxes on a quarterly basis and will appear on the W-2 (Wage and Tax Statement) form for each employee.

STATE WITHHOLDING CERTIFICATE

It is optional for an employer to withhold taxes from an employee's paycheck. If an employer and employee decide to withhold state income taxes, then the state's registration form should be completed by contacting the state's withholding agency. This provides an employer with an ID number, a coupon booklet, and instructions on how to submit withholding taxes according to the state's laws. This number will also appear on Form W-2 for each employee.

STATE NEW HIRE REPORT

New hire reporting is a process by which an employer has to register any newly hired employee with the state within a certain time of the hire date. This report usually gives contact and basic identification information for each new employee to the state's department of labor, which then transmits the report to the National Directory of New Hires (NDNH). (The most common use of this information is to help the child support collection unit track down debtors for child support payments.)

WORKERS' COMPENSATION AND DISABILITY INSURANCE

Most states require household employers to carry a workers' compensation and/or disability policy if employing a full-time or part-time person. These policies provide compensation to an employee who is injured on the job. It is recommended that even if your state does not require employers to have a policy, you should consider obtaining appropriate coverage for peace of mind. Some states also require insurance coverage for non occupational injury or illness.

If you do not cover yourself for an employee injury, you set yourself up for possibly a very costly lawsuit if your nanny, eldercare provider, housekeeper, or other employee is injured on the job. Homeowner's insurance policies often *do not* cover these situations. With the proper insurance coverage, you will protect yourself and your home—while also protecting your employee from the added costs of the injury and potential loss of work.

> ## Q&A
>
> *Q. Must I carry workers' compensation insurance on full-time and part-time household employees?*
> *A. Most states require employers to carry a workers' compensation and/or disability policy for any person employed fulltime or part-time. Workers' compensation policies protect the employer from lawsuits and liability in case an employee is injured in the home while performing her or his job duties. Workers' compensation also protects the employee, who, if hurt on the job, can collect certain medical and wage-loss compensation. Even if your state does not require you to carry workers' compensation/disability insurance, it is a very good idea to do so.*

Record Retention

An employer should make sure that all hiring, tax, and payroll documentation regarding an employee's hire, including all IRS and state forms, is kept in a safe place. It is recommended that these forms be kept on file for at least five years, in case the IRS or Department of Justice needs to check who is, or has been, employed by the employer.

Comply with Tax Laws

GTM Household Employment Experts™, which provides tax and payroll services to household employers through its EasyPay Service, estimates that employers can expect to pay 9%–12% of the employee's gross pay for the following:

- federal unemployment insurance (0.8%);
- Social Security and Medicare (7.65%);
- state unemployment insurance (about 2%-4% in most states); and,
- other state and local taxes (e.g., employment training or workforce taxes).

GTM estimates that based on average salaries, employees can expect to pay 10%–30% of their gross pay for:

- Social Security and Medicare (7.65%);
- other state and local taxes (e.g., disability), if applicable; and,
- federal and state income taxes, if they choose (estimated at 15%–25%).

Although tempting to many, not paying taxes is illegal. By not paying an employee lawfully, the employer is liable for all unpaid taxes, interests, and penalties, and may face a potential jail term.

Federal Taxes

There are several federal taxes that apply to the household employer's payroll. Known as *payroll taxes*, these federal taxes are paid to the federal government via the employee's pay and are established to protect the employer and employee in the event the employee is no longer employed by the employer. For instance, if the employee is no longer needed by the employer, he or she may be covered by federal unemployment insurance. It is important to be aware of all federal, state, and local taxes applicable to you as an employer. Key federal taxes include Social Security, federal income tax, and the Federal Unemployment Tax Act (FUTA).

SOCIAL SECURITY

Social Security tax, otherwise known as Old Age Survivor's Disability Insurance (OASDI), is required to be paid by both the employer and the employee. Each pays half of the Social Security taxes owed to the federal government. This calculates to 6.2% each of the employee's gross salary (6.2% for the employee is withholding, 6.2% from the employer is a matching contribution, totaling 12.4%). The tax is capped at a gross salary of $94,200 in a calendar year as of 2006 (for both the employee and employer).

Paying into Social Security is an important benefit to your employee, as it provides retirement coverage when he or she becomes older. Protection for his or her future years is a valuable benefit, and shows your employee that you respect his or her position.

MEDICARE

Like Social Security, Medicare taxes require the employer and employee to contribute equally. This tax is 2.9%, so both pay 1.45% of the employee's gross salary. There is no salary limit earned for this tax.

As with Social Security, Medicare is an important benefit for your employee to have when he or she is older and retired, providing basic medical insurance when many need it the most.

FEDERAL INCOME TAX

Withholding federal income tax (FIT) from an employee's paycheck is optional, but if agreed to by employer and employee, then the employer must withhold income taxes based on the employee's completion of W-4. This is an employee-only withholding, and the employer does not incur any additional expenses. The FIT amount owed by each employee varies according to his or her income and filing status.

Paying federal income tax from each paycheck helps the employee disburse payment across the year, and not face paying the total federal income tax all at once. It also ensures that both employer and employee are complying with the law.

Federal Unemployment Tax Act

If an employer pays cash wages to a household employee, totaling $1,000 or more in any calendar quarter, then he or she is responsible for paying the *Federal Unemployment Tax Act* (FUTA). This is an employer tax and is not withheld from an employee's pay. It is calculated on the first $7,000 of gross wages per employee at the tax rate of 0.8%, if an employer has paid his or her state unemployment taxes on time. An employer must report FUTA with the Schedule H form, which is filed with his or her 1040 personal income tax return.

Federal unemployment, while an employer tax, benefits an employee if he or she finds him- or herself to be out of work.

> ## Q&A
>
> Q. *Is there a difference between being covered by Social Security and being eligible for Social Security?*
> A. *Yes, and it is significant. To be eligible for Social Security, an employee must work forty calendar quarters to be fully insured and eligible for retirement, disability, death, and survivor benefits. To be covered, you must work at least ten calendar quarters to be insured and eligible for limited death benefits.*

State and Local Tax Laws

Along with federal taxes, household employers are responsible for complying with their state and local tax laws. Be sure that you cover all payroll taxes—federal, state, and local.

State Unemployment Insurance

State unemployment insurance is an employer tax and is normally due on a quarterly basis. Unemployment insurance contributions are accumulated in every state's unemployment insurance fund for workers who can claim eligibility. State unemployment insurance is generally calculated between 2%–4% on a certain amount of each employee's gross wages for the calendar year, which varies state by state. For example, for new employers, Virginia's state unemployment insurance is set at 2.5% on the first $8,000 per employee, whereas Arizona requires 2.7% on the first $7,000 (in 2006).

Unemployment is an important factor for any worker. Sometimes, a new employee just does not work out, or perhaps circumstances change and you no longer need a nanny or other household worker. Unemployment insurance would protect your nanny and his or her family, paying a percent of their income, until he or she is hired elsewhere and no longer needs assistance.

STATE WITHHOLDING TAXES

State withholding taxes are employee income taxes based on filing status and wage level. This practice is not required, unless agreed upon by the employer and employee, but it generally helps employees distribute their owed income taxes throughout the year at regular intervals, rather than requiring a total payment at the end of the tax year. The employee may want the employer to withhold state income taxes from his or her paycheck.

Also, much like federal taxes, paying state withholding taxes documents an employee's legal employment history and is critical in their establishing and improving themselves financially. In addition, just like federal taxes, payment throughout the year helps pay taxes at a more manageable level, and not face a total sum payment once per year.

Q&A

Q. I am a housekeeper and my employer is paying my Social Security and Medicare but has asked me if I would like income taxes withheld. I am uncertain whether to have income tax withheld from my paycheck. What is the best scenario?

A. What is best depends on you. First, please know that choosing to withhold income tax from your paycheck is not the same as choosing whether to pay it. You must pay it. The option you ask about is whether you want your employer to withhold income tax from your paycheck or you want to pay the income tax yourself. So, this becomes a budgeting and convenience issue. We strongly discourage employees from trying to pay taxes on their own.

DISABILITY INSURANCE

Some states may require the employer to withhold additional taxes or insurances from the employee's pay. For example, both New Jersey and California have a state disability tax. The California State Disability Insurance (SDI) is a partial wage-replacement insurance plan for California workers. The SDI program is state mandated and funded through employee payroll deductions. It provides affordable, short-term benefits to eligible workers who suffer a loss of wages when they are unable to work due to a non-work related illness or injury, or a medically disabling condition from pregnancy or childbirth.

Q&A

Q. I am nervous about dealing with the IRS and all federal, state, and local tax forms that I need to complete. What can I do to ensure that I'm doing all I need to be doing, particularly since two friends of mine do not file the same paperwork that I do?

A. Given the circumstances, you're right to be anxious. Following all tax requirements can be confusing and time consuming, but it must be done. Refer to IRS Publication 926 and Publication 15, as well as relevant state and local labor and tax guides. Many household employers contract with payroll services firms like GTM to handle taxes and paperwork and to consult with experts regarding the precise, timely, and lawful handling of wages. Many who choose not to adhere to the tax law unfortunately risk heavy penalties and jail. Paying a household employee under the table puts the household employee in a very vulnerable spot, as he or she is without the protection of unemployment insurance, Social Security, and so on. The important thing is to make sure you pay the correct taxes.

LOCAL TAX

Some localities require an employer to withhold local income tax, based on either the place of employment or residence of the employee. Such localities include some in Ohio and Pennsylvania, as well as New York City.

Paying an Employee

Unless an employer already has a firm idea of when he or she wants an employee to be paid, it is probably best to talk to the employee to see what best suits his or her needs and to agree on a regular pay interval. Generally, workers must be paid at least twice a month; however, some states require a weekly pay frequency for household employment.

Wages should always be paid by check so both the employer and the employee have an earnings and deduction record for the current pay period and year-to-date accumulated totals (see Appendix D for a sample *Paycheck and Payroll Earnings Statement*.) The amount on the check should always be net (after all applicable taxes are withheld). An employer can also offer the option of direct deposit, which is a convenient payment method for both the employer and the employee.

Reporting and Filing Payroll Taxes

There are two options for filing federal payroll taxes: annually or quarterly. Household employers must report and file all federal taxes by using Schedule H, which is an annual reconciliation form that is used by the employer to report to the IRS wages paid to the household employee throughout the year.

Alternatively, employers may pay estimated taxes on a quarterly schedule to help alleviate the tax burden at the end of the year. In addition, Schedule H must be filed annually with the employer's personal tax return. To do this, an employer will need to file the 1040 Estimated Tax Form. This calculates an estimate of the following:

- employee federal income tax (FIT);
- employer and employee Social Security and Medicare; and,
- employer federal unemployment tax (FUTA).

This sum is an estimated amount for each quarter. The due dates for submitting this form are explained in the table below.

Facts & Figures

FILING FEDERAL TAXES

Quarter	Due
First (January–March)	April 15
Second (April–May)	June 15
Third (June–August)	September 15
Fourth (September–December)	January 15

If the estimated tax payments are not made quarterly, then an employer may want to arrange to have additional federal income taxes withheld from his or her own salary. This will help to avoid owing a significant sum on his or her personal tax return and also to avoid a possible 10% "under payment" penalty.

Each year, an employer must provide employees with Form W-2 (Wage and Tax Statement) on or before January 31. This provides a breakdown of all withholding and income throughout the previous calendar year and helps the employee submit her or his individual income tax forms.

By February 28 (or March 31 if the W-2 is filed electronically), the employer must also file the employer copy of the employee's W-2 and W-3 (a Wage Transmission report) forms to the Social Security Administration. A W-3 is a reconciliation of all W-2s for each employee, even if only employing one employee.

It is extremely important for your employee to be able to prove that he or she has a source of income in establishing credit, getting a loan or a credit card, or benefiting from any tax credits. Plus, both employer and employee may benefit from tax credits: an employer may benefit from credits and from a dependent care account at work, while an employee may benefit from the federal earned income tax credit.

FILING STATE TAXES

Most states require the quarterly filing of state taxes (state unemployment and other taxes). Unfortunately, state tax quarters do not coincide with federal tax quarters. Instead, states require taxes to be submitted every three months—typically one month after the quarter ends. After an employer has registered with the state to file taxes, the state sends blank quarterly forms with instructions. If an employer uses a payroll service, then he or she may avoid the hassle of signing checks and filing taxes accurately and timely.

If they so choose, the employer and the employee may file state income taxes (state withholding taxes) that are typically due each quarter. However, each state has specific filing frequencies based on how much income tax is withheld. The amount withheld from an employee's wages during a quarter generally determines the filing frequency in any given state (semiweekly, monthly, quarterly,

> **Q&A**
>
> *Q. What state taxes am I required to pay as a household employer?*
> *A. State employment laws are similar for a worker in the home or in the corporate office. All states have a state unemployment insurance tax, which employers must pay. This amount is a percentage (2%–4%) of the household employee's gross salary and is capped at an annual wage amount. For example, Illinois requires 3.3% on the first $9,000 of the gross wage per employee. Some states, such as California and New Jersey, require the employee to contribute a small amount to disability or unemployment out of her or his own gross pay in addition to employer payments.*

annually). When an employer registers with the state, state tax officials will inform her or him of the filing frequency. Another way to determine filing frequency is to refer to the welcome letter in the correspondence received with the state withholding income number.

Facts & Figures

FILING STATE TAXES

Quarter	Due
First (January–March)	April 30
Second (April–June)	July 31
Third (July–September)	October 31
Fourth (October–December)	January 31

Although these dates do apply for most states, they can vary from state to state. Be sure to double-check your state's due dates.

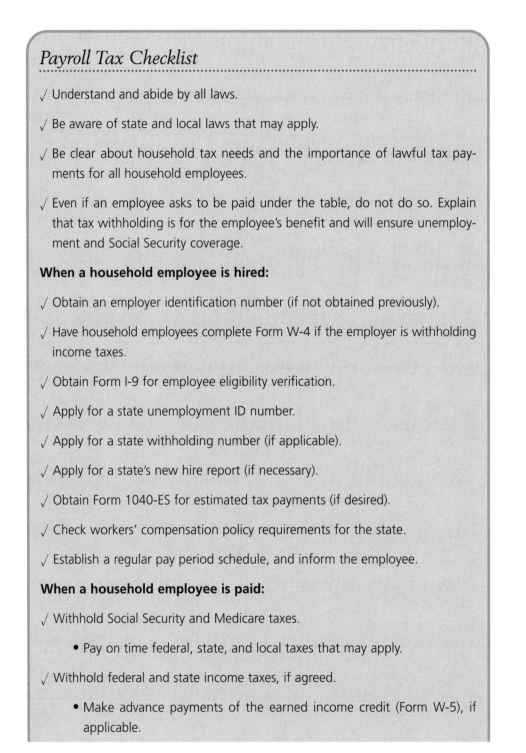

Payroll Tax Checklist

√ Understand and abide by all laws.

√ Be aware of state and local laws that may apply.

√ Be clear about household tax needs and the importance of lawful tax payments for all household employees.

√ Even if an employee asks to be paid under the table, do not do so. Explain that tax withholding is for the employee's benefit and will ensure unemployment and Social Security coverage.

When a household employee is hired:

√ Obtain an employer identification number (if not obtained previously).

√ Have household employees complete Form W-4 if the employer is withholding income taxes.

√ Obtain Form I-9 for employee eligibility verification.

√ Apply for a state unemployment ID number.

√ Apply for a state withholding number (if applicable).

√ Apply for a state's new hire report (if necessary).

√ Obtain Form 1040-ES for estimated tax payments (if desired).

√ Check workers' compensation policy requirements for the state.

√ Establish a regular pay period schedule, and inform the employee.

When a household employee is paid:

√ Withhold Social Security and Medicare taxes.

   • Pay on time federal, state, and local taxes that may apply.

√ Withhold federal and state income taxes, if agreed.

   • Make advance payments of the earned income credit (Form W-5), if applicable.

√ Send copy A of Form W-2 with Form W-3 to the Social Security Administration by February 28 (or March 31 if filing electronically) each year.

√ File Schedule H with the employer's federal income tax return (Form 1040) by April 15 each year.

√ Keep records in a safe place for five years.

Source: IRS Publication 926 Household Employer's Tax Guide.

For an easy-to-follow step-by-step tax guide, see Appendix A on page 221.

State tax form checklists can be found at **www.taxadmin.org/fta/link**.

9

Health and Safety Rules and Tips

A satisfying workplace is only obtained in a healthy and safe environment. This chapter discusses the Occupational Safety and Health Act (OSHA) and other safety issues within the household that will help make the workplace a better and safer one.

Occupational Safety and Health Act

The *Occupational Safety and Health Act* (OSHA) ensures that employers provide employees with a workplace that is free from recognized hazards that cause or could cause serious harm or death to employees. It is applicable to everyone except to sole proprietors and those employing family members in a business or on a farm. Under OSHA, employers must provide safety training to employees, inform employees about hazardous chemicals to which they may be exposed, and notify regulators about workplace accidents.

Under OSHA, employers must follow requirements to ensure a healthy work environment, which include providing training, medical examinations, and recordkeeping. Some employer requirements follow.

- Provide a workplace free from serious hazards, and comply with OSHA rules and regulations.
- Ensure that employees have and use safe tools and equipment.
- Use color codes, posters, labels, or signs to warn employees of potential hazards.

Q&A

Q. I recently argued with my full-time nanny about what I needed to provide her with to care for my five-year-old daughter with chicken pox. The nanny was concerned that she was exposed to the illness and was carrying it home to her husband, who had never had chicken pox. What types of protective gear am I liable for?

A. Every employer in the United States must ensure that a workplace—even one in the home—is a safe and healthy environment in which to work. As a household employer, you could provide your housekeeper with gloves and a face mask when using a chemical cleaner; gardener with eye goggles and ear plugs when using landscaping equipment; eldercare worker with medical gloves when injecting medication; or, your child care worker with medical gloves and a face mask when caring for a child with the flu, measles, chicken pox, and so on. Such universal precautions are standard in any work environment and are an ideal topic for employers to discuss with employees during the development of a work agreement and review of the employee handbook.

- Establish or update operating procedures, and communicate them to employees.
- Keep records of work-related injuries and illnesses. (Employers with ten or fewer employees and employers in certain low-hazard industries are exempt from this OSHA requirement.)

Some OSHA workplace concerns include:
- exposure to hazardous chemicals;
- first aid and medical treatment required as a result of a workplace injury;
- noise levels;
- protective gear (i.e., goggles, work shoes, and ear protectors);
- workplace temperatures and ventilation; and,
- safety training.

Because OSHA is so broadly written, household employers may want to contact a local OSHA office to determine specific requirements. Housekeepers might be instructed to wear protective gloves when in contact with cleaning solvents, or gardeners might be instructed to wear goggles and earplugs when performing landscaping work with certain equipment.

Employers also must follow OSHA record-keeping rules, which include maintaining a log of workplace injuries that require treatment beyond first aid.

A good practice is for employers to keep a written safety policy in the employee handbook, which could offer instructions on where the house's first aid kit is kept, a list of emergency service telephone numbers, protective gear required for specific tasks, and an employee requirement to report all health and safety issues immediately to the employer. In addition, the safety policy could provide instructions that improper use of equipment (i.e., using equipment for purposes other than what it is intended or using equipment that is not properly connected) is prohibited within the household.

Along with federal OSHA requirements, an employer may need to meet state and local health and safety requirements. To obtain information on state and local requirements, contact your state and local health departments, chambers of commerce, business bureaus, and so on.

Home Safety

Aside from federal, state, and local laws governing a healthy and safe workplace, household employers may take some basic steps to ensure household safety. These home safety measures apply to any home or household member, but can easily apply to household workers. This list is not exhaustive, but it does offer some general guidelines that employers may want to consider for their home.

NOTE: *According to the International Nanny Association, auto accidents are probably the most common type of claim involving a nanny and his or her employer. So, employers need to fully understand what and who is covered by their insurance policies. To be safe, employers may want to consider adding the nanny or other household worker to his or her auto insurance policy.*

Home Safety Checklist

There are many measures you can make to ensure that your home is safe, and an easy checklist reviewed occasionally can help you protect your family, friends, employees, and visitors from injury and harm.

Kitchen

√ Are the exhaust hood and duct on the kitchen stove cleaned frequently?

√ Are cleaners, disinfectants, poisons, and so on stored away from food and out of children's reach?

√ Are utensils and knives stored neatly and kept out of children's reach?

√ Are pot and pan handles turned away from stove fronts?

√ Are cupboard contents stored neatly to prevent falling?

√ Are spills wiped up immediately?

√ Are plastic grocery and shopping bags out of children's reach?

Entrances and stairways

√ Are entrances, halls, and stairways adequately lighted to prevent trips and falls?

√ Are steps well maintained?

√ Are steps cleared of objects and tripping hazards? Are there at least two exits that are designated fire exits and always kept clear?

√ Is a child's gate used at the top and bottom of stairs if a toddler is living in the home? (Accordion-type gates are dangerous; children's heads can easily get trapped in them.)

√ Are steps and railings sturdy and in good condition?

Living areas

√ Are electrical cords kept away from carpets? Are cords in good condition (not frayed or overloaded)?

√ Are long electrical blinds and drapery cords beyond a child's reach? (Excess cord can be bound with a twist-tie, or a holder or spool specially designed to hide the extra cord.)

√ Are all wires in the house properly insulated?

√ Are there safety outlet covers in all of the unused electrical outlets?

√ Are throw rugs secured to prevent tripping?

√ Is furniture kept away from windows to prevent children from falling out? (Window screens will not prevent a child from falling out of the window.)

√ Are sharp furniture edges covered?

√ Are radiators and pipes covered to protect against burns?

√ Are lamps located near beds to prevent tripping in the dark?

√ Is there ample walking space between furniture and objects?

√ Are all plants safe? (Some plants are toxic and need to be placed out of children's reach.)

Bathrooms

√ Are medicines and vitamins stored out of children's reach?

√ Is the home's hot water temperature set at the safe temperature of 120°F? (If the temperature cannot be altered [i.e., rented homes], then install an anti-scald device on the faucet.)

√ Is there a toilet-lid locking device in households with small children?

Nursery

√ Does the crib mattress snugly fit against the crib's sides? (No more than two fingers' distance should exist between the mattress and the crib railing.)

√ Are crib bars two inches or less apart? (Any more space and a child could be caught or strangled between the crib's bars.)

√ Are crib side rails kept up?

Garage

√ Are all tools, including those used for gardening, automotive, and lawn care, stored in a locked container?

√ Are recycling containers holding glass and metal far from children's reach?

Yard

√ Is outdoor play equipment safe with no loose parts or rust?

√ Are surfaces around swing sets and play equipment soft to absorb shock from falls? (Good surface equipment can be sand or wood chips. Concrete and packed dirt are not adequate to absorb shock from falls.)

√ Is access to the swimming pool blocked for small children? Are dangerous cleaning chemicals kept locked away?

Fire Safety Checks

√ Are there smoke and carbon monoxide detectors on each level of the home and near the sleeping area? Are detectors checked monthly to ensure that they are operating? Are batteries replaced at least once a year?

√ Are detectors cleaned monthly to clear away dust and cobwebs?

√ Are detectors replaced every ten years? (Detectors become less sensitive over time.)

√ Does the home have one or more fire extinguishers and do all household members know how to operate them? (The local fire department can provide training on how to properly use an extinguisher.)

√ Does the home have an automatic sprinkler system? (Automatic sprinkler systems are a good consideration—even in the home.)

√ Is there a clearly written fire escape plan for the home? Is the plan practiced at least twice a year?

Home Security

Nothing is more important than protecting loved ones. Keeping a household and the family safe and sound can be complicated, expensive, and involved. Depending on the nature of the household and the location, an employer should make sure that the employee hired is aware of all necessary security systems, keys and locks, spotlights, and video surveillance that may be required knowledge for the job. For example, if the employer is away during the day, the employee should know how to lock up the house, turn on the alarm system, and so forth. It is advised that the employee have his or her own security code, if possible. It is a good idea, during the orientation of the employee in the first few days, to go over all security procedures and what needs to be checked if the house is left unattended during the day (closing and locking windows, locking doors, turning lights on, setting the alarm system, and so on).

SECURITY PROFESSIONAL

If full-time personal security protection is warranted, then identifying the security professional for use in the household is not as difficult as it may seem. Some overall areas to consider include:

- experience in personal protection, business security, and estate and asset protection;

Q&A

Q. I am a busy mother and working professional in New York, and I employ both a full-time child care provider and occasional baby-sitters. To what extent does my auto insurance protect me and my employees when they use my car during their work hours?

A. Check with your insurance agent about what your particular policy covers. Major liability could exist if your household employee is not properly covered under the household's auto insurance policy. While states' and carriers' requirements vary, the following is a summary of New York's auto insurance.

For occasional users (baby-sitters) driving the family's car, protection is offered through the liability and medical insurance segments of the insured's (the family's) car insurance. An occasional user driving his or her own vehicle is protected under the liability and medical insurance segments of the employee's car insurance.

A regular user (full-time child care provider) driving your car should be listed as a driver with the insurance company. This protects the employer in the event that an accident occurs when the employee is driving the family's car. An employer who does not notify his or her insurance agent of the regular user risks the insurer not renewing the insurance policy.

- background in estate management practices, public relations, entertainment methodology, and personnel management; and,
- personal demeanor, including personable countenance, flexibility, and discretion.

A professional should have this experience and skill set before being considered for a household security position. Without them, the individual is either lacking the security skills necessary to protect the household or is missing the public relations skills needed to interact in a smooth, balanced, and relaxed manner with both the client and the household staff.

Facts & Figures

IDENTIFYING PERFORMANCE BEHAVIOR ISSUES

Performance	Behavior
Inconsistent work quality	Frequent financial problems
Poor concentration	Avoiding friends and colleagues
Lowered productivity	Blaming others for own problems
Increased absenteeism	Complaints about own home life
Unexplained disappearances from job site	Deterioration in personal appearance
Carelessness, mistakes, judgment errors	Complaints of vaguely-defined illness
	Needless risk taking
	Disregard for safety

A Drug-Free Workplace

A written drug-free workplace policy is the basis of the workplace's drug-free program. Included in the employee handbook, the policy needs to clearly state why the policy is being implemented—to ensure a safe and healthy workplace. Prohibited behaviors should be clearly outlined within the policy. Use, at a minimum, language that states that the use, possession, transfer, or sale of illegal drugs or controlled substances by employees is prohibited. Include consequences, such as immediate dismissal, but take care that these consequences are consistent with other existing personnel policies, and of course, any applicable laws. For instance, if a personnel policy states that any illegal act performed by an employee on workplace premises will result in immediate dismissal, then it follows that any illegal drugs or controlled substances found on the employee will result in immediate dismissal.

In the drug-free workplace policy, an employer may want to include information on drug testing. While most private employers have the right to test for a wide variety of substances, federal, state, and local regulations may apply. However, according to the U.S. Department of Labor, employers who drug test without a drug-testing policy are exposed to liability. Employers may request that employees take a drug test after a job is offered and that employment is contingent upon a successful outcome. Local drug stores sell drug testing kits for about $20.

According to the U.S. Department of Labor, employers may be able to identify workers with substance abuse problems by noting aspects of their performance and behavior. While these symptoms may not mean that a worker has an alcohol or a drug abuse problem, employers should be alert to any of these aspects, outlined on page 174.

> ## Our Advice
>
> *"Intelligence is recognizing possibilities; wisdom is preparing for those possibilities. The wise take steps before an unsavory event occurs. Well-planned security measures cause the nefarious to look elsewhere for their illicit gains. Thus, the wise protect their families and loved ones."*
> —Barry Wilson
>   President/Certified Protection
>   Specialist
>   Anlance Protection, Ltd.

Remember, it is not the employer's job to diagnose substance abuse, but it *is* the employer's job to ensure health and safety within the work environment. Clear and firm communication with the employee focused on his or her job performance is key, as is explaining the drug-free workplace policy, performance policies, and what will occur when performance expectations are not met.

Some states have workplace-related substance abuse laws. To learn what states mandate, go to **www.dol.gov/workingpartners**.

Q&A

Q. *How can I tell whether my nanny is using drugs?*

A. *There are some signs and behaviors you can watch for to detect or raise your suspicion regarding drug use, or other questionable behavior, by your nanny. Signals to watch for include:*

- *frequent requests for early dismissal or time off;*
- *frequent lateness or unreliability;*
- *inconsistent work performance and behavior;*
- *exhibited confusion, memory lapses, or difficulty recalling details and difficulty following directions;*
- *progressive deterioration of personal appearance and hygiene; and,*
- *anxiety, moodiness, and personality changes.*

It is a fairly standard business practice for new hires to take a drug test and for employers to ask employees to repeat drug tests periodically.

Workers' Compensation

Many states require an employer to pay workers' compensation insurance. An employee can receive workers' compensation benefits to replace income and to cover medical expenses resulting from work-related illness or injury. Employers need to exercise caution—if state law requires workers' compensation insurance, be aware that a household liability insurance policy will not cover any injuries, court awards, or any other penalties.

The following states require workers' compensation insurance coverage for full-time and part-time household employees: Alabama, California, Colorado, Connecticut, Delaware, Florida, Georgia, Hawaii, Illinois, Iowa, Kansas, Maryland, Maine, Michigan, Minnesota, New Hampshire, New Jersey, New York, Ohio, Oklahoma, South Dakota, Montana, and Washington.

Some individual local and state workers' compensation requirements directly refer to household employees (i.e., domestic workers).

- **Maryland workers' compensation requirements**
  Under Maryland workers' compensation provisions, any domestic worker whose earnings from a private employer are $750 or more in any calendar quarter, may choose with the employer for the employee to be covered by workers' compensation, even if the individual does not meet the state earnings requirement.

- **New York workers' compensation and disability**
  New York State requires employers cover workers' compensation and disability coverage for domestic workers who work a minimum of forty hours per week for the same employer. For more, go to **www.labor.state.ny.us/formsdocs/wp/LS210.PDF.**
- **Washington, D.C. worker's compensation requirements**
  Washington, D.C. calls for employers to carry workers' compensation coverage for domestic workers employed by the same employer at least 240 hours during a calendar year.

As always, you need to be aware of all statutes and requirements—federal, state, and local. It is best to consult your insurance agent and state insurance department, as many states offer employers a state insurance fund option, and laws requiring coverage may change.

Facts & Figures

WORKERS' COMPENSATION BY STATE

Alabama	An employer may provide voluntary coverage.
Alaska	Any domestic worker except part-time baby-sitters, cleaning persons, harvest help, and similar part-time or transient help.
Arizona	An employer may provide voluntary coverage.
Arkansas	An employer may provide voluntary coverage.
California	Any domestic worker—including one who cares for and supervises children—employed fifty-two or more hours, or who earned $100 or more, during ninety calendar days immediately preceding date of injury or last employment exposing such worker to the hazards of an occupational disease. Excludes workers employed by a parent, spouse or child whose duties are related to ownership, maintenance, or use of residential dwelling by the owner or occupant.
Colorado	Any domestic worker employed forty or more hours per week or five or more days per week by one employer.

Connecticut	Any domestic worker employed more than twenty-six hours per week by one employer.
Delaware	Any household worker who earns $750 or more in any three-month period from a single private home or household.
District of Columbia	One or more domestic workers employed by the same employer for 240 or more hours during a calendar quarter.
Florida	An employer may provide voluntary coverage.
Georgia	An employer may provide voluntary coverage.
Hawaii	Any worker employed solely for personal, family, or household purposes, whose wages are $225 or less during the current calendar quarter and during each completed calendar quarter of the preceding twelve-month period.
Idaho	An employer may provide voluntary coverage.
Illinois	Any worker or workers employed for a total of forty or more hours per week for a period of thirteen or more weeks during a calendar year by any household or residence.
Indiana	An employer may provide voluntary coverage.
Iowa	Any employee working in or about a private dwelling (who is not a regular household member) whose earnings are $1,500 or more during the twelve consecutive months prior to an injury.
Kansas	Any domestic worker if the employer had a total gross payroll for the preceding calendar year of more than $20,000 for all workers under his or her employ.
Kentucky	Two or more domestic workers regularly employed in a private home forty or more hours a week. (The law has no numerical exemption for general employments.)
Louisiana	Specifically excludes domestic household employees.
Maine	An employer may provide voluntary coverage.
Massachusetts	Domestic workers employed sixteen or more hours per week by an employer.
Maryland	Any domestic worker whose earnings are $750 or more in any calendar quarter from a private household.

	Domestic servants and their employers jointly may elect for the employee to be covered, even if the individual does not meet the earnings requirement.
Michigan	Any household domestic worker except those employed for less than thirty-five hours per week for thirteen weeks or longer during the preceding fifty-two weeks.
Minnesota	Any domestic worker who earns $1,000 or more in any three-month period or who has earned $1,000 or more in the same single, private household.
Mississippi	An employer may provide voluntary coverage.
Missouri	Specifically excludes domestic household employees.
Montana	An employer may provide voluntary coverage.
Nebraska	An employer may provide voluntary coverage.
Nevada	Specifically excludes domestic household employees.
New Hampshire	All domestic workers.
New Jersey	Domestic workers are covered the same as all other employees.
New Mexico	An employer may provide voluntary coverage.
New York	Any domestic worker employed (other than those employed on a farm) by the same employer for a minimum of forty hours a week.
North Carolina	Covers domestic service if employer employs more ten full-time non-seasonal laborers.
North Dakota	An employer may provide voluntary coverage.
Ohio	Any household worker who earns $160 or more in cash in any calendar quarter from a single household.
Oklahoma	Any person employed as a domestic worker if the employer had a gross annual payroll in the preceding calendar year of $10,000 or more for such workers.
Oregon	An employer may provide voluntary coverage.
Pennsylvania	An employer may provide voluntary coverage.
Puerto Rico	Any domestic worker regularly employed by the same employer.
Rhode Island	An employer may provide voluntary coverage.
South Carolina	Four or more domestic workers except those whose

	employer had a total annual payroll during the previous calendar year of less than $3,000.
South Dakota	Any domestic worker employed more than twenty hours in any calendar week and for more than six weeks in any thirteen-week period.
Tennessee	An employer may provide voluntary coverage.
Texas	An employer may provide voluntary coverage.
Utah	Any domestic worker regularly employed for forty or more hours per week by the same employer.
Vermont	An employer may provide voluntary coverage.
Virginia	Specifically excludes domestic household employees.
Virgin Islands	An employer may provide voluntary coverage.
West Virginia	An employer may provide voluntary coverage.
Washington	Two or more domestic workers if regularly employed in a private home four or more hours per week. (The law has no numerical exception for general employment.)
Wisconsin	An employer may provide voluntary coverage.
Wyoming	Specifically excludes domestic household employees.

Source: January 1, 2005 Branch of Planning, Policy, and Review, Office of Workers' Compensation Programs, U.S. Department of Labor

CASE STUDY

ILO MILTON
PRESIDENT
FAMILYWISE, INC.
BEDFORD, NY
GTM PARTNER AGENCY

When clients and candidates ask Ilo Milton about the advantage of above the table pay, she readily describes a real-life incident that puts it all into perspective.

A family and its nanny mutually agreed that the nanny would be paid off the books. The nanny, playing with the two boys she was hired to care for, tripped, fell, and severely injured her back—requiring at least three weeks of bed rest and subsequent physical therapy.

Since the employee was paid off the books, she was not covered by workers' compensation insurance. The nanny expected her employer to pay her full salary while she recovered—and even asked the employer to illegally submit a liability claim against the homeowners' insurance.

"All were complicit in going outside of the law," said Milton. "The family was terrified the nanny would sue. The nanny thought the family should pay her while she was out of work. The solution would have been easy if the nanny was on the books." The family felt that the nanny was trying to take advantage of them without taking on any of the risks. They did not feel that they could trust the nanny any longer.

So the family paid the nanny—who no longer works through FamilyWise—four weeks' severance pay, and then replaced her.

"Everyone took a risk here," noted Milton. "While I have my belief that all should pay on the books, people live at their own risk tolerance level. I'm certain [this story] has an impact. It makes household employers aware of the realities and possibilities."

As a household employer, you should ensure that you are adequately covered in the event that an accident occurs in the workplace. Most states require a workers' compensation insurance policy that covers accident-related medical expenses, and even if you do not meet the required standard for your state, you should consider obtaining a workers' compensation policy. Many household employers fail to see that an attempt to save a few dollars in the short-term could result in a huge liability later, putting stress on both the employer and the employee.

—Guy

Health and Safety Rules and Tips Checklist

From time to time, incidents will occur with employees. It is a good practice to document the incident and discuss the matter with the employee in hopes to correct the behavior. (See page 278 in Appendix E for a sample of an *Incident Report*.)

√ Establish a safety policy, and provide protective gear and equipment.

√ Enforce universal precautions and use of safety equipment.

√ Conduct a home safety check to ensure a safe household and healthy work environment.

√ Check with an auto insurance company if your employee is going to be driving your dependents.

√ Call an insurance agent or the state insurance department for the contact information for your area's workers' compensation administration.

√ Find out if your state requires workers' compensation insurance coverage and if it offers a state insurance fund option.

√ Injuries happen. Consider workers' compensation insurance coverage even if it is not mandated by your state or locality.

10

Illegal Discrimination in the Home

The U.S. government enforces many laws and regulations that protect workers against discrimination. Many laws are implemented at both the federal and state levels, and employers need to be aware of all laws and regulations affecting them, including federal, state, and local. Often, antidiscrimination laws are required for businesses with a specific number of workers. Although many federal laws require five, fifteen, or even twenty employees for a law to apply, discrimination laws (especially state and local laws) could apply to household employers. A common best practice is to set fair hiring and employment procedures as if they do apply to the workplace. This creates a professional hiring attitude, while also designating the household as an equitable, unbiased work environment.

Federal law prohibits discrimination on the basis of:

- race, color, religion, sex, and national origin (Title VII of the Civil Rights Act);
- age (Age Discrimination in Employment Act);
- pregnancy (Pregnancy Discrimination Act);
- citizenship (Immigration Reform and Control Act);
- gender (Equal Pay Act);
- disability (Americans with Disabilities Act);
- union membership (National Labor Relations Act); and,
- bankruptcy (Bankruptcy Code).

In some circumstances, federal law may also be interpreted to prohibit discrimination against workers based on other factors, such as testing HIV positive, alcoholism, marital status, and obesity.

Federal Laws

The U.S. Civil Rights Act of 1964 (Title VII) protects employees from being discriminated against based on their race, color, religion, sex, or national origin. Federal law also prohibits discrimination based on age, pregnancy, disability, and U.S. citizenship status.

While Title VII applies only to those who employ fifteen or more people, all household employers should act fairly to avoid any workplace discrimination charge. Remember, federal, state, and local laws may apply. For more information, go to the Equal Employment Opportunity Commission (EEOC) website at **www.eeoc.gov**.

IMMIGRATION REFORM AND CONTROL ACT OF 1986

The Immigration Reform and Control Act of 1986 (IRCA) requires employers to ensure that employees hired are legally authorized to work within the United States by verifying the identity and employment eligibility of all new employees. At the same time, the law prohibits employers from committing document abuse or discrimination on the basis of citizenship status. Households with three or fewer employees are not subject to the IRCA's mandates.

Document Abuse

All U.S. citizens, legal immigrants, and certain other groups are protected from document abuse under IRCA. According to the U.S. Department of Justice's Office of Special Counsel, document abuse occurs when an employer (or potential employer) asks an employee (or an employee candidate) to produce a specific document to establish employment authorization, rather than allowing the employee to select what document to produce from the list of acceptable documents under IRCA. It can also occur if an employer or potential employer requests a different document other than the one the employee has selected from the authorized list. In addition, document abuse includes an employer's (or a potential employer's) rejection of valid documents that appear genuine and related to the individual. For instance, document abuse can occur when an employer requires an immigrant employee to produce upon hire proof of employment eligibility but then refuses to accept, such as an unrestricted Social Security card, requiring instead the employee's green card, despite the Social Security card's legitimate appearance and the employee's name on it.

The employee must produce proof of employment eligibility and identity within three business days after she or he begins work.

Proof of employment eligibility may be a green card or any U.S. Citizenship and Immigration Services (USCIS)-issued document. According to IRCA, employers must accept any document or combination of documents listed on the USCIS Form I-9 to establish identity and employment eligibility. Such documents can include:

> ### Our Advice
>
> *"All of us really do have two selves: our public selves and our home selves. It's the home self psyche that the household employee deals with. I remind my clientele that even though their home is their private domain, it is now also the work environment of another. As private employers, they have an obligation to provide a safe and healthy work environment, abiding by labor laws, at a minimum, but also establishing clear professional boundaries."*
> —Leann Brambach
>   Owner/Operator
>   Home Details Inc.
>   Seattle, WA

- a U.S. passport, an alien registration receipt card, or a permanent resident card (Form I-551);
- an unexpired foreign passport containing an I-551 stamp; or,
- an unexpired employment authorization document issued by the USCIS that contains a photograph (forms I-766, I-688, I-688A, or I-688B).

The list of documents to establish employment eligibility and identity is extensive. For a complete list of I-9 acceptable documents and for more information on Form I-9, go to **www.uscis.gov** or **www.gtm.com/resourcecenter**, or see Appendix E for a sample I-9 Form.

Employers who have failed to complete Form I-9 will be sanctioned by the USCIS if they hire aliens not authorized to work within the United States. Fines may range from $250 to $10,000 per unauthorized alien. An employer demonstrating a persistent pattern of hiring unauthorized aliens may face a maximum six-month prison sentence. However, an employer who has completed Form I-9 correctly for an employee is protected from liability, even if the employee turns out to be not authorized to work. The nature of the documents that are acceptable under Form I-9 does mean that, on occasion, an alien without work authorization will be able to produce documents that comply with Form I-9, even though the alien is, indeed, not authorized to work.

Citizenship Discrimination

Title VII of the Civil Rights Act of 1964, the Immigration Reform and Control Act of 1986 (IRCA), and other antidiscrimination laws prohibit discrimination against individuals employed in the United States based on citizenship. However, all workers must have legal authorization to work in the United States. Title VII applies to employers with fifteen or more employees, and IRCA covers employers with four or more employees. Although many household employers with one or two household employees may not be required to follow the antidiscrimination rules put forth by these laws, it is best practice not to discriminate against any person lawfully admitted to the United States and authorized to work within the United States.

State and Local Laws

Some states and localities protect employees with separate laws. For instance, the California Department of Fair Employment and Housing (DFEH) protects all workers from discrimination in all aspects of employment, including hiring, firing, and terms and conditions. While Title VII generally exempts employers with fourteen or fewer employees, the California FEHA applies to employers with five or more employees.

Another example is the City of New York's Local Law No. 33 (see p. 40), which requires that licensed employment agencies provide to applicants for employment (as household employees) a written statement of employee rights and employer obligations under local, state, and federal law. Passed in 2003, the law is premised on the legislative finding that "the majority of domestic or household employees in New York City are immigrant women of color who, because of race and sex discrimination, language barriers, and immigration status, are probably vulnerable to unfair labor practices."

All employers must comply with all laws pertaining to them—federal, state, and local. As you have already read, the local law often supercedes the federal and the onus is on you, the employer, to know *all* the laws and regulations by which to operate your household employment. For instance, the District of Columbia Discrimination Regulation applies to all employers— any employer with one or more employee—and prohibits discrimination based upon the actual or perceived race, color, religion, national origin, sex, age, marital status, personal appearance, sexual orientation, family responsibilities, disability, matriculation, or political affiliation of any individual.

Sexual Harassment

Sexual harassment policies stipulate that no employee should be subject to unwelcome verbal or physical conduct that is sexual in nature or that shows hostility to the employee because of his or her gender. Sexual harassment can have devastating effects on the workplace. Therefore, household employers needs to take every step necessary to prohibit sexual harassment from occurring. Many workplaces have a zero tolerance policy, which means an employer will not tolerate any sexual harassment whatsoever.

It is best for an employer to include an antiharassment/antidiscrimination policy in his or her employee handbook, which specifically addresses sexual harassment. According to the "Quick Reference to Sexual Harassment Prevention Training," published by CCH, Inc., such a policy needs to clearly state that:

- all employees and employers within the household are expected to treat one another with respect;
- the employer will act immediately upon learning of a sexual harassment complaint. An employee should promptly file a complaint if the employee is made to feel uncomfortable or finds behavior unwelcome, offensive, or inappropriate. A complaint may be made formally or informally. The law stipulates that the perception of misbehavior must be reasonable. Employers need to assure employees that all complaints of sexual harassment will be handled as confidentially as possible;

- the employer mandates a workplace free from all forms of discrimination; and,
- everyone within the household is expected to act respectfully in order to enjoy a positive working environment.

An employer must be prepared to respond to sexual harassment in the workplace—just as he or she is responsible for preventing any harassment or discrimination within the workplace. The employee handbook should cover the employer's sexual harassment policy, and should include what is prohibited behavior in the workplace and what actions will be taken when a sexual harassment complaint is filed. In addition, the policy must state that no employee will experience retaliation for submitting a sexual harassment complaint.

Americans with Disabilities Act

The *Americans with Disabilities Act* (ADA) prohibits discrimination against any qualified person with a disability. If an applicant is qualified to perform the job or can perform the work with reasonable accommodation, the ADA requires employers to consider that applicant equally with other non-disabled, qualified applicants. The ADA prohibits discrimination on the basis of disability in all employment practices—not only hiring and firing. Employment practices covered under the ADA include recruitment, pay, hiring, firing, promotions, job assignments, training, leave, layoffs, benefits, and all other employment-related activities.

Under the ADA, employers ensure people with disabilities:

- have an equal opportunity to apply for jobs and to work in jobs for which they are qualified;
- have an equal opportunity to be promoted;
- have equal access to benefits and privileges offered to other employees; and,
- are not harassed because of their disability.

The ADA covers employers with fifteen or more employees, as well as applicable employment agencies. However, all employers should be aware of ADA regulations.

Under the ADA:

- a person with a disability is defined as someone who has a physical or mental impairment that substantially limits one or more of the major life activities of such individual (e.g., walking, seeing, hearing, speaking), has a record of such an impairment, or is regarded as having such an impairment;
- a qualified employee or applicant with a disability is someone who satisfies skill, experience, education, and other job-related requirements of the position held or sought and who can perform the position's essential functions with or without reasonable accommodation;
- reasonable accommodation may include (but is not limited to) making existing facilities readily accessible to and usable by people with disabilities, such as a specially designed computer keyboard or software, or perhaps just lowering a bulletin board to make it readable or lowering a paper cup dispenser in the employee break room for all to easily reach. Other accommodations could include allowing an employee to begin work at 10 a.m. instead of 9 a.m. in order for her or him to attend physical therapy appointments; and,
- reasonable accommodation must be made if it would not impose undue hardship on an employer's business. Under the ADA, *undue hardship* is defined as an action requiring significant difficulty or expense when considered with an employer's size and financial resources, and the nature and structure of the business' operation. According to the federal government, most accommodations are not expensive. The government estimates that the median cost of accommodation is about $240. In addition, to help businesses offset the cost of accommodations, tax credits may apply, such as the ADA Tax Incentives and the Small Business Tax Credit.

The ADA offers equal access and opportunities to people with disabilities. It does not offer people with disabilities an unfair advantage; an employer may hire a person without a disability who is more qualified than another applicant with a disability. While the ADA prohibits employers from asking about a disability, employers may ask whether an applicant will require a reasonable accommodation if it seems likely that he or she may need it. It is generally unlawful for an employer to ask an applicant whether she or he is disabled or to inquire about the nature or severity of her or his disability. Also, it is unlawful for an employer to require an applicant to take a medical examination before a job offer is made. However, an employer *can* ask an applicant questions about his or her ability to perform job-related functions (as long as the questions are not phrased in terms of a disability). The ADA strictly limits questioning; employers may first check with an ADA specialist to determine what is allowable under the law.

Go to **www.eeoc.gov** or **www.ada.gov** for more information, or call the ADA Information Line at 800-514-0301, where an ADA specialist may be reached. Information on the ADA and its tax codes and incentives may be reached at **www.irs.gov** or 800-829-1040 or 202-622-3120.

Employers also should be aware of state and local laws pertaining to employment discrimination on the basis of disability. For instance, the Massachusetts Commission Against Discrimination (state law Chapter 151B) works with the federal ADA to protect people with disabilities against employment discrimination. However, the Massachusetts law also extends to prohibit disability discrimination in housing, public accommodations, and credit.

A household employer needs to be cautious about imposing certain requirements on the position. He or she may prefer to employ an older, unmarried, Christian woman, but implementing such preferences may violate federal, state, and local law.

Equal Employment Opportunity Commission

The federal *Equal Employment Opportunity Commission* (EEOC) enforces most federal laws prohibiting job discrimination. These laws include the following:

- Title VII of the Civil Rights Acts of 1964, outlawing job discrimination based on race, color, religion, sex, or national origin;
- Equal Pay Act of 1963, protecting against sex-based wage discrimination for men and women performing substantially the same work in the same establishment;
- Age Discrimination in Employment Act of 1967, protecting people age 40 or older; and,

- Titles I and V of the Americans with Disabilities Act of 1990, prohibiting discrimination against qualified individuals with disabilities in employment. (see p.188.)

These laws offer a wide range of protection to employees. EEOC oversees and coordinates the large majority of federal equal employment opportunity regulations, practices, and policies. Some antidiscrimination laws apply to employers with at least four employees, while some apply only to employers with fifteen or more employees. (Household employment agencies may be subject to many of these laws; therefore, discrimination by such agencies is illegal.) Even employers not subject to antidiscrimination laws should use such laws as guidelines to ensure equal opportunity employment. In all, the federal antidiscrimination laws and the EEOC work to outlaw discrimination in employment, including hiring, firing, compensation, promotions, layoffs, recruitment, testing, job advertisements, use of company facilities, fringe benefits, retirement plans, disability leaves, and other terms and conditions of employment. Employers are required to post notices to all employees advising them of their rights under these laws.

It is important to note that Title VII of the Civil Rights Act of 1964 prohibits intentional discrimination and practices that have the effect of discrimination against individuals because of their race, color, national origin, religion, or sex.

STATE AND LOCAL AGENCIES

The EEOC has cooperative relationships with the vast majority of the state and local Fair Employment Practices Agencies (FEPAs). The EEOC and FEPAs have work share agreements that separate common workload to avoid duplication of charge processing. (Go to **www.eeoc.gov** or call 800-669-4000 for more information.)

Common Sense Practices

Some common sense practices can help employers prevent illegal discrimination in the workplace, such as:

- treat all employees equally;
- hire, promote, and fire without bias;

- review employment policies for unfair and negative impact on a protected class (i.e., race, religion, ethnicity, gender, age, disability, or pregnancy);
- eliminate any unfair or negative policies or practices;
- take immediate action to eliminate discriminatory conduct, including inappropriate comments or behavior;
- encourage diversity; and,
- never retaliate against an employee for filing a discrimination complaint—it is illegal.

Household employers struggle with their home being a personal residence, and at the same time, a workplace for others. Be aware of any discrimination laws in your state or locality and how they apply to you, then implement employment practices to avoid the inconvenience of arguments or a lawsuit. The employment practices should be listed in the employee handbook.

Discrimination Checklist

√ Know all discrimination laws and regulations that apply to the household workplace—federal, state, and local.

√ Establish and enforce zero tolerance for unlawful activities and behaviors such as sexual harassment.

√ Be prepared to respond to any complaint of sexual harassment. While your employee handbook covers your zero tolerance policy, be prepared on how you will handle this sensitive issue.

√ Establish and implement procedures for dealing with illegal discrimination, and document them in the employee handbook.

√ Keep in mind that many employment agencies are subject to equal employment opportunity law and may not legally discriminate on the employer's behalf.

√ Be aware of the potential for document abuse and take care to verify a document's validity.

Termination, Resignation, and Saying Good-bye

All good things, and possibly some bad things, must come to an end. One of the most difficult aspects of being an employer is to face the end of an employee relationship, whether terminating an employee or dealing with a resignation.

There are certain ways to handle the end of a relationship, which should be provided in the household's employee handbook and the work agreement, and should be consistent with relevant laws. The best strategy that any employer can use when terminating an employee, accepting an employee's resignation, or saying good-bye to an employee is to address the situation as soon as possible and to be honest.

Always end an employee relationship professionally. Deal with it head-on and without delay. Often, an employer's first instinct to terminate an employee should be acted upon, since it is seldom that the employer's perspective or situation changes.

At-Will Employment

Typically, an employee works at the will of the employer, known as at-will employment, unless a contract has been signed for a fixed term of employment. *At-will employment* means that the employer can fire the employee at any time, and that the employee can quit at any time.

Many employers ensure that they can apply at-will employment to their household by including as part of the job application an at-will employment statement, which the applicant usually initials or signs to acknowledge that he or she has read it and understands that he or she will be an at-will employee if hired. In addition, employers should include at-will employment language in job offer letters, employee handbooks, and termination letters. Without an at-will statement, the household employee's work agreement stipulates what was agreed upon regarding when employment ends.

In the United States, at-will employees can be terminated for good, bad, or no cause. Three exceptions to the rule are:

1. violation of the state's public policy;
2. an implied contract for employment was established; and,
3. an implied covenant of good faith and fair dealing was established.

For information on how laws regarding termination apply to each state, go to **http://csi.toolkit.cch.com/text/P05_8101.asp**.

Facts & Figures

REASONS NANNIES LEAVE JOBS

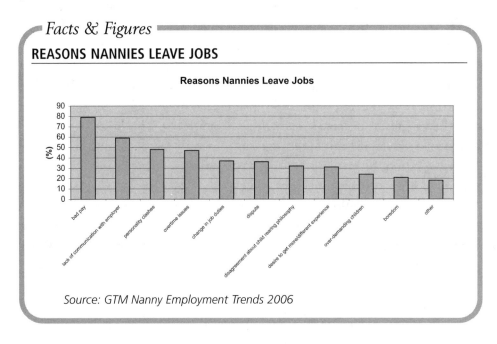

Source: GTM Nanny Employment Trends 2006

Termination

Firing an employee is an uncomfortable situation for many employers and their employees. Unless carefully done, firing an employee also can be downright dangerous for the employer. Be prepared to show support and documentation to prove legitimate cause for termination—and take care that all employees are treated equally.

First, carefully review the initial offer letter, any employment contract, handbook, appraisals, and so on for written agreements. Have the signed work agreement in hand. The work agreement should include described reasons for termination, as well as cause for mandated immediate termination clauses for any illegal or inappropriate behavior on the employee's part.

"It is best to terminate employees in a two-step process," said the president of an East Coast nanny placement agency. "First, talk to the employee about the issue, and give him or her time to improve or change. Explain that noncompliance can result in termination. Document the conversation, providing a copy to the employee. If the situation changes in a positive way, the employer avoids turnover. If the situation remains unchanged, termination is justified." Second chances, though, should never be considered if the employee has broken the law, or put the family home or household members in danger.

In addition, the employee handbook should have stipulated a progressive process for the employer to take to attempt to improve employee performance through the job performance evaluation. An employee who previously was made aware of unsatisfactory performance or incidents through *Incident Reports* (p.278), and who knows his or her performance does not meet the employer's approval, also knows that he or she risks termination. The progressive discipline method works well and provides the employer with a record of the employee's performance issues. The progress usually entails a verbal warning, then a written warning if the problem persists, and lastly, termination. Not only does this method help protect the employer from legal action, it also provides the employee with fair warning about unsatisfactory job performance and possible termination if performance is not improved.

When an employee leaves employment, stipulate in a termination letter the exact time and date of termination, what is included in the final paycheck, when that paycheck will be issued, and other appropriate information. Also, some employers request that the employee return the employee handbook, which was stipulated in the statement release that was signed when the employee was issued the handbook. (See Appendix D for a sample *Termination of Employment to Household Employee Letter*.)

Facts & Figures

RED FLAGS WHEN ASSESSING TERMINATION

- Is it discriminatory?
- Is it on a whim?
- Is it to head off potential blackmail?
- Is it for financial hardship or difficulties?
- Is it because the employee is pregnant?
- Is it because the employee is involved with union activities?
- Is it because the employee is performing military service?
- Is it for any non-job-related activity?

Facts & Figures

TERMINATION BEST PRACTICE

DO

- Be prepared and be consistent.
- Have an adult witness present.
- Meet without children or dependents around.
- Be concise and to the point.
- Focus on measurable behavior (preferably written documentation).
- Allow for an employee response to avoid one-way communication.
- State twice the decision to terminate.
- Inform the employee of the severance policy and unemployment compensation option.
- Avoid any lead time between firing and departing—the best time to set a termination meeting is at the end of the workday.
- Reiterate the confidentiality agreement that the employee signed at the beginning of employment. Inform the employee that what he or she has learned about the family is very private, and that confidentiality was agreed upon for the term of employment, as well as after employment ended.
- Collect from the employee security codes, keys, car seats, and other family items.
- Escort the employee from the premises.

DO NOT

- Delay—an employer's first hunch is usually the right one.
- Apologize, ramble, or speak in generalities. You should speak directly and keep only to the facts.
- Make it a one-way conversation—allow the employee to provide feedback.
- Threaten an employee.
- Provide false hope—make the break clean.
- Withhold financial or insurance benefits.
- Hold a termination meeting in isolation or in public.
- Have children present.
- Provide prior notice of termination plans.
- Allow the employee to depart with employer/household belongings.

Exit Interview/Termination Meeting

The best practice is to hold a termination meeting, during which the employer states the reason for termination, reviews any severance package offerings, and provides the employee with an opportunity to voice his or her views. Always have a concisely written letter prepared at the time of termination. (See Appendix D for a sample *Termination of Employment Letter.*) Avoid lengthy explanations or apologies—be as straightforward as possible when explaining why the termination action is being taken. Keep your discussion short and to the point. Also, at the meeting have a prepared list of employer property and a deadline for its return. In some circumstances, unreturned property may be deducted from the final paycheck after the stated deadline has passed. Be sure to notify the employee that she or he may apply for unemployment insurance to determine whether if she or he is eligible. Often it is suggested that a third party perform exit interviews, which may be a placement agency or a service such as GTM Household Employment Experts™ Household HR Helpdesk, or that a disinterested person be present. (See Appendix B for a sample list of exit interview questions.)

An effective exit interview can provide constructive feedback to allow an employer to improve the employment environment for future employees. State laws vary on what constitutes legal practice when terminating an employee. (Go to **www.dol.gov** to determine which termination laws are enforced in specific states.) In addition, state laws vary in regard to when an

Q&A

Q. How do I handle questions about a household employee no longer working for me?

A. The norm is that most employers talk freely about their previous employees to agencies and other employers. However, when providing references, always stick to the facts—and only the facts. Avoid stating your opinion or hearsay/gossip. Use the personnel file to help you answer reference questions, such as dates of employment and the employee's title or position.

Note: It is an accepted business practice to provide references with only a former employee's dates of employment and her or his title/position. However, this is not a common practice in household employment. Often families feel responsible to other families to provide references for the employee and insight into her or his job performance. When providing references, employers should remember that offering this information is generally at their discretion.

employer is required to provide employees with their final paychecks, as well as whether the employer is mandated to pay an employee for unused vacation time, and so on. Contact the state labor department's wage and hour division for more information.

Finally, consider offering the employee a severance package with a release of future claims contingency. Common severance is one week's pay for each year the employee has worked in the household, with a minimum of two weeks.

After the exit interview, the employer should write up what was discussed during the interview and file this with the termination letter in the employee's personnel file.

COBRA

Under the *Consolidated Omnibus Budget Reconciliation Act* (COBRA), employers with twenty or more employees who offer an employee health plan must offer employees and former employees the option of continuing their health care coverage if coverage is lost or reduced. This COBRA coverage is only available when coverage is lost because of certain events. While COBRA seldom applies to household employment because of the *twenty or more employees* stipulation, state and local laws may offer employees similar rights regardless of the number of employees. Under COBRA, coverage must be identical coverage provided to those beneficiaries not receiving COBRA. Employers need to be aware of their own state requirements and may contact their health plan administrator or their state insurance department to learn more.

Facts & Figures

WHAT TO THINK ABOUT WHEN CONSIDERING TERMINATING AN EMPLOYEE

- Is the reason to terminate an employee job-related?
- Does it relate to absenteeism?
- Is it due to work quality?
- Will it ensure the safety of the family and the household?
- Is it the result of the employee's failure to perform tasks?
- Is the reason to terminate related to misconduct?
- Is it the result of theft?
- Is it because the employee is regularly tardy for work?
- Is the employee neglecting her or his duties?
- Has the employee misused family or household property?

CASE STUDY

Pat Cascio
Owner/Operator
Morningside Nannies, LP
Houston, TX
(President, International Nanny Association)
GTM Partner Agency

Pat Cascio of Morningside Nannies has a wealth of experience and a plethora of tales to tell regarding household employment. She lists one incident as "a classic case of the worst employer."

A nanny living outside the home, who had been employed for seven months, slipped on her employer's kitchen floor while caring for the family's one-year-old child. Her injury, a broken ankle, was so significant that she called her employer, who arrived home in fifteen minutes but refused to assist her. In fact, the nanny remained on the kitchen floor until her own son arrived to transport her to the hospital emergency room for treatment. (The nanny's ankle was set in a cast for three weeks, and then she required three weeks of physical therapy after the cast was removed.) The day after the injury, the employer, who had no workers' compensation insurance and was concerned about liability, fired the nanny over the telephone, offering no reason for the termination. In addition, the employer withheld payment for work the nanny performed during that pay period.

Upon intervention by the nanny's son, the employer paid the nanny for the two days she worked but refused to pay for the workday on which the nanny was injured; paid one week's severance (not two weeks', as stipulated in the signed employment agreement); and, agreed to write a recommendation letter only after the nanny signed a statement saying she would not sue the employer.

The nanny, who had no health insurance, paid for all medical expenses without any assistance from the employer. As a result of the injury and termination, the nanny was unemployed for two months.

According to Cascio, employers need to be educated about the possible occurrence of injury to employees in their household. "I recommend they be willing to help with medical bills or provide health insurance," she said. "They should also be educated in regard to wrongful termination issues, as the nanny could have sued on both accounts."

Household employers must have a sound termination policy, which is outlined in the employee handbook. As an employer is not required to offer any explanation by law, it is helpful to provide closure to an employee, providing some items for her or him to improve upon for her or his next position and preventing any future problems or retaliation due to a feeling of mistreatment, and so on. Again, paying taxes, having the proper workers' compensation and unemployment insurance, and paying the employee for all work hours helps eliminate the liability for the employer and employee.
—Guy

Mini-COBRA

Mini-COBRA allows employees and their families to continue health insurance coverage with small group carriers. Mini-COBRA closely mirrors the benefits required by the federal COBRA and has been adopted by many states, allowing small group coverage to be extended to those who would previously would have lost coverage.

Although COBRA and mini-COBRA are very similar, some differences exist. While COBRA is a federal law, not enforced by the Division of Insurance, Mini-COBRA is a state law, enforced by the Division of Insurance. Generally, COBRA applies to health plans with twenty or more employees. Mini-COBRA generally applies to group health plans with two to nineteen employees. Finally, COBRA applies to self-funded plans, but Mini-COBRA does not.

Facts & Figures

ELIGIBILITY FOR MINI-COBRA AND COBRA BY STATE

State	Business Size Covered by Mini-COBRA	Time Period of Continued Coverage under mini-COBRA	Business Size Covered by COBRA	Time Period of Continued Coverage under COBRA
Alabama	N/A	N/A	20+	18 months*
Alaska	N/A	N/A	20+	18 months*
Arizona	N/A	N/A	20+	18 months*
Arkansas	2-19	4 months	20+	18 months*
California	2-19	18 months	20+	18 months*
Colorado	2-19	18 months	20+	18 months*
Connecticut	2-19	18 months*	20+	18 months*
Delaware	N/A	N/A	20+	18 months*
District of Columbia	N/A	N/A	20+	18 months*
Florida	2-19	18 months	20+	18 months*
Georgia	2-19	3 months	20+	18 months*
Hawaii	N/A	N/A	20+	18 months*
Idaho	N/A	N/A	20+	18 months*
Illinois	2-19	9 months	20+	18 months*
Indiana	N/A	N/A	20+	18 months*
Iowa	2-19	9 months	20+	18 months*
Kansas	2-19	6 months	20+	18 months*
Kentucky	2-19	18 months	20+	18 months*
Louisiana	2-19	12 months	20+	18 months*
Maine	2-19	12 months	20+	18 months*
Maryland	2-19	18 months	20+	18 months*
Massachusetts	2-19	18 months*	20+	18 months*
Michigan	N/A	N/A	20+	18 months*
Minnesota	2-19	18 months	20+	18 months*
Mississippi	2-19	12 months	20+	18 months*

State	Business Size Covered by Mini-COBRA	Time Period of Continued Coverage under mini-COBRA	Business Size Covered by COBRA	Time Period of Continued Coverage under COBRA
Missouri	2-19	9 months	20+	18 months*
Montana	N/A	N/A	20+	18 months*
Nebraska	2-19	6 months**	20+	18 months*
Nevada	2-19	18 months*	20+	18 months*
New Hampshire	2-19	18 months	20+	18 months*
New Jersey	2-19	12 months	20+	18 months*
New Mexico	2-19	6 months	20+	18 months*
New York	2-19	18 months*	20+	18 months*
North Carolina	2-19	18 months	20+	18 months*
North Dakota	2-19	39 weeks	20+	18 months*
Ohio	2-19	6 months	20+	18 months*
Oklahoma	2-19	1 month	20+	18 months*
Oregon	2-19	6 months	20+	18 months*
Pennsylvania	N/A	N/A	20+	18 months*
Rhode Island	2-19	18 months	20+	18 months*
South Carolina	2-19	6 months	20+	18 months*
South Dakota	2-19	18 months*	20+	18 months*
Tennessee	2-19	3 months	20+	18 months*
Texas	2-19	6 months	20+	18 months*
Utah	2-19	6 months	20+	18 months*
Vermont	2-19	6 months	20+	18 months*
Virginia	N/A	N/A	20+	18 months*
Washington	N/A	N/A	20+	18 months*
West Virginia	2-19	18 months	20+	18 months*
Wisconsin	2-19	18 months	20+	18 months*
Wyoming	2-19	12 months	20+	18 months*

*In some cases, coverage may extend to 36 months.

**In some cases, coverage may extend to 12 months.

Source: Kaiser Family Foundation

MAXIMUM PERIOD OF CONTINUED COVERAGE AND ITS EXTENSION

Under COBRA, continuation of health care coverage is mandated by the U.S. Department of Labor and available for a limited period of time, generally a maximum period of eighteen months or thirty-six months, as a result of a qualifying event. However, an employer may provide longer coverage periods, however, beyond the maximum period mandated by the federal government. The length of time depends on a second qualifying event's type.

To be eligible for an extension of the maximum period—generally from eighteen months to thirty-six months—an employee (or his or her qualified beneficiary) must be disabled or experience a second qualifying event.

- *Disabled.* If any member or beneficiary of the health plan coverage is disabled (as defined by the Social Security Association), *all* of the qualified beneficiaries already receiving coverage continuation (as a result of the first qualifying event) as stipulated by COBRA are entitled to an eleven-month extension for a maximum total period of twenty-nine months of continued coverage. The qualified beneficiary must meet requirements set forth by the U.S. Social Security Administration strictly for this disability extension. For in-depth information on COBRA, refer to the DOL booklet, "An Employee's Guide to Health Benefits Under COBRA."

- *Second qualifying event.* An employee already receiving an eighteen-month period of continuation coverage may become entitled to another eighteen-month extension for a total maximum period of thirty-six months of continued coverage. A second qualifying event may be the death of a covered employee, divorce or legal separation of a covered employee and his or her spouse, an employee becoming entitled to Medicare, or a loss of a dependent child. The second qualifying event can be a second only if it would have caused lost coverage under the plan in the absence of the first qualifying event.

Under COBRA, the cost of continued coverage via the extensions may be increased.

Facts & Figures

COBRA COVERAGE EXTENSION QUALIFYING EVENTS AND MAXIMUM TIME PERIOD OF CONTINUED COVERAGE

Qualifying Event	Qualified Beneficiaries	Maximum Time Period of Continued Coverage
Termination (for reasons other than gross miscon-duct) or reduction in hours of employment	Employee Spouse Dependent child	18 months*
Employee enrollment in Medicare	Spouse Dependent child	36 months
Divorce or legal separation	Spouse Dependent child	36 months
Death of employee	Spouse Dependent child	36 months
Loss of dependent child (as defined by dependent child status under the plan)	Dependent child	36 months

*In certain circumstances, coverage may be extended.

Source: U.S. Labor Department's An Employee's Guide to Health Benefits Under COBRA.

The U.S. Department of Labor offers an employer and employee hotline at 866-444-3272, and further information on COBRA and mini-COBRA may be obtained at **www.dol.gov/ebsa**.

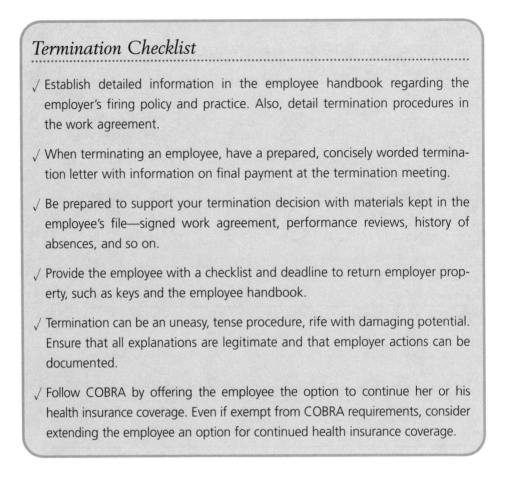

Termination Checklist

√ Establish detailed information in the employee handbook regarding the employer's firing policy and practice. Also, detail termination procedures in the work agreement.

√ When terminating an employee, have a prepared, concisely worded termination letter with information on final payment at the termination meeting.

√ Be prepared to support your termination decision with materials kept in the employee's file—signed work agreement, performance reviews, history of absences, and so on.

√ Provide the employee with a checklist and deadline to return employer property, such as keys and the employee handbook.

√ Termination can be an uneasy, tense procedure, rife with damaging potential. Ensure that all explanations are legitimate and that employer actions can be documented.

√ Follow COBRA by offering the employee the option to continue her or his health insurance coverage. Even if exempt from COBRA requirements, consider extending the employee an option for continued health insurance coverage.

Resignation

Employees should be guided by an employer's preference when he or she resigns from his or her position. Common employment practice is for the employee to provide the employer with two weeks' notice. It would be advantageous for the employer to specify resignation expectations upon an employee's hire in the work agreement and the employee handbook. Be sure to include both employee and employer requirements to be followed when resigning.

In household employment, thirty days' notice is often preferred, due to the lengthy time involved in hiring and replacing household help, and because there is not often other staff employed (unless part of a bigger household estate) where someone else can pick up the resigned employee's duties while a replacement is found.

Facts & Figures

ITEMS TO INCLUDE IN A RESIGNATION POLICY

- Specify the length of time preferred by the employer for the employee to give notice of resignation and if the employer will accept a verbal or written resignation.

- Detail what happens if an employee provides more than the minimum amount of notice. Let the employee know that you, as the employer, reserve the right to evaluate whether the additional notice is necessary and will confirm the final date of employment.

- Detail what happens if an employee provides little or no notice (for example, ineligibility for rehire, no references will be provided, etc.).

- Specify conditions. For example, if an employee fails to report to work for a certain period of time (typically three days) without notifying the employer, the employer will consider that to be the employee's voluntary resignation.

- State whether the employee will be eligible for pay for unused accrued time off and provide information on when a final paycheck will be received, when benefits will end, and so on. (Typically, benefits end on the last day of the month in which termination becomes effective.)

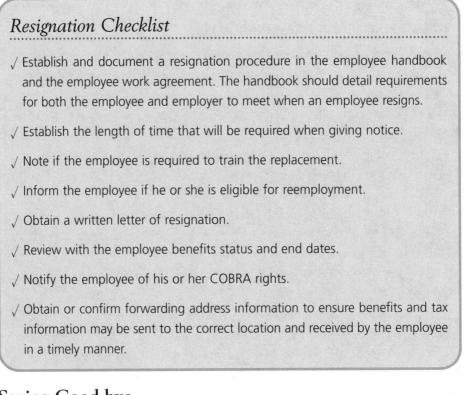

Resignation Checklist

√ Establish and document a resignation procedure in the employee handbook and the employee work agreement. The handbook should detail requirements for both the employee and employer to meet when an employee resigns.

√ Establish the length of time that will be required when giving notice.

√ Note if the employee is required to train the replacement.

√ Inform the employee if he or she is eligible for reemployment.

√ Obtain a written letter of resignation.

√ Review with the employee benefits status and end dates.

√ Notify the employee of his or her COBRA rights.

√ Obtain or confirm forwarding address information to ensure benefits and tax information may be sent to the correct location and received by the employee in a timely manner.

Saying Good-bye

Some households make an employee's good-bye an event, involving the entire family in a dinner celebration or a night of reminiscing. Some employers provide the employee with an album with stories and photos, while others may provide a more businesslike gift, such as a watch or a plaque. The point is that some good-byes are natural, and just because the employee is leaving, the household need not lose all contact with her or him. It is merely a change in the relationship; perhaps something that goes from full-time contact as an employee to occasional visits as a guest or a friend.

Of course, good-byes affecting children have more of an impact. The household employer should be involved in communicating an employee's departure plans with the household. Household employers may want to work with a departing nanny or other household employee to explain to children why the employee is leaving employment, what his or her plans are and how the change may affect the children and the household. Recognize that there can be a positive ending when one employee leaves, and take the necessary time to prepare the household for a new hire.

Good-bye Checklist

√ Make sure you receive any items that were given to the employee during the course of his or her employment, including car and house keys, passes to any country clubs or pools, gas card, car seats, garage door openers, cell phone, and so on.

√ Discuss COBRA with the employee. (see p.200.)

√ If the employee would like, provide a letter of reference.

√ If the employee had worked with an agency, notify the agency of the situation.

√ Conduct an exit interview.

Glossary

A

at-will employment. At-will employment allows an employer to hire an employee any time, and the employee can quit at any time.

au pair (foreign). An au pair is a foreign national living in the United States as part of the host family who receives a small stipend in exchange for babysitting and help with housework. Legally authorized to live and work in the United States for up to one year in order to experience American life, an au pair may or may not have previous childcare experience.

B

baby-sitter. A baby-sitter provides supervisory, custodial care of children on an irregular basis. No special training or background is expected.

butler. According to the International Guild of Professional Butlers Household Employee Definitions, a butler uses his or her skills and attitude to provide service to his employer. Attitude is defined as energy, commitment, and attention to detail while striving for perfection. The butler role fills myriad services, including: overseeing and scheduling all household help and contracted vendors; keeping household budgets; managing inventories; greeting callers; managing household, family, and estate security; organizing and overseeing events and parties held in the household; serving meals and drinks; and, many other supervisory and hands-on tasks to operate the household professionally and efficiently.

C

Consolidated Omnibus Reconciliation Act (COBRA). The federally mandated Consolidated Omnibus Reconciliation Act (COBRA) requires employers with twenty or more employees to offer an option of continued health care coverage after an employee and/or his plan beneficiaries experience a qualifying event, such as if an employee is terminated from his or her position, COBRA allows he or she to continue health coverage through his or her present plan. (Please also see mini-COBRA.)

cook. In contrast to the chef, a cook is homeschooled, typically very talented in the local cuisine, and not responsible for creating the menu. Prepared meals are often house favorites. A cook cleans and serves like a chef.

couples. Couples work together to provide a service package and offer a great variety of skills and talents. Two broad categories of couples are domestic couples and house manager couples. The major difference between the two types of couples is educational and private service experience along with the sophistication of their employment situations and salary history.

D

domestic couples. Domestic couple teams are generally inside/outside teams: one partner may cook and clean while the other handles all outside work. The tasks involved incorporate aspects of the maid, housekeeper, houseman, house manager, and gardener roles.

doula. Doula, a word from ancient Greek, today refers to a person experienced in childbirth who provides continuous support to the mother before, during, and for several weeks after childbirth.

driver. A licensed professional who drives the employer to and from all specified destinations. A driver may also be responsible for maintenance of the employer's vehicles.

E

earned income credit (EIC). EIC, which is claimed on an employee's federal income tax return, reduces his or her tax or allows him or her to receive a payment from the IRS.

eldercare provider. A generic term referring to someone who helps an elderly person with daily care, health care, financial matters, companionship, and social activity. An eldercare provider may offer this assistance for payment or voluntarily.

estate manager or executive estate manager. A true estate manager is typically responsible for a substantial property(ies) and aircraft, yachts, and other employer personal interests. Management authority over inside and outside staffs and operations is held at varying degrees, depending on the employer. The executive estate manager refers to the highest level in this category, and, in complex situations, is similar to the chief executive officer in the corporate world. Some key tasks include: developing personnel and financial management plans, as well as written position descriptions, standards of quality and operating manuals; providing overall leadership to household service staff; organizing, planning and evaluating all estate job activities; providing primary human resources for estate employees; coordinating and monitoring all property(ies) building, development and maintenance; coordinating and monitoring all contracted services such as security, outside cleaning services, etc.; and, effectively communicating with employer.

G

gardener. A gardener tends to the landscaping, lawn, and outside environment of the employer's property.

gentleman's gentleman. The gentleman's gentleman provides similar services as the butler, but with service focused on the gentleman employer.

governess. Traditionally an educated person (minimum of a bachelor's degree), the governess is employed by families for the full- or part-time at-home education of school-age children. A governess functions as a teacher and is not usually concerned with domestic work or the physical care of younger children.

H

Health Insurance Portability and Accountability Act of 1996 (HIPPA). HIPPA amended the Employee Retirement Income Security Act (ERISA) to provide new rights and protections for participants and beneficiaries in group health plans.

health maintenance organization (HMO). A health maintenance organization (HMO) is a plan that provides medical services to its members for a fixed, prepaid premium and requires members to use only the plan's participating (or networked) providers.

home health care. Home health care is professional health care, provided under the direction of a physician and in the patient's home, and is a viable and often preferable alternative for those people who do not need 24-hour supervision or an extended hospitalization to recover.

homemaker service. For people who are unable to perform daily household duties and who have no available help, a homemaker service includes light housekeeping, laundry, limited personal care, grocery shopping, meal preparation, and other shopping assistance.

house manager couples. House manager couples are less hands-on than domestic couples and more managerial. While they may handle cooking and/or service, house manager couples manage service delivery per house standards. Often, one partner performs personal assistant duties while the other handles butler or house manager tasks.

household employer. Per the IRS, a household employer is an individual who employs housekeepers, maids, gardeners, and others who work around that individual's private residence.

household manager. The household manager is another term for a butler with few subtle differences, such as a butler is knowledgeable and sophisticated in the finer details of privilege and wealth, particularly in the area of wines and food. A household manager usually oversees staff in one residence, greets callers, assists in staff training, schedules and coordinates staff, plans and organizes parties and events in the home, serves meals and drinks, and may be involved in many more functions akin to a butler's responsibilities.

hours worked. According to the U.S. Fair Labor Standards Act, in general, hours worked include all time an employee must be on duty, on the employer's premises, or at any other prescribed workplace.

housekeeper. The housekeeper handles general cleaning, laundry, ironing, mending, and other basic household functions.

I
individual health plan. An individual health plan is for people not connected to an employer, such as self-employed people who have no other employees.

immigrant. Per the U.S. Justice Department, an immigrant is a foreign national who is authorized to live and work permanently in the United States.

in-home child care. A situation in which a caregiver cares for children in his or her home.

M
maids. Parlor maids, scullery maids, kitchen maids, laundry maids, house maids, and ladies' maids refer to various positions in a staffed home. A maid performs specialized tasks, primarily care and cleaning duties, and is often associated with a particular area of the home.

migrant worker. A worker who travels from one area to another in search of work.

mini-COBRA. Mini-COBRA (Consolidated Omnibus Reconciliation Act) allows employees and their families to continue health insurance coverage with small group carriers, firms with two to nineteen employees. (Please see COBRA.)

N
nanny. Livein or liveout, a nanny works in the household to undertake all tasks related to the care of children. Duties are generally restricted to childcare and the domestic tasks related to childcare. May or may not have had any formal training, though often has a good deal of actual experience. Nanny's work week ranges from 40–60 hours per week, and a nanny usually works unsupervised.

nursery nurse. The nursery nurse is a title used in Great Britain for a person who has received special training and preparation in caring for young children, in or out of the home. The nursery nurse may livein or liveout, works independently, and is responsible for everything related to childcare. Duties are generally restricted to childcare and the domestic tasks related to childcare, and the work week is usually 50–60 hours per week. In addition to specialized training, the nursery nurse successfully passed Great Britain's certification examination of the National Nursery Examination Board.

P

parent/mother's helper. Lives in or lives out and works to provide full-time childcare and domestic help for families in which one parent is home most of the time. The parent/mother's helper may be left in charge of the children for brief periods of time and may or may not have previous childcare experience.

personal assistant. The personal assistant is a key position in the private life of household employer and performs a broad category of services. Generally, the personal assistant focuses on handling: the employer's correspondence and communications; staff coordination; travel planning; errands; and, odd jobs.

personal time off. Personal time off (PTO) refers to all the time offered to the employee for time off or work benefits.

preferred provider plan (PPO). A preferred provider plan (PPO) is a managed care health plan that contracts with providers. Plan members are offered a financial incentive to use providers on the plan's network but are able to see nonnetwork providers as well.

private/personal chef. A private/personal chef is professionally trained and seasoned in the various cuisines, and caters to the preferences, tastes, and diets of his or her employers. The private/personal chef: performs or cooks in the home, as well as on a family-owned yacht and aircraft; may serve meals and refreshments; and, cleans the kitchen and related facilities such as coolers and freezers.

S

security professional. An individual who is responsible for household security, including household property and personal security.

U

U.S. citizen. Per the U.S. Justice Department, citizens include people who are born in the United States, Puerto Rico, Guam, the Northern Mariana Islands, and the U.S. Virgin Islands, as well as others who obtain U.S. citizenship.

U.S. national. Per the U.S. Justice Department, U.S. nationals include people born in America Samoa, including Swains Island.

W

workweek. According to the U.S. Fair Labor Standards Act, a workweek is a period of 168 hours during seven consecutive 24-hour periods.

Tax Information

Useful tools for employers to have on hand include a tax calendar and a household employer's tax and payroll guide. The tax calendar lists important dates, such as due dates for quarterly tax filings and due dates for tax form filings. The tax and payroll guide for household employers is a valuable resource in determining what and when federal and state employment taxes must be withheld. The most up-to-date calendar and guide may be found at **www.gtm.com/resourcecenter**.

Employer Tax Responsibility Calendar

Due Date	Item
January 15	Fourth federal estimated taxes (1040-ES)
January 31	Fourth quarter state income taxes
	Fourth quarter unemployment taxes
February 2	W-2 form(s) mailed to employee(s)
February 28	W-3 and W-2 forms for previous year to be filed with the Social Security administration
April 15	First federal estimated taxes (1040-ES)
	Schedule H with Form 1040 for wages paid during pervious year
April 30	First quarter state income taxes
	First quarter state unemployment taxes
June 15	Second federal estimated taxes (1040-ES)
July 31	Second quarter state income taxes
	Second quarter state unemployment taxes
September 15	Third federal estimated taxes (1040-ES)
October 31	Third quarter state income taxes
	Third quarter state unemployment taxes

Tax & Payroll Guide for Household Employers

GTM
household employment experts™

Whether you employ a nanny, housekeeper, eldercare worker or other household professional, here is a step-by-step guide for you to use when setting up and administering your employee's payroll and taxes.

Understanding the Laws

Step 1 – Determine if you have an employee or independent contractor

Household professionals include nannies, home health aides, private nurses, cooks, gardeners, caretakers, and other similar domestic workers. The main difference between an employee and a contractor is that an employee operates under the control and supervision of his/her employer (you), and a contractor retains all control over himself and his services. For example, a nurse who has her own company and comes by once a week to provide medical services to an aging parent is a contractor; a nanny who cares for your children in your home is an employee. For more information contact the IRS at (800) 829-1040 and order publication 926.

Step 2 – Research Tax Laws

The IRS states that anyone who pays an individual $1,500 or more in gross wages during the calendar year legally employs a household employee and must comply with all state and federal tax laws.

Household Employ er Taxes
Employers can expect to pay 9-11% of their employee's gross pay, including:
- Federal and state unemployment insurance (about 2-4% for most states)
- 50% of Social Security and Medicare (7.65%)
- Other state taxes where required, such as employment training or work force taxes

Household Employ ee Taxes
Employees can expect to pay 15-20% of their gross wages, including:
- Federal and state income taxes (not required, but advised)
- 50% of Social Security and Medicare (7.65%)
- Other state taxes where required, such as Disability Insurance

For more information contact the IRS at (800) 829-1040, and visit GTM's new Net to Gross Tax Calculator.

Step 3 – Follow Payroll Regulations

According to the Federal Labor Standards Act, all household employees must be paid at least minimum wage ($5.15/hour — higher in some states), however, benefits such as room and board can account for a portion of that wage. There is no limit to the number of hours an employee can work – provided there is mutual agreement. However, overtime may be required in your state. Paid vacations, holidays and sick days are not required by law.

Filing the Paperwork

Step 4 – Submit Federal and State Forms

- Complete SS4 Form for an Employer ID # (download at www.GTM.com/resourcecenter)

- Register for State Unemployment ID # (contact state for form)

- Register for State Withholding Tax ID # (contact state for form)

- Complete your State New Hire Report (contact state for form)

- Have employee complete W-4 Form (download at www.GTM.com/resourcecenter and keep on file)

- Have employee complete I-9 Form (download at www.GTM.com/resourcecenter and keep on file)

Step 5 – Add Workers' Compensation to Your In-surance Policy

Most states require household employers to carry a workers' compensation and/or disability policy if you employ someone on a full or part-time basis. These policies will cover you from lawsuits and liability in the event that your employee is injured on the job. If your state requires this, you can either contact your state's insurance fund or your homeowner's insurance company. GTM strongly recommends that even if you're not required to have a policy, you obtain one anyway.

For more information, visit www.GTM.com or call 1 -888-4-EASYPAY today

Step 6 – Set Up Dependent Care Assistance

You can pay your household employee with pre-taxed funds through an employer-sponsored Dependent Care Assistance Program (DCAP), if your employer offers this plan. This plan allows you to set aside up to $5,000 per year "tax free" money that you can use to pay for your childcare or eldercare. Contact your employer's Human Resources department for more details.

Complying with Payroll and Tax Laws

Step 7 – Calculate Withholding Taxes

Weekly Gross Pay   = _____

Social Security
& Medicare Taxes   Less: _____
(7.65% of Gross Salary)

Federal, State & Local
Income Taxes   Less: _____
(Estimated 10-20%)*

Net (take-home) Pay   = _____

Varies based on state, gross pay and withholding allowance.

Example: *$400 gross salary per week x 22.65% (7.65%+15%) = $309.40 weekly NET (take-home) salary*

In addition to paying your employee a weekly gross salary, household employers have their own payroll taxes that need to be calculated weekly and paid on a quarterly basis to the IRS and your state.

Weekly Gross Pay   = _____

Social Security
& Medicare Taxes   + _____
(7.65% of Gross Salary)

Federal Unemployment
Insurance (0.80%)   + _____

State Unemployment
Insurance (2-4%)*   + _____

Total Weekly Costs   = _____

Varies from state to state.

Example: *$400 gross salary per week x 11.45 (7.65%+.8%+ 3%) = $445.80 weekly total costs*

* *Also found online at www.GTM.com/resourcecenter*

Step 8 – Distribute Paychecks Regularly

You have the option of paying your employee weekly, bi-weekly, monthly or at any other agreed upon interval. Wages should always be paid via check so both parties have a record, and the amount should always be net (after all applicable taxes are withheld). You can also offer the option for direct deposit (check with your bank for details).

Step 9 – File Payroll Taxes Every Quarter

January
15th   4th quarter estimated taxes due
31st   4th quarter Income and State Unemployment Taxes Due
31st   W-2 forms mailed to employees

February
28th   W-3 and/or W-2 forms to be filed with the Social Security Administration

April
15th   1st quarter estimated Taxes Due
15th   Schedule H of Form 1040 for wages paid from January-December of previous year due
30th   1st quarter Income and State Unemployment Taxes due

June
15th   2nd federal estimated payment due

July
31st   2nd quarter Income and State Unemployment Taxes due

September
15th   3rd estimated tax payment due

October
31st   3rd quarter Income and State Unemployment Taxes due

GTM is the most established household payroll and tax service in the U.S., serving families who employ household professionals since 1985. With EasyPay^{SM}, we'll help you eliminate penalties, interest or costs of unnecessary accounting and legal fees. We'll show you how to qualify for significant tax breaks and credits and, because our associates stay informed on new and changing tax laws, we'll keep you up to date on all state and federal regulations.

For more information, visit www.GTM.com or call 1-888-4-EASYPAY today

Interview Questions

The following are lists of questions to ask during a candidate interview. They cover a range of areas—from questions relating to general employment to questions regarding behavior and ethics. A prepared list of questions helps to keep the interview on track and helps to ensure that all questions and topics are covered. A list of interview questions is also beneficial when multiple candidates are interviewed, as it allows the employer to make fair and accurate comparisons and considerations by examining different candidates' answers and responses to the same questions.

Very similar to interview questions for job applicants, the exit interview questions help the employer keep on track and ensure all questions are answered. An exit interview is your opportunity to learn what works and what needs improving within the household, and how the employee viewed the job and the household. After the exit interview, the employer should write up his or her notes from the discussion and attach the completed exit interview questions form and write-up with the termination letter. Both are filed in the employee's personnel file.

Interview Questions

General:

- What made you choose this particular field of work?
- What motivates you at work? What is important to you about the household you work for? In the past, in what ways how have you demonstrated that you care about the work you do?
- What do you feel is the greatest strength that you bring to your job or your work? What is an area(s) in which you need or would like to improve? How do you plan to address this?
- How would you describe your ideal working conditions?
- What are your career plans for the future?

Educational Background:

- What is your educational background?
- How would you rate yourself academically?
- What are you doing now to develop your knowledge or talents? What have you done in the past to expand your knowledge in your field?
- What do you do to keep informed in your field?
- Tell me about a mistake you have made, in your current or previous positions, and what you did to resolve it.

Work History:

- Why are you leaving your current position (or why did you leave your most recent position)?
- Of your previous positions, which did you like the best and why? Which did you like the least? Which motivated you the most?
- Describe your relationship with the last household. What do you think that your employer or manager would say about your job performance?
- At work, what have been your major work accomplishments? What are you most proud of in regards to past experience and why?
- Describe your working relationships with others.

Behavior:

- Name a specific problem you faced on the job. How did you resolve it?
- Describe a time when you had to go above and beyond the call of duty to get the job done.
- What frustrates you about your job? How did you handle it and what was the result?
- What was the toughest decision that you had to make recently in your job? What was it, why was it difficult, and how did you handle the situation?
- Describe how you solved a problem in a unique way.

Ethical:

- What process do you use to resolve an ethical dilemma? What, if anything, would you have done differently?
- Tell us when it was necessary to make an exception to the rules to get something accomplished.

Learning Orientation:

- What do you feel is a specific weakness of yours and how did you overcome it? Be specific.

Results Focused:

- What is an accomplishment that you are especially proud of?

Change Orientation:

- Describe a time when you were faced with a change in your work environment. What was it and how did you handle it?
- Think of a situation in which when you were provided with very little instruction on how to perform a task. How did you proceed?

Exit Interview Questions

Today's date_____

Date employment began_____

Date employment ended_____

1. Why are you leaving your household position?
2. What will you be doing when you leave your position?
3. If you are to be employed in another household position, please explain why.
4. How would you rate the job? Excellent Good Average Fair Poor
   If average or less, why?

5. How would you rate the family? Excellent Good Average Fair Poor
   If average or less, why?

6. Did you have written job description? Yes No
7. Did you have a written work agreement? Yes No
8. What were your duties?
9. What problem(s) did you encounter in the job/household?
10. If you were in the same situation again, would you accept a position with this family? Yes No
11. Would you recommend that other household employees work for this family? Yes No
    If no, why not?

12. Would you consider working as a household employee again in the future if applicable? Yes No
13. What would you suggest the household improve upon?
14. Other Comments:_____

_____   _____

Household Employee Signature   Date

Work days/schedule_____

Name of household employer_____

Resources

W hat follows are links and telephone numbers where you can find a wealth of information on various topics, including hiring and discrimination laws, payroll taxes and wages, unemployment insurance, and state and federal requirements for hiring household help. In addition, there are links to several organizations that provide information on nanny tips and practices as well as agency information. For your state's contact information on tax withholding, unemployment insurance, new hire reporting, and workers' compensation, visit **www.sphinxlegal.com/extras/nanny**.

Resources and References

<small>WEBSITES</small>

GTM Household Employment Experts
www.gtmhouseholdemploymentexperts.com

Alliance of Professional Nanny Agencies
www.theapna.org

Americans with Disabilities
www.ada.gov

Internal Revenue Service
www.irs.gov

International Guild of Professional Butlers
www.butlersguild.com

International Nanny Association
www.nanny.org

National Association of Nannies
www.nannyassociation.com

National Household Employment Association (NHEA)
www.thenhea.org

Social Security Administration
www.ssa.gov

U.S. Citizenship and Immigration Services
www.uscis.gov

U.S. Department of Agriculture
www.usda.gov/wps/portal/usdahome

U.S. Equal Employment Opportunity Commission
www.eeoc.gov

U.S. Department of Labor
www.dol.gov

U.S. Department of Labor Wage and Hour Division
www.dol.gov/esa/whd

TELEPHONE NUMBERS

GTM Household Employment Experts
888-432-7972

American with Disabilities Act Specialist
800-514-0301

IRS Small Business
800-829-3676

IRS Tax Questions
800-829-1040

IRS Taxpayer Advocate
877-777-4778

Social Security Number Verification
800-772-1213

U.S. Citizenship and Immigration Services Office of Business Liaison
800-357-2099

U.S. Equal Employment Opportunity Commission
(call is automatically directed to the nearest EEOC Field Office)
800-669-4000

U.S. Department of Justice National Customer Service Center
800-375-5283

U.S. Department of Labor Wage and Hour Toll-Free Information and Helpline
866-4USWAGE
(866-487-9243)

Sample Forms

The following forms may be helpful in your nanny hire. Use them as they are or adapt them to serve your household.

OFFER LETTER FOR HOUSEHOLD EMPLOYMENT

Confidential
(Date)
Mary Poppins
123 Main Street
Chicago, IL, 12345

Dear Mary,

To confirm our conversation of earlier today, _____ (date), I am pleased to offer you the full-time position of nanny with our family. We would like you to start work on _____ (date). Your hours will be Monday through Friday, 8:15 a.m. until 5:30 p.m. Your compensation package is as follows.

- **Compensation:**
  $10 per hour
  Overtime $15 per hour
  $493.75 gross per week for 46.25 hours
  Paid weekly through GTM's EasyPay® service

- **Benefits:** (after 60 days of employment)
  Paid Health Insurance for a single individual of either major medical,
      HMO, or PPO
  Health Reimbursement Account
  Guardian Dental Insurance coverage
  IRA retirement plan participation, 3% family contribution

- **Vacation:**
  two weeks after 60 days of employment
  ✦ one week—employer choice
  ✦ one week—employee choice

- **Personal/Sick:**
  three personal days and two sick days per year after 60 days of employment

- **Holidays:**
  six holidays plus three floating (family choice) after 60 days of employment

We are happy you have accepted our offer, and we look forward to you joining our family. Please call me with any questions. Otherwise, we look forward to seeing you to finalize some customary paperwork, on _____ (date). Please return this letter to the address noted above to confirm your acceptance of this position.

Sincerely,

Household Employer

Accepted by

_____   _____
Candidate Name   Date

All household employees are employed at-will. This employment is at the discretion of the employer and the employee. Employment may terminate with or without notice or cause. Employees are also free to end employment at any time, for any reason, with or without notice.

REJECTION LETTER TO CANDIDATE

[Date]

Dear _____,

Thank you for your interest in employment with our household. We have reviewed your application and carefully considered your qualifications. At this time, we have selected another candidate for the position.

We will retain your application and if we need additional information concerning your qualifications, we will contact you.

Sincerely,

Household Employer

NANNY JOB DESCRIPTION

Summary
To provide child care to the _____ Household's children, in a loving, secure, positive and responsible manner following the parents ideologies of discipline and child rearing as requested.

Essential Functions
- Interact with the children keeping in mind developmental issues.
- Read interesting and stimulating stories.
- Respond with thoughtful answers to questions.
- Help the children solve problems.
- Maintain the children's cleanliness: hands and face, soiled clothing.
- Be able to handle emergency situations calmly with swiftness and reassurance.
- Provide daily communication with the parents regarding the children: good occurrences and any problems or concerns.
- Keep the children safe at all times inside and outside the house.
- Manage the home, including light housework and picking up after the children and in their play area.
- Provide nutritional meal planning, including snacks for the children and, on occasion, for the family.
- Provide exhilarating, thought-provoking learning recreation.
- Provide teaching methods to children.
- Be dependable and flexible with schedule. Notify the family well in advance of any needed time off.
- Take direction from the parents and maintain a patient, understanding and cheerful demeanor with a good sense of humor.
- Adhere to the Employer/Household Employee Work Agreement.

Nonessential Functions
- Assist in managing the home by helping with family laundry, housekeeping—including vacuuming and dusting, and family meal preparation.
- Purchasing children's clothing.
- Assist with errands such as grocery shopping, pick up/drop off dry cleaning.

Knowledge, Skills, Abilities
- Basic knowledge of CPR and First Aid.
- Knowledge of child development issues, such as age appropriate activities and nutrition.
- Basic reading and writing skills.
- Ability to follow written and oral instructions.
- Ability to be active with the children (i.e., standing, walking, bending, kneeling, lifting, climbing stairs).
- Knowledge of operating home electronics and kitchen appliances.
- Safe driving skills and child seat safety.

Supervisory Responsibilities
None

Working Conditions
The job will be performed at the primary residence of the _____ Household.

(Use this section to give guidelines and describe your home and its layout, provisions for food, any pets in the house, whether or not a vehicle will be provided to use while working, etc.)

Minimum Qualifications
- A high school diploma or equivalent preferred.
- Must be at least 18 years old.
- Must have a valid drivers license.
- Previous childcare experience with references.

Success Factors
- A warm, caring and compassionate personality with a love of children.
- Follow direction well but also take initiative when needed.
- Possess schedule flexibility.

HOUSEKEEPER JOB DESCRIPTION

Summary
To do anything necessary to maintain an impeccable appearance in the _____ home and to ensure the value of the possessions trusted in your care.

Essential Functions
- Conduct a scheduled cleaning of the house.
- Vacuum and clean the floors, carpets, and area rugs.
- Dust and polish all surfaces.
- Do all family laundry and ironing.
- Coordinate the drop off and pick up of all dry cleaning.
- Schedule all linen changes.
- Keep a household maintenance report.
- Track inventory of all household cleaning products.

Nonessential Functions
- Care and maintenance of fine china, silver and crystal.
- Assist with serving responsibilities for dinner parties or other events in the home.
- Keep floral arrangements fresh throughout the house.
- Run errands.
- Conduct household shopping.

Knowledge, Skills, Abilities
- Have knowledge of and understand the need for quartering/zoning a home.
- Have the ability to track which rooms must be detail-cleaned several time a month and which may be detail-cleaned only once a month.
- Possess knowledge of various cleaning products and know which work most effectively on specific surfaces.
- Have the ability to follow a schedule and work efficiently and effectively.
- Have strong communication skills.

Supervisory Responsibilities
None

Working Conditions
The job will be performed at the primary residence of the _____
Household.

(Here you can describe your home—its layout and square footage, additional residences to be managed, housing accommodations, etc.)

Minimum Qualifications
- Previous experience working in private service as a housekeeper.
- Professional references.

Success Factors
- Meticulous attention to detail.
- Follows direction well and takes initiative to ensure the highest standards are met.

ELDERCARE PROVIDER/COMPANION JOB DESCRIPTION

Summary
Assist employer in maintaining an independent life and provide the best care when independent living is no longer possible.

Essential Functions
- Assist in preparing and serving meals
- Light cleaning duties
- Driving
- Bathing
- Helping to dress
- Run errands
- Grocery shopping

Nonessential Functions
- Accompanying employer to events and appointments
- Traveling with employer

Knowledge, Skills, Abilities
- Basic nursing skills
- Knowledge of first aid and CPR
- Ability to perform everyday activities/movements (i.e., lifting, standing, walking, bending, kneeling, climbing stairs)
- Safe driving skills
- Knowledge of operating home electronics and kitchen appliances
- Knowledge of medication administration (i.e., following dosage schedule and amount)

Supervisory Responsibilities
None

Working Conditions
The job will be based from the primary residence of the _____ household.

Minimum Qualifications
- Degree in social work or related field, or equivalent field experience
- First aid and CPR certification or training

Success Factors
- Possess a calming and accommodating personality
- Patience and ability to be flexible
- Warm and friendly disposition

MAINTENANCE WORKER JOB DESCRIPTION

Summary

Responsible for the performance of specialized maintenance and repair operations. Expected to plan details of projects and carry them out to completion.

Essential Functions

- Provides maintenance in such areas as skilled and semiskilled electrical, plumbing, painting, roof repair, carpentry, etc.
- Inspects safety of all equipment, machinery and tools.
- Operates power driven and motorized equipment.
- Performs skilled work in the maintenance, repair, alteration, and remodeling of the residence.
- Performs rough and finished carpentry.
- Performs bench carpentry using shop equipment and power tools such as drills, saws, sanders, planers, air nailers, routers, and radial arm saws.
- Assembles, installs, and repairs pipes, fittings and fixtures of water, heating, and drainage systems.
- Performs preventative maintenance and minor repairs on cooling and air distribution systems.
- Pour concrete to make floors, walkways, pads or other projects.
- Repairs or replaces leaking and defective roofing.
- Repairs doors, door checks, and locks.
- Repairs window frames, tables, chairs and other related objects.
- Mixes prepared paint and paints a variety of surfaces both inside and outside the residence using brushes, spray guns, and rollers.
- Makes routine electrical repairs such as replacing lighting fixtures, electrical outlets, appliances, light switches.
- Estimates and orders materials and supplies.
- Ensures the proper inventory controls are in place for various materials and supplies.
- Cleans equipment and work areas.

Nonessential Functions

- Assists in the maintenance of grounds.

Knowledge, Skills, Abilities

- Knowledge of methods, practices, tools and materials used in building maintenance and repair work.
- Knowledge of occupational hazards and necessary safety precautions applicable to maintenance work.
- Knowledge of the general repair of large equipment, and experience in repairing such equipment.
- Skill in the use and care of tools and equipment necessary to perform various maintenance and repair tasks.
- Ability to operate, install, and repair all equipment in a safe and efficient manner.
- Ability to plan and organize the proper performance of a variety of construction, maintenance and repair tasks.
- Use graphic instructions such as blueprints, layouts, or other visual aids.
- Ability to follow oral and written instructions, working independently while performing major repairs and overhauls.
- Calculate cost, labor and material estimates by performing arithmetic functions such as addition, subtraction, multiplication, division, and algebra.
- Establish priorities for own workload based upon such factors as need for immediate action, work objectives, work schedule, knowledge or future needs, etc.

Supervisory Responsibilities

- Directs the work of other skilled or semi-skilled staff for specified projects.

Working Conditions

- While performing the duties of this job, the employee is frequently exposed to fumes or airborne particles and toxic or caustic chemicals.
- Employee may be exposed to excessive dust, mold, or mildew.
- Duties to be performed are both outside and inside in varying conditions including extreme heat, extreme cold and wet and/or humid, etc.

- While performing the duties of this job, the employee is regularly required to stand, walk, use hands and arms to operate tools and equipment, climb, crouch or stoop, and lift/carry objects weighing up to 40 pounds.

Minimum Qualifications

- Successful completion of a standard high school program supplemented by trade school courses.
- Three years of skilled level experience in building maintenance and repair work, with a high level of proficiency in at least two of the building trades.
- Any reasonable combination of knowledge, skills, abilities, training and experience may be supplemented.

Success Factors

- Listens and gets clarification, when needed. Responds well to questions.
- Demonstrates accuracy and thoroughness.
- Follows policies and procedures; completes tasks correctly and on time.

PAYCHECK AND PAYROLL EARNINGS STATEMENT

DO NOT ACCEPT THIS CHECK without confirming presence of Artificial Watermark on back. Other security features are listed on back.

Household Employer
123 Main Street
New York, NY 10028

Bank Name

13
1000

Check Date 4/16/2004   Check Number 10006

Pay *Nine Hundred Sixty Dollars and Twenty-Seven Cents*

$******960.27

To the Order of:

0001 10006

PAY ONLY

Alice Nelson
123 Main Street
New York, NY 10028

Authorized Signature

⑈⑈0 10006⑈⑈ ⑈000000000⑈ 12345⑈⑈

Alice Nelson

Company	Period Begin	Division
Household	4/3/2004	
Number	Period End	Branch
0001	4/16/2004	
Social Security #	Check Date	Department
123-45-6789	4/16/2004	
Hire Date	Check Number	Team
1/1/2004	10006	

Household Employer

Personal 24.00-2.00=22.00 HOURS
Sick 7.00-0.50=6.50 HOURS
Vacation 35.00-10.00=25.00 HOURS

Earnings

Description	Location / Job	Rate	Hours	Current	Year To Date
Salary					1100.00
Hourly Rate 1		12.00	80.00	960.00	960.00
Overtime Rate1		18.00	24.00	432.00	432.00
Milege Reimb		12.00	0.00	13.44	26.88
MEMOS					
HRA			0.00	25.00	50.00

Deductions

Description	Current	Year To Date
Fed (S/1) (2392.00)	158.38	269.15
OASDI (2492.00)	86.30	154.50
Medicare (2492.00)	20.18	36.13
NY (S /1) (2392.00)	55.65	91.54
New York City Res.(2418.88)	34.66	58.19
Life Insurance	10.00	20.00
Health Insurance	30.00	60.00
Simple IRA	50.00	100.00

Total Earnings			104.00	1405.44	2518.88

Total Deductions	445.17	789.51

NET PAY	960.27	Total Direct Deposits	0.00	Check Amount	960.27	1729.37

TERMINATION OF EMPLOYMENT TO
HOUSEHOLD EMPLOYEE LETTER

Date _____

Dear _____,

As we have discussed, your employment with our household will terminate at the close of business on _____. You are entitled to the following benefits, per our household's policy:

1. Your salary will be continued through _____.
2. Your health insurance benefits will continue through _____. Beyond that date, your rights to continue coverage under COBRA will be provided to you under separate cover.
3. You will be paid for your unused, accrued vacation and personal time.
4. You may be entitled to unemployment insurance. It's your responsibility to contact the local office of unemployment to understand your entitled benefits, if any.

Should you have further questions, you may contact _____ at _____.

Sincerely,

Household Employer

All household employees are employed at-will. This employment is at the discretion of the employer and the employee. Employment may terminate with or without notice or cause.

Employees are also free to end employment at any time, for any reason, with or without notice.

(NOTE: Certain states require "service letters" which must also include a reason for the termination. If this is the case in your state, or if you wish to document the reason(s), make sure to include only verifiable facts.)

Forms

This appendix contains various forms that you may use in the course of your household employment.

Department of Homeland Security
U.S. Citizenship and Immigration Services

OMB No. 1615-0047; Expires 03/31/07
Employment Eligibility Verification

INSTRUCTIONS
PLEASE READ ALL INSTRUCTIONS CAREFULLY BEFORE COMPLETING THIS FORM.

Anti-Discrimination Notice. It is illegal to discriminate against any individual (other than an alien not authorized to work in the U.S.) in hiring, discharging, or recruiting or referring for a fee because of that individual's national origin or citizenship status. It is illegal to discriminate against work eligible individuals. Employers **CANNOT** specify which document(s) they will accept from an employee. The refusal to hire an individual because of a future expiration date may also constitute illegal discrimination.

Section 1- Employee.
All employees, citizens and noncitizens, hired after November 6, 1986, must complete Section 1 of this form at the time of hire, which is the actual beginning of employment. **The employer is responsible for ensuring that Section 1 is timely and properly completed.**

Preparer/Translator Certification. The Preparer/Translator Certification must be completed if Section 1 is prepared by a person other than the employee. A preparer/translator may be used only when the employee is unable to complete Section 1 on his/her own. However, the employee must still sign Section 1 personally.

Section 2 - Employer.
For the purpose of completing this form, the term "employer" includes those recruiters and referrers for a fee who are agricultural associations, agricultural employers or farm labor contractors.

Employers must complete Section 2 by examining evidence of identity and employment eligibility within three (3) business days of the date employment begins. If employees are authorized to work, but are unable to present the required document(s) within three business days, they must present a receipt for the application of the document(s) within three business days and the actual document(s) within ninety (90) days. However, if employers hire individuals for a duration of less than three business days, Section 2 must be completed at the time employment begins. **Employers must record: 1)** document title; **2)** issuing authority; **3)** document number, **4)** expiration date, if any; and **5)** the date employment begins. Employers must sign and date the certification. Employees must present original documents. Employers may, but are not required to, photocopy the document(s) presented. These photocopies may only be used for the verification process and must be retained with the I-9. **However, employers are still responsible for completing the I-9.**

Section 3 - Updating and Reverification.
Employers must complete Section 3 when updating and/or reverifying the I-9. Employers must reverify employment eligibility of their employees on or before the expiration date recorded in Section 1. Employers **CANNOT** specify which document(s) they will accept from an employee.

- If an employee's name has changed at the time this form is being updated/reverified, complete Block A.
- If an employee is rehired within three (3) years of the date this form was originally completed and the employee is still eligible to be employed on the same basis as previously indicated on this form (updating), complete Block B and the signature block.
- If an employee is rehired within three (3) years of the date this form was originally completed and the employee's work authorization has expired **or** if a current employee's work authorization is about to expire (reverification), complete Block B and:

- examine any document that reflects that the employee is authorized to work in the U.S. (see List A **or** C),
- record the document title, document number and expiration date (if any) in Block C, and
- complete the signature block.

Photocopying and Retaining Form I-9. A blank I-9 may be reproduced, provided both sides are copied. The Instructions must be available to all employees completing this form. Employers must retain completed I-9s for three (3) years after the date of hire or one (1) year after the date employment ends, whichever is later.

For more detailed information, you may refer to the Department of Homeland Security (DHS) Handbook for Employers, (Form M-274). You may obtain the handbook at your local U.S. Citizenship and Immigration Services (USCIS) office.

Privacy Act Notice. The authority for collecting this information is the Immigration Reform and Control Act of 1986, Pub. L. 99-603 (8 USC 1324a).

This information is for employers to verify the eligibility of individuals for employment to preclude the unlawful hiring, or recruiting or referring for a fee, of aliens who are not authorized to work in the United States.

This information will be used by employers as a record of their basis for determining eligibility of an employee to work in the United States. The form will be kept by the employer and made available for inspection by officials of the U.S. Immigration and Customs Enforcement, Department of Labor and Office of Special Counsel for Immigration Related Unfair Employment Practices.

Submission of the information required in this form is voluntary. However, an individual may not begin employment unless this form is completed, since employers are subject to civil or criminal penalties if they do not comply with the Immigration Reform and Control Act of 1986.

Reporting Burden. We try to create forms and instructions that are accurate, can be easily understood and which impose the least possible burden on you to provide us with information. Often this is difficult because some immigration laws are very complex. Accordingly, the reporting burden for this collection of information is computed as follows: **1)** learning about this form, 5 minutes; **2)** completing the form, 5 minutes; and **3)** assembling and filing (recordkeeping) the form, 5 minutes, for an average of 15 minutes per response. If you have comments regarding the accuracy of this burden estimate, or suggestions for making this form simpler, you can write to U.S. Citizenship and Immigration Services, Regulatory Management Division, 111 Massachusetts Avenue, N.W., Washington, DC 20529. OMB No. 1615-0047.

NOTE: This is the 1991 edition of the Form I-9 that has been rebranded with a current printing date to reflect the recent transition from the INS to DHS and its components.

EMPLOYERS MUST RETAIN COMPLETED FORM I-9
PLEASE DO NOT MAIL COMPLETED FORM I-9 TO ICE OR USCIS

Form I-9 (Rev. 05/31/05)Y

Department of Homeland Security
U.S. Citizenship and Immigration Services

OMB No. 1615-0047; Expires 03/31/07
Employment Eligibility Verification

Please read instructions carefully before completing this form. The instructions must be available during completion of this form. ANTI-DISCRIMINATION NOTICE: It is illegal to discriminate against work eligible individuals. Employers CANNOT specify which document(s) they will accept from an employee. The refusal to hire an individual because of a future expiration date may also constitute illegal discrimination.

Section 1. Employee Information and Verification. To be completed and signed by employee at the time employment begins.

Print Name: Last	First	Middle Initial	Maiden Name

Address (Street Name and Number)	Apt. #	Date of Birth (month/day/year)

City	State	Zip Code	Social Security #

I am aware that federal law provides for imprisonment and/or fines for false statements or use of false documents in connection with the completion of this form.

I attest, under penalty of perjury, that I am (check one of the following):

☐ A citizen or national of the United States
☐ A Lawful Permanent Resident (Alien #) A _____
☐ An alien authorized to work until _____
(Alien # or Admission #) _____

Employee's Signature	Date (month/day/year)

Preparer and/or Translator Certification. *(To be completed and signed if Section 1 is prepared by a person other than the employee.) I attest, under penalty of perjury, that I have assisted in the completion of this form and that to the best of my knowledge the information is true and correct.*

Preparer's/Translator's Signature	Print Name

Address (Street Name and Number, City, State, Zip Code)	Date (month/day/year)

Section 2. Employer Review and Verification. To be completed and signed by employer. Examine one document from List A OR examine one document from List B and one from List C, as listed on the reverse of this form, and record the title, number and expiration date, if any, of the document(s).

List A	OR	List B	AND	List C
Document title:				
Issuing authority:				
Document #:				
Expiration Date (if any):				
Document #:				
Expiration Date (if any):				

CERTIFICATION - I attest, under penalty of perjury, that I have examined the document(s) presented by the above-named employee, that the above-listed document(s) appear to be genuine and to relate to the employee named, that the employee began employment on *(month/day/year)* _____ **and that to the best of my knowledge the employee is eligible to work in the United States. (State employment agencies may omit the date the employee began employment.)**

Signature of Employer or Authorized Representative	Print Name	Title

Business or Organization Name	Address (Street Name and Number, City, State, Zip Code)	Date (month/day/year)

Section 3. Updating and Reverification. To be completed and signed by employer.

A. New Name (if applicable)	B. Date of Rehire (month/day/year) (if applicable)

C. If employee's previous grant of work authorization has expired, provide the information below for the document that establishes current employment eligibility.

Document Title: _____ Document #: _____ Expiration Date (if any): _____

I attest, under penalty of perjury, that to the best of my knowledge, this employee is eligible to work in the United States, and if the employee presented document(s), the document(s) I have examined appear to be genuine and to relate to the individual.

Signature of Employer or Authorized Representative	Date (month/day/year)

NOTE: This is the 1991 edition of the Form I-9 that has been rebranded with a current printing date to reflect the recent transition from the INS to DHS and its components.

Form I-9 (Rev. 05/31/05)Y Page 2

LISTS OF ACCEPTABLE DOCUMENTS

LIST A		LIST B		LIST C
Documents that Establish Both Identity and Employment Eligibility	**OR**	**Documents that Establish Identity**	**AND**	**Documents that Establish Employment Eligibility**

LIST A — Documents that Establish Both Identity and Employment Eligibility

1. U.S. Passport (unexpired or expired)

2. Certificate of U.S. Citizenship (Form N-560 or N-561)

3. Certificate of Naturalization (Form N-550 or N-570)

4. Unexpired foreign passport, with I-551 stamp or attached Form I-94 indicating unexpired employment authorization

5. Permanent Resident Card or Alien Registration Receipt Card with photograph (Form I-151 or I-551)

6. Unexpired Temporary Resident Card (Form I-688)

7. Unexpired Employment Authorization Card (Form I-688A)

8. Unexpired Reentry Permit (Form I-327)

9. Unexpired Refugee Travel Document (Form 1-571)

10. Unexpired Employment Authorization Document issued by DHS that contains a photograph (Form I-688B)

LIST B — Documents that Establish Identity

1. Driver's license or ID card issued by a state or outlying possession of the United States provided it contains a photograph or information such as name, date of birth, gender, height, eye color and address

2. ID card issued by federal, state or local government agencies or entities, provided it contains a photograph or information such as name, date of birth, gender, height, eye color and address

3. School ID card with a photograph

4. Voter's registration card

5. U.S. Military card or draft record

6. Military dependent's ID card

7. U.S. Coast Guard Merchant Mariner Card

8. Native American tribal document

9. Driver's license issued by a Canadian government authority

For persons under age 18 who are unable to present a document listed above:

10. School record or report card

11. Clinic, doctor or hospital record

12. Day-care or nursery school record

LIST C — Documents that Establish Employment Eligibility

1. U.S. social security card issued by the Social Security Administration (other than a card stating it is not valid for employment)

2. Certification of Birth Abroad issued by the Department of State (Form FS-545 or Form DS-1350)

3. Original or certified copy of a birth certificate issued by a state, county, municipal authority or outlying possession of the United States bearing an official seal

4. Native American tribal document

5. U.S. Citizen ID Card (Form I-197)

6. ID Card for use of Resident Citizen in the United States (Form I-179)

7. Unexpired employment authorization document issued by DHS (other than those listed under List A)

Illustrations of many of these documents appear in Part 8 of the Handbook for Employers (M-274)

Form **SS-8**
(Rev. June 2003)
Department of the Treasury
Internal Revenue Service

Determination of Worker Status for Purposes of Federal Employment Taxes and Income Tax Withholding

OMB No. 1545-0004

Name of firm (or person) for whom the worker performed services	Worker's name

Firm's address (include street address, apt. or suite no., city, state, and ZIP code)	Worker's address (include street address, apt. or suite no., city, state, and ZIP code)

Trade name	Telephone number (include area code) ( )	Worker's social security number

Telephone number (include area code) ( )	Firm's employer identification number	Worker's employer identification number (if any)

If the worker is paid by a firm other than the one listed on this form for these services, enter the name, address, and employer identification number of the payer.

Important Information Needed To Process Your Request

We must have your permission to disclose your name and the information on this form and any attachments to other parties involved with this request. **Do we have your permission to disclose this information?** . . . . ☐ **Yes** ☐ **No**
If you answered "No" or did not mark a box, we will not process your request and will not issue a determination.

You must answer ALL items OR mark them "Unknown" or "Does not apply." If you need more space, attach another sheet.

A This form is being completed by: ☐ Firm ☐ Worker; for services performed _____ to _____ .

(beginning date)   (ending date)

B Explain your reason(s) for filing this form (e.g., you received a bill from the IRS, you believe you received a Form 1099 or Form W-2 erroneously, you are unable to get worker's compensation benefits, you were audited or are being audited by the IRS). _____
_____
_____
_____
_____

C Total number of workers who performed or are performing the same or similar services _____ .

D How did the worker obtain the job? ☐ Application ☐ Bid ☐ Employment Agency ☐ Other (specify) _____ .

E Attach copies of all supporting documentation (contracts, invoices, memos, Forms W-2, Forms 1099, IRS closing agreements, IRS rulings, etc.). In addition, please inform us of any current or past litigation concerning the worker's status. If no income reporting forms (Form 1099-MISC or W-2) were furnished to the worker, enter the amount of income earned for the year(s) at issue $ _____ .

F Describe the firm's business. _____
_____
_____
_____

G Describe the work done by the worker and provide the worker's job title. _____
_____
_____
_____

H Explain why you believe the worker is an employee or an independent contractor. _____
_____
_____
_____

I Did the worker perform services for the firm before getting this position? . . . . ☐ **Yes** ☐ **No** ☐ **N/A**
If "Yes," what were the dates of the prior service? _____
If "Yes," explain the differences, if any, between the current and prior service. _____
_____
_____
_____

J If the work is done under a written agreement between the firm and the worker, attach a copy (preferably signed by both parties). Describe the terms and conditions of the work arrangement. _____
_____

For Privacy Act and Paperwork Reduction Act Notice, see page 5.   Cat. No. 16106T   Form **SS-8** (Rev. 6-2003)

Form SS-8 (Rev. 6-2003)   Page **2**

Part I   Behavioral Control

1   What specific training and/or instruction is the worker given by the firm? ....
....

2   How does the worker receive work assignments? ....
....

3   Who determines the methods by which the assignments are performed? ....

4   Who is the worker required to contact if problems or complaints arise and who is responsible for their resolution? ....
....

5   What types of reports are required from the worker? Attach examples. ....
....

6   Describe the worker's daily routine (i.e., schedule, hours, etc.). ....
....
....

7   At what location(s) does the worker perform services (e.g., firm's premises, own shop or office, home, customer's location, etc.)? ....
....

8   Describe any meetings the worker is required to attend and any penalties for not attending (e.g., sales meetings, monthly meetings, staff
meetings, etc.). ....

9   Is the worker required to provide the services personally?   .   .   .   .   ☐ **Yes**   ☐ **No**

10 If substitutes or helpers are needed, who hires them? ....

11 If the worker hires the substitutes or helpers, is approval required?   .   .   .   .   ☐ **Yes**   ☐ **No**
If "Yes," by whom? ....

12 Who pays the substitutes or helpers? ....

13 Is the worker reimbursed if the worker pays the substitutes or helpers?   .   .   .   .   ☐ **Yes**   ☐ **No**
If "Yes," by whom? ....

Part II   Financial Control

1   List the supplies, equipment, materials, and property provided by each party:
The firm ....
The worker ....
Other party ....

2   Does the worker lease equipment?   .   .   .   .   ☐ **Yes**   ☐ **No**
If "Yes," what are the terms of the lease? (Attach a copy or explanatory statement.) ....
....

3   What expenses are incurred by the worker in the performance of services for the firm? ....
....

4   Specify which, if any, expenses are reimbursed by:
The firm ....
Other party ....

5   Type of pay the worker receives: ☐ Salary   ☐ Commission   ☐ Hourly Wage   ☐ Piece Work
☐ Lump Sum   ☐ Other (specify)
If type of pay is commission, and the firm guarantees a minimum amount of pay, specify amount $ _____ .

6   Is the worker allowed a drawing account for advances?   .   .   .   .   ☐ **Yes**   ☐ **No**
If "Yes," how often? ....
Specify any restrictions. ....

7   Whom does the customer pay?   .   .   .   .   ☐ Firm   ☐ Worker
If worker, does the worker pay the total amount to the firm?   ☐ **Yes**   ☐ **No**   If "No," explain. ....

8   Does the firm carry worker's compensation insurance on the worker?   .   .   .   .   ☐ **Yes**   ☐ **No**

9   What economic loss or financial risk, if any, can the worker incur beyond the normal loss of salary (e.g., loss or damage of equipment,
material, etc.)? ....
....

Form **SS-8** (Rev. 6-2003)

Form SS-8 (Rev. 6-2003)   Page **3**

Part III   **Relationship of the Worker and Firm**

1   List the benefits available to the worker (e.g., paid vacations, sick pay, pensions, bonuses). ....
....

2   Can the relationship be terminated by either party without incurring liability or penalty?   .   .   .   .   ☐ **Yes**   ☐ **No**
    If "No," explain your answer. ....

3   Does the worker perform similar services for others?   .   .   .   .   ☐ **Yes**   ☐ **No**
    If "Yes," is the worker required to get approval from the firm?   .   .   .   .   ☐ **Yes**   ☐ **No**
4   Describe any agreements prohibiting competition between the worker and the firm while the worker is performing services or during any later
    period. Attach any available documentation.   ....
....

5   Is the worker a member of a union?   .   .   .   .   ☐ **Yes**   ☐ **No**
6   What type of advertising, if any, does the worker do (e.g., a business listing in a directory, business cards, etc.)? Provide copies, if applicable.
....

7   If the worker assembles or processes a product at home, who provides the materials and instructions or pattern? ....
....

8   What does the worker do with the finished product (e.g., return it to the firm, provide it to another party, or sell it)? ....
....

9   How does the firm represent the worker to its customers (e.g., employee, partner, representative, or contractor)? ....
....

10 If the worker no longer performs services for the firm, how did the relationship end? ....
....

Part IV   **For Service Providers or Salespersons**—Complete this part if the worker provided a service directly to
                 customers or is a salesperson.

1   What are the worker's responsibilities in soliciting new customers? ....
....

2   Who provides the worker with leads to prospective customers? ....
3   Describe any reporting requirements pertaining to the leads. ....
....

4   What terms and conditions of sale, if any, are required by the firm? ....
5   Are orders submitted to and subject to approval by the firm?   .   .   .   .   ☐ **Yes**   ☐ **No**
6   Who determines the worker's territory? ....
7   Did the worker pay for the privilege of serving customers on the route or in the territory?   .   .   .   .   ☐ **Yes**   ☐ **No**
    If "Yes," whom did the worker pay? ....
    If "Yes," how much did the worker pay?   .   .   .   . $ _____ .
8   Where does the worker sell the product (e.g., in a home, retail establishment, etc.)? ....
....

9   List the product and/or services distributed by the worker (e.g., meat, vegetables, fruit, bakery products, beverages, or laundry or dry cleaning
    services). If more than one type of product and/or service is distributed, specify the principal one. ....
....

10 Does the worker sell life insurance full time?   .   .   .   .   ☐ **Yes**   ☐ **No**
11 Does the worker sell other types of insurance for the firm?   .   .   .   .   ☐ **Yes**   ☐ **No**
    If "Yes," enter the percentage of the worker's total working time spent in selling other types of insurance.   .   .   . _____ %
12 If the worker solicits orders from wholesalers, retailers, contractors, or operators of hotels, restaurants, or other similar
    establishments, enter the percentage of the worker's time spent in the solicitation.   .   .   .   . _____ %
13 Is the merchandise purchased by the customers for resale or use in their business operations?   .   .   .   .   .   .   ☐ **Yes**   ☐ **No**
    Describe the merchandise and state whether it is equipment installed on the customers' premises. ....
....

Part V   **Signature** (see page 4)

Under penalties of perjury, I declare that I have examined this request, including accompanying documents, and to the best of my knowledge and belief, the facts
presented are true, correct, and complete.

Signature ▶ _____   Title ▶ _____   Date ▶ _____
                       (Type or print name below)

                                                                                                              Form **SS-8** (Rev. 6-2003)

Form SS-8 (Rev. 6-2003)

General Instructions

Section references are to the Internal Revenue Code unless otherwise noted.

Purpose

Firms and workers file Form SS-8 to request a determination of the status of a worker for purposes of Federal employment taxes and income tax withholding.

A Form SS-8 determination may be requested only in order to resolve Federal tax matters. If Form SS-8 is submitted for a tax year for which the statute of limitations on the tax return has expired, a determination letter will not be issued. The statute of limitations expires 3 years from the due date of the tax return or the date filed, whichever is later.

The IRS does not issue a determination letter for proposed transactions or on hypothetical situations. We may, however, issue an information letter when it is considered appropriate.

Definition

Firm. For the purposes of this form, the term "firm" means any individual, business enterprise, organization, state, or other entity for which a worker has performed services. The firm may or may not have paid the worker directly for these services. **If the firm was not responsible for payment for services, be sure to enter the name, address, and employer identification number of the payer on the first page of Form SS-8 below the identifying information for the firm and the worker.**

The SS-8 Determination Process

The IRS will acknowledge the receipt of your Form SS-8. Because there are usually two (or more) parties who could be affected by a determination of employment status, the IRS attempts to get information from all parties involved by sending those parties blank Forms SS-8 for completion. The case will be assigned to a technician who will review the facts, apply the law, and render a decision. The technician may ask for additional information from the requestor, from other involved parties, or from third parties that could help clarify the work relationship before rendering a decision. The IRS will generally issue a formal determination to the firm or payer (if that is a different entity), and will send a copy to the worker. A determination letter applies only to a worker (or a class of workers) requesting it, and the decision is binding on the IRS. In certain cases, a formal determination will not be issued. Instead, an information letter may be issued. Although an information letter is advisory only and is not binding on the IRS, it may be used to assist the worker to fulfill his or her Federal tax obligations.

Neither the SS-8 determination process nor the review of any records in connection with the determination constitutes an examination (audit) of any Federal tax return. If the periods under consideration have previously been examined, the SS-8 determination process will not constitute a reexamination under IRS reopening procedures. Because this is not an examination of any Federal tax return, the appeal rights available in connection with an examination do not apply to an SS-8 determination. However, if you disagree with a determination and you have additional information concerning the work relationship that you believe was not previously considered, you may request that the determining office reconsider the determination.

Completing Form SS-8

Answer all questions as completely as possible. Attach additional sheets if you need more space. Provide information for all years the worker provided services for the firm. Determinations are based on the entire relationship between the firm and the worker.

Additional copies of this form may be obtained by calling 1-800-829-4933 or from the IRS website at **www.irs.gov.**

Fee

There is no fee for requesting an SS-8 determination letter.

Signature

Form SS-8 must be signed and dated by the taxpayer. A stamped signature will not be accepted.

The person who signs for a corporation must be an officer of the corporation who has personal knowledge of the facts. If the corporation is a member of an affiliated group filing a consolidated return, it must be signed by an officer of the common parent of the group.

The person signing for a trust, partnership, or limited liability company must be, respectively, a trustee, general partner, or member-manager who has personal knowledge of the facts.

Where To File

Send the completed Form SS-8 to the address listed below for the firm's location. However, for cases involving Federal agencies, send Form SS-8 to the Internal Revenue Service, Attn: CC:CORP:T:C, Ben Franklin Station, P.O. Box 7604, Washington, DC 20044.

Firm's location:	Send to:
Alaska, Arizona, Arkansas, California, Colorado, Hawaii, Idaho, Illinois, Iowa, Kansas, Minnesota, Missouri, Montana, Nebraska, Nevada, New Mexico, North Dakota, Oklahoma, Oregon, South Dakota, Texas, Utah, Washington, Wisconsin, Wyoming, American Samoa, Guam, Puerto Rico, U.S. Virgin Islands	Internal Revenue Service SS-8 Determinations P.O. Box 630 Stop 631 Holtsville, NY 11742-0630
Alabama, Connecticut, Delaware, District of Columbia, Florida, Georgia, Indiana, Kentucky, Louisiana, Maine, Maryland, Massachusetts, Michigan, Mississippi, New Hampshire, New Jersey, New York, North Carolina, Ohio, Pennsylvania, Rhode Island, South Carolina, Tennessee, Vermont, Virginia, West Virginia, all other locations not listed	Internal Revenue Service SS-8 Determinations 40 Lakemont Road Newport, VT 05855-1555

Instructions for Workers

If you are requesting a determination for more than one firm, complete a separate Form SS-8 for each firm.

 Form SS-8 is not a claim for refund of social security and Medicare taxes or Federal income tax withholding.

If the IRS determines that you are an employee, you are responsible for filing an amended return for any corrections related to this decision. A determination that a worker is an employee does not necessarily reduce any current or prior tax liability. For more information, call 1-800-829-1040.

Time for filing a claim for refund. Generally, you must file your claim for a credit or refund within 3 years from the date your original return was filed or within 2 years from the date the tax was paid, whichever is later.

Filing Form SS-8 does not prevent the expiration of the time in which a claim for a refund must be filed. If you are concerned about a refund, and the statute of limitations for filing a claim for refund for the year(s) at issue has not yet expired, you should file **Form 1040X,** Amended U.S. Individual Income Tax Return, to protect your statute of limitations. File a separate Form 1040X for each year.

On the Form 1040X you file, do not complete lines 1 through 24 on the form. Write "Protective Claim" at the top of the form, sign and date it. In addition, you should enter the following statement in Part II, Explanation of Changes to Income, Deductions, and Credits: "Filed Form SS-8 with the Internal Revenue Service Office in (Holtsville, NY; Newport, VT; or Washington, DC; as appropriate). By filing this protective claim, I reserve the right to file a claim for any refund that may be due after a determination of my employment tax status has been completed."

Filing Form SS-8 does not alter the requirement to timely file an income tax return. Do not delay filing your tax return in anticipation of an answer to your SS-8 request. In addition, if applicable, do not delay in responding to a request for payment while waiting for a determination of your worker status.

Instructions for Firms

If a **worker** has requested a determination of his or her status while working for you, you will receive a request from the IRS to complete a Form SS-8. In cases of this type, the IRS usually gives each party an opportunity to present a statement of the facts because any decision will affect the employment tax status of the parties. Failure to respond to this request will not prevent the IRS from issuing a determination letter based on the information he or she has made available so that the worker may fulfill his or her Federal tax obligations. However, the information that you provide is extremely valuable in determining the status of the worker.

If **you** are requesting a determination for a particular class of worker, complete the form for **one** individual who is representative of the class of workers whose status is in question. If you want a written determination for more than one class of workers, complete a separate Form SS-8 for one worker from each class whose status is typical of that class. A written determination for any worker will apply to other workers of the same class if the facts are not materially different for these workers. Please provide a list of names and addresses of all workers potentially affected by this determination.

If you have a reasonable basis for not treating a worker as an employee, you may be relieved from having to pay employment taxes for that worker under section 530 of the 1978 Revenue Act. However, this relief provision cannot be considered in conjunction with a Form SS-8 determination because the determination does not constitute an examination of any tax return. For more information regarding section 530 of the 1978 Revenue Act and to determine if you qualify for relief under this section, you may visit the IRS website at **www.irs.gov.**

Privacy Act and Paperwork Reduction Act Notice. We ask for the information on this form to carry out the Internal Revenue laws of the United States. This information will be used to determine the employment status of the worker(s) described on the form. Subtitle C, Employment Taxes, of the Internal Revenue Code imposes employment taxes on wages. Sections 3121(d), 3306(a), and 3401(c) and (d) and the related regulations define employee and employer for purposes of employment taxes imposed under Subtitle C. Section 6001 authorizes the IRS to request information needed to determine if a worker(s) or firm is subject to these taxes. Section 6109 requires you to provide your taxpayer identification number. Neither workers nor firms are required to request a status determination, but if you choose to do so, you must provide the information requested on this form. Failure to provide the requested information may prevent us from making a status determination. If any worker or the firm has requested a status determination and you are being asked to provide information for use in that determination, you are not required to provide the requested information. However, failure to provide such information will prevent the IRS from considering it in making the status determination. Providing false or fraudulent information may subject you to penalties. Routine uses of this information include providing it to the Department of Justice for use in civil and criminal litigation, to the Social Security Administration for the administration of social security programs, and to cities, states, and the District of Columbia for the administration of their tax laws. We may also disclose this information to Federal and state agencies to enforce Federal nontax criminal laws and to combat terrorism. We may provide this information to the affected worker(s) or the firm as part of the status determination process.

You are not required to provide the information requested on a form that is subject to the Paperwork Reduction Act unless the form displays a valid OMB control number. Books or records relating to a form or its instructions must be retained as long as their contents may become material in the administration of any Internal Revenue law. Generally, tax returns and return information are confidential, as required by section 6103.

The time needed to complete and file this form will vary depending on individual circumstances. The estimated average time is: **Recordkeeping,** 22 hrs.; **Learning about the law or the form,** 47 min.; and **Preparing and sending the form to the IRS,** 1 hr., 11 min. If you have comments concerning the accuracy of these time estimates or suggestions for making this form simpler, we would be happy to hear from you. You can write to the Tax Products Coordinating Committee, Western Area Distribution Center, Rancho Cordova, CA 95743-0001. **Do not** send the tax form to this address. Instead, see **Where To File** on page 4.

WORK AGREEMENT SAMPLE

This Agreement is made and entered into on _____(date), between _____ (employer) residing at _____ _____ and _____ (employee) resid- ing at _____.

Recitals

1. Employer is an individual and a "Household Employer," resident of _____(state), and over the age of 18.
2. Employee is an individual, resident of _____(state), and over the age of 18.
3. Employee is willing to be employed by Employer, and Employer is willing to employ Employee, on the terms and conditions set forth in this Agreement.

A. Employment

1. Employment under this agreement is to begin on _____ and continue unless sooner terminated as provided herein.
2. Subject to the supervision and control of Employer, Employee shall perform the usual and customary duties of _____, including but not limited to that of those described in the written job description.
3. Employee shall work at the convenience of Employer, arriving and leaving at times to be specified by Employer. Employee shall not be required to work more than _____ hours per week, but may consent to do so.

B. Compensation

1. Subject to the following provisions of this agreement, the Employer agrees to pay the Employee a gross compensation hourly rate of $_____.
2. Employer shall deduct and withhold appropriate amounts from Employee's gross pay as required by federal and state laws.
3. Employer shall pay Employee on a (weekly _____) basis on the Friday of each week.

4. Employee shall receive an overtime wage of 1.5 times the usual gross hourly rate for each hour worked exceeding 40 hours per week. At the Employer's option, the Employer may compensate Employee by either paying overtime or by giving Employee compensatory time off, during the same pay period.

5. Employer, at its own discretion, may agree to increase Employee's hourly gross compensation from time to time in writing.

C. Benefits

1. Employee is entitled to _____ days of paid vacation annually. The vacation must be scheduled 30 days in advance and agreed to by employer. Vacation is based upon normal payment for a 40-hour workweek.

2. Employee will receive _____ days per year as paid sick time. Sick time may not be accumulated from year to year. Sick time benefits cannot be taken in cash compensation and are forfeited on termination of employment.

D. Terms And Conditions Of Employment

1. Employee may not drink alcohol, use illegal drugs or smoke while on duty for the employer.

2. Employer shall provide Employee with a petty cash fund for job related expenses. Employer shall reimburse Employee upon providing Employer with a complete expense report with related receipt(s). Reimbursements will be made weekly.

3. Employment with the Household employer lends itself to intimate and sensitive information. Therefore, Household employee agrees to treat household information as private and confidential both during and after his/her employment tenure. Household employee agrees that no information pertaining to the household, such as the home's security system code or a password for childcare drop offs, is to be repeated inside or outside of the worksite. This applies to any information that is discussed by parties within the household, as well. In addition, Household employee agrees not to discuss his/her salary and benefits with other household employees. Household employee acknowledges that a violation of this rule of conduct will be grounds for early dismissal.

E. Termination Of Agreement

1. Employer may terminate employment by Employee for violation of paragraph D-1.
2. Employer may terminate employment by Employee for failure to perform the duties set forth in the job description and employee handbook.
3. Termination means that benefits in paragraph C cease as of the date of termination.
4. Agreement may be ended by mutual agreement.
5. Employment is at the discretion of employer and employee. Either party may terminate this agreement with or without notice or cause.

F. Modification And Interpretation

1. The job description may change by mutual consent.
2. Each party expects that Employee will conform to the custom and practice of the _____ (household employment, e.g., Chef, nanny, butler).

G. Applicable Laws

1. The provisions of this agreement shall be construed in accordance with the laws of the state of _____.

_____   _____
Household employer   Date

_____   _____
Household employee   Date

(NOTICE: the information in this sample is designed to provide an outline that you can follow when formulating personnel plans. Due to the variances of many local, city, county and state laws, we recommend that you seek professional legal counseling before entering into any agreement.)

GENERAL APPLICATION FOR EMPLOYMENT

_____   _____

Name Last   First   Middle   Previous Name(s) if any

_____

Address Number   Street   City   State   ZIP Code

_____   _____

Telephone   Email address

_____   _____

Driver's License #   State

EDUCATION

Name/ Location of School	Degree Earned	Type	Year Graduated	Major
Grade School _____	Y N	_____	_____	_____
High School _____	Y N	_____	_____	_____
Vocational School _____	Y N	_____	_____	_____
College _____	Y N	_____	_____	_____
Graduate School _____	Y N	_____	_____	_____

Courses in Child Development, Education

Extracurricular Activities

EMPLOYMENT HISTORY (*Starting with current to most recent, list all previous positions. Explain any gap between employment in the space provided.*)
DATES   EMPLOYED   EMPLOYER   PHONE   POSITION HELD
1. _____
2. _____
3. _____
Explanation of any gaps in employment

_____

BACKGROUND

A. Have you ever been convicted of a crime? [ ] No [ ] Yes
   If yes, explain the nature of the offense, date and court location. _____
   _____

B. Have you had any traffic citations, (including speeding tickets, DWI or
   DUI convictions) in the past five years? [ ] No [ ] Yes
   If yes, list all traffic citations for the past five years, including speeding
   tickets, DWI or DUI convictions. _____

Is your driver's license currently valid, not under a suspension or revoked?
[ ] Yes [ ] No
Explain: _____
In what other states have you had a driver's license? _____
_____

| State | License numbers (if known) |

C. List all addresses you have lived at for the past five years.

Address	County	State	Dates
1.			
2.			
3.			

AVAILABILITY/COMPENSATION

When can you start work? _____
Are you willing to make a one-year commitment? [ ] Yes [ ] No
What days and hours are you available to work? _____
_____

Gross hourly rate requested $_____ per _____
What benefits do you desire? _____

STATEMENT

I have not withheld any information a reasonable person would expect a prospective candidate to provide. I have been honest in revealing and explaining any undesirable background information. I do certify that all information noted here is true to the best of my knowledge.

I authorize full disclosure and release to any duly authorized agent of the Household employer of all information and records both public and private, including, but not limited to, criminal and financial history, as required to conduct a complete background investigation. I hereby release all persons and agencies from any liability associated with such disclosure. I understand such information may be duplicated and given to any prospective client seeking to hire me, and I hereby authorize this.

I also specifically request that all agencies and references fully cooperate with this investigation and provide the requested information.

_____   _____

Applicant Signature   Date

ADDITIONAL APPLICATION QUESTIONS
SPECIFIC TO JOB TYPE

Additional application questions to use when hiring a NANNY.
- Do you have an educational background in child development?
- How many years of childcare experience do you have?
- What age will you care for?
- How many children will you care for?
- Have you experience in caring for multiples?
    - ✦ Would you care for sick children?
    - ✦ Would you care for children with special needs?
    - ✦ Will you assist with homework?
- Will you tutor science?
- Reading?
- Foreign language?
- What childcare tasks are you willing to perform?
- Why are you interested in working in childcare?
- With respect to childcare, what activities would you organize on a daily or weekly basis?
- What is your philosophy on discipline?
- If you were a parent looking for a childcare provider, what characteristics would you look for in a provider? What would be most important to you in hiring a nanny or childcare provider?
- What are the most important characteristics you believe lend to a successful relationship between a childcare provider and parents?
- Briefly tell us about your family life (i.e., your parents, siblings, and/or children you have raised).

Additional application questions to use when hiring an ELDERCARE PROVIDER.

- Do you have experience working with an elderly or disabled person?
- How many years?
- Do you have experience working in a private household?
- How many years?
- What elder care responsibilities are you willing to perform?
  - ✦ What household responsibilities are you willing to perform or assist with?
  - ✦ Are you able to lift heavy objects (50 lbs or more)?
- Have you had medical training in transferring?
- Are you able to transfer someone from a wheelchair into a car?
- Are you able to transfer someone from a wheelchair into a bed?
- How do you handle someone who is angry, fearful, or upset?
- How do you handle someone who is downcast or depressed?
- Do you have experience caring for someone with mental problems, such as depression, dementia, or loss of memory? Please explain:
- Why do you want to work in eldercare?

Additional application questions to use when hiring a HOUSEKEEPER.
- What formal experience do you have as a housekeeper?
- How many years experience do you have in a private household?
- What is the largest property you have ever cleaned (sq. ft.)?
- Which housekeeping tasks are you willing to perform?
    - Which laundry tasks are you willing to perform?
    - Which ironing tasks are you willing to perform?
- Check ONE of the following that best describes your housekeeping standards:
    - ____ I have sloppy housekeeping standards
    - ____ I am a messy but happy housekeeper
    - ____ My housekeeping standards are average
    - ____ I am a neat and orderly housekeeper
- What are your housekeeping standards?
    - ____ I must have orderliness to function
    - ____ I always perform every task scrupulously and thoroughly.
- Please rate yourself on the following skills, using a 0-10 scale with 10 being the highest/best and 0 being the lowest/worst.
    - ____ Computer use
    - ____ Cooking
- Communication
    - Problem solving
    - Organizational
- Will you prepare meals for (please check all that apply):
    - ____ My employer's children only
    - ____ My employer's immediate family living within the household
    - ____ My employer's immediate family and household staff
    - ____ My employer's children and their playmates
    - ____ My employer's guests
    - ____ Any person within the household at that meal time, excluding vendors, service professionals and repairmen
    - ____ Anyone my employer requests me to feed
- Are you willing to work in a home with a child?
- What ages?
- How many?
- What is your personal style of service?

Additional application questions to use when hiring a HOUSEHOLD MANAGER.

- Do you have formal experience as a household manager?
- How many years experience do you have in a private household?
- What is the largest property you have ever managed (sq. ft.)?
    - ✦ What is the largest size of household staff you have managed?
    - ✦ What household management tasks are you willing to perform?
    - ✦ Please rate yourself on the following skills, using a 0-10 scale with 10 being the highest/best and 0 being the lowest/worst.

    ____ Communication

    ____ Problem solving

    ____ Formal service

    ____ Social etiquette

    ____ Personnel management

    ____ Leadership
- Fiscal management
- Negotiating skills
- Computer skills
    - ✦ Please describe your computer skills and list which programs you are proficient with. _____

    _____
- Are you willing to work in a home with a child?
- What ages?
- How many?
- What is your personal style of service?
- What is your style of management?
- Please describe any experience you have working with contractors.
- Please describe the kinds of household duties you are not willing to perform.

CONFIDENTIALITY / NONDISCLOSURE AGREEMENT

This Agreement (this "Agreement") is made effective as of _____
___, 20__, by and between _____,
("Household employer"), of _____, [address] of the
_____ Household and _____, ("the
Household employee").

A. Household employer is a private household with an employment position.
B. Household employer desires to have services of the Household employee.
C. Household employee is willing to be employed by Household employer.

Therefore, the parties agree as follows:

1. CONFIDENTIALITY. Employment with the Household employer lends
   itself to intimate and sensitive information. Therefore, Household
   employee agrees to treat household information as private and confidential both during and after his/her employment tenure. Household
   employee agrees that no information pertaining to the household, such as
   the home's security system code or a password for childcare drop offs, is
   to be repeated inside or outside of the worksite. This applies to any information that is discussed by parties within the household, as well. In addition, Household employee agrees not to discuss his/her salary and benefits with other household employees. Household employee acknowledges
   that a violation of this rule of conduct will be grounds for early dismissal.

2. UNAUTHORIZED DISCLOSURE OF INFORMATION. If it appears
   that Household employee has disclosed (or has threatened to disclose)
   Information in violation of this Agreement, Household employer shall be
   entitled to a Court injunction to restrain Household employee from dis-
   closing, in whole or in part, such Information, or from providing any services to any party to whom such Information has been disclosed or may be
   disclosed. Household employer shall not be prohibited by this provision
   from pursuing other remedies, including a claim for losses and damages.

3. CONFIDENTIALITY AFTER TERMINATION OF SERVICES. The confidentiality provisions of this Agreement shall remain in full force and effect for a one-year period after the termination of Household employee's services.

4. APPLICABLE LAW. The laws of the State of _____ shall govern this Agreement.

Household employer

By _____ Date _____

AGREED TO AND ACCEPTED.

Household employee

By _____ Date _____

EMPLOYEE HANDBOOK ACKNOWLEDGEMENT RECEIPT

Date: _____

I acknowledge that I have received a copy of the household employee handbook, and that I am responsible for reading and understanding the information set forth within the handbook. I understand that I am responsible for returning the employee handbook to my employer upon my resignation or termination of employment.

Employee Name (please print): _____

Employee Signature: _____

EXPENSE REPORT OF HOUSEHOLD EMPLOYEE
MILEAGE REIMBURSEMENT WORKSHEET

DATE	Day	Meals	Food & Grocery	Transport & Travel	Supplies	Equipment & Tool	Entertainment	Other
Totals								

MILEAGE REIMBURSEMENT WORKSHEET

	Sunday	Monday	Tuesday	Wednesday	Thursday	Friday	Saturday
Date							
# of Miles							
Reimbursement Rate (_¢/mile)							
Total							

SUBTOTAL	**$**	
Less advance	$	
Less pre-paid expenses	$	
Total due employee	$	

REMEMBER: Attach Travel Authorization form and itinerary.

Approved by:

_____

Household employee

_____

Household employer

MEDICAL CARE RELEASE FORM

I, _____, (parent/guardian) authorize the following household employee, _____, to act on my behalf in the care of my dependent(s). The above person has my authority to request emergency health and/or medical services for my dependent in case of a health emergency.

Primary Physician:_____

Dependent Name: _____ DOB _____
Known Allergies _____

Dependent Name: _____ DOB _____
Known Allergies _____

Dependent Name: _____ DOB _____
Known Allergies _____

_____
Parent/Guardian Signature   Telephone   Date

MEDICATION PERMISSION

I give my permission that _____,
who is caring for my dependent, give my dependent the following medication.

Dependent's name:

_____

_____

Medication:

_____

_____

Condition for which medication is prescribed:

_____

_____

Instructions for use:

Dosage _____

Time(s) _____

_____

_____

Prescribing Physician Name:

_____

Telephone:

_____

Possible side effects to be aware of:

_____

_____

_____

Parent/Guardian Signature   Date

Form W-4 (2006)

Purpose. Complete Form W-4 so that your employer can withhold the correct federal income tax from your pay. Because your tax situation may change, you may want to refigure your withholding each year.

Exemption from withholding. If you are exempt, complete only lines 1, 2, 3, 4, and 7 and sign the form to validate it. Your exemption for 2006 expires February 16, 2007. See Pub. 505, Tax Withholding and Estimated Tax.

Note. You cannot claim exemption from withholding if (a) your income exceeds $850 and includes more than $300 of unearned income (for example, interest and dividends) and (b) another person can claim you as a dependent on their tax return.

Basic instructions. If you are not exempt, complete the **Personal Allowances Worksheet** below. The worksheets on page 2 adjust your withholding allowances based on itemized deductions, certain credits, adjustments to income, or two-earner/two-job situations. Complete all worksheets that apply. However, you may claim fewer (or zero) allowances.

Head of household. Generally, you may claim head of household filing status on your tax return only if you are unmarried and pay more than 50% of the costs of keeping up a home for yourself and your dependent(s) or other qualifying individuals. See line **E** below.

Tax credits. You can take projected tax credits into account in figuring your allowable number of withholding allowances. Credits for child or dependent care expenses and the child tax credit may be claimed using the **Personal Allowances Worksheet** below. See Pub. 919, How Do I Adjust My Tax Withholding, for information on converting your other credits into withholding allowances.

Nonwage income. If you have a large amount of nonwage income, such as interest or dividends, consider making estimated tax payments using Form 1040-ES, Estimated Tax for Individuals. Otherwise, you may owe additional tax.

Two earners/two jobs. If you have a working spouse or more than one job, figure the total number of allowances you are entitled to claim on all jobs using worksheets from only one Form W-4. Your withholding usually will be most accurate when all allowances are claimed on the Form W-4 for the highest paying job and zero allowances are claimed on the others.

Nonresident alien. If you are a nonresident alien, see the Instructions for Form 8233 before completing this Form W-4.

Check your withholding. After your Form W-4 takes effect, use Pub. 919 to see how the dollar amount you are having withheld compares to your projected total tax for 2006. See Pub. 919, especially if your earnings exceed $130,000 (Single) or $180,000 (Married).

Recent name change? If your name on line 1 differs from that shown on your social security card, call 1-800-772-1213 to initiate a name change and obtain a social security card showing your correct name.

Personal Allowances Worksheet (Keep for your records.)

A Enter "1" for **yourself** if no one else can claim you as a dependent . . . . **A** _____

B Enter "1" if:
- You are single and have only one job; or
- You are married, have only one job, and your spouse does not work; or
- Your wages from a second job or your spouse's wages (or the total of both) are $1,000 or less.

} . . **B** _____

C Enter "1" for your **spouse.** But, you may choose to enter "-0-" if you are married and have either a working spouse or more than one job. (Entering "-0-" may help you avoid having too little tax withheld.) . . . . . . **C** _____

D Enter number of **dependents** (other than your spouse or yourself) you will claim on your tax return . . . . . . **D** _____

E Enter "1" if you will file as **head of household** on your tax return (see conditions under **Head of household** above) . **E** _____

F Enter "1" if you have at least $1,500 of **child or dependent care expenses** for which you plan to claim a credit . . **F** _____
(**Note.** Do **not** include child support payments. See **Pub. 503,** Child and Dependent Care Expenses, for details.)

G **Child Tax Credit** (including additional child tax credit):
- If your total income will be less than $55,000 ($82,000 if married), enter "2" for each eligible child.
- If your total income will be between $55,000 and $84,000 ($82,000 and $119,000 if married), enter "1" for each eligible child plus "1" **additional** if you have four or more eligible children. **G** _____

H Add lines A through G and enter total here. (**Note.** This may be different from the number of exemptions you claim on your tax return.) ▶ **H** _____

For accuracy, complete all worksheets that apply.
{
- If you plan to **itemize or claim adjustments to income** and want to reduce your withholding, see the **Deductions and Adjustments Worksheet** on page 2.
- If you have **more than one job** or are **married and you and your spouse both work** and the combined earnings from all jobs exceed $35,000 ($25,000 if married) see the **Two-Earner/Two-Job Worksheet** on page 2 to avoid having too little tax withheld.
- If **neither** of the above situations applies, **stop here** and enter the number from line H on line 5 of Form W-4 below.

------------------------------------ **Cut here and give Form W-4 to your employer. Keep the top part for your records.** ------------------------------------

Form **W-4**	**Employee's Withholding Allowance Certificate**	OMB No. 1545-0074
Department of the Treasury Internal Revenue Service	▶ Whether you are entitled to claim a certain number of allowances or exemption from withholding is subject to review by the IRS. Your employer may be required to send a copy of this form to the IRS.	2006

1 Type or print your first name and middle initial.	Last name		2 Your social security number

Home address (number and street or rural route)		3 ☐ Single ☐ Married ☐ Married, but withhold at higher Single rate.
		Note. If married, but legally separated, or spouse is a nonresident alien, check the "Single" box.
City or town, state, and ZIP code		4 If your last name differs from that shown on your social security card, check here. You must call 1-800-772-1213 for a new card. ▶ ☐

5 Total number of allowances you are claiming (from line **H** above **or** from the applicable worksheet on page 2) **5** _____

6 Additional amount, if any, you want withheld from each paycheck . . . . **6** $ _____

7 I claim exemption from withholding for 2006, and I certify that I meet **both** of the following conditions for exemption.
- Last year I had a right to a refund of **all** federal income tax withheld because I had **no** tax liability **and**
- This year I expect a refund of **all** federal income tax withheld because I expect to have **no** tax liability.

If you meet both conditions, write "Exempt" here . . . . ▶ **7** _____

Under penalties of perjury, I declare that I have examined this certificate and to the best of my knowledge and belief, it is true, correct, and complete.

Employee's signature
(Form is not valid unless you sign it.) ▶ _____ Date ▶ _____

8 Employer's name and address (Employer: Complete lines 8 and 10 only if sending to the IRS.)	9 Office code (optional)	10 Employer identification number (EIN)

For Privacy Act and Paperwork Reduction Act Notice, see page 2.   Cat. No. 10220Q   Form **W-4** (2006)

Form W-4 (2006)   Page **2**

Deductions and Adjustments Worksheet

Note. Use this worksheet *only* if you plan to itemize deductions, claim certain credits, or claim adjustments to income on your 2006 tax return.

1   Enter an estimate of your 2006 itemized deductions. These include qualifying home mortgage interest, charitable contributions, state and local taxes, medical expenses in excess of 7.5% of your income, and miscellaneous deductions. (For 2006, you may have to reduce your itemized deductions if your income is over $150,500 ($75,250 if married filing separately). See *Worksheet 3* in Pub. 919 for details.) . . .   **1** $ _____

2   Enter: { $10,300 if married filing jointly or qualifying widow(er)
        $ 7,550 if head of household
        $ 5,150 if single or married filing separately } . . . .   **2** $ _____

3   **Subtract** line 2 from line 1. If line 2 is greater than line 1, enter "-0-" . . . .   **3** $ _____

4   Enter an estimate of your 2006 adjustments to income, including alimony, deductible IRA contributions, and student loan interest   **4** $ _____

5   **Add** lines 3 and 4 and enter the total. (Include any amount for credits from *Worksheet 7* in Pub. 919) .   **5** $ _____

6   Enter an estimate of your 2006 nonwage income (such as dividends or interest) . . . .   **6** $ _____

7   **Subtract** line 6 from line 5. Enter the result, but not less than "-0-" . . . .   **7** $ _____

8   **Divide** the amount on line 7 by $3,300 and enter the result here. Drop any fraction . . . . . .   **8**   _____

9   Enter the number from the **Personal Allowances Worksheet**, line H, page 1 . . . .   **9**   _____

10   **Add** lines 8 and 9 and enter the total here. If you plan to use the **Two-Earner/Two-Job Worksheet**, also enter this total on line 1 below. Otherwise, **stop here** and enter this total on Form W-4, line 5, page 1 .   **10**   _____

Two-Earner/Two-Job Worksheet (See *Two earners/two jobs* on page 1.)

Note. Use this worksheet *only* if the instructions under line H on page 1 direct you here.

1   Enter the number from line H, page 1 (or from line 10 above if you used the **Deductions and Adjustments Worksheet**)   **1**   _____

2   Find the number in **Table 1** below that applies to the **LOWEST** paying job and enter it here . . . .   **2**   _____

3   If line 1 is **more than or equal to** line 2, subtract line 2 from line 1. Enter the result here (if zero, enter "-0-") and on Form W-4, line 5, page 1. **Do not** use the rest of this worksheet . . . .   **3**   _____

Note. If line 1 is *less than* line 2, enter "-0-" on Form W-4, line 5, page 1. Complete lines 4–9 below to calculate the additional withholding amount necessary to avoid a year-end tax bill.

4   Enter the number from line 2 of this worksheet . . . .   **4**   _____

5   Enter the number from line 1 of this worksheet . . . .   **5**   _____

6   **Subtract** line 5 from line 4 . . . .   **6**   _____

7   Find the amount in **Table 2** below that applies to the **HIGHEST** paying job and enter it here . . . .   **7** $ _____

8   **Multiply** line 7 by line 6 and enter the result here. This is the additional annual withholding needed .   **8** $ _____

9   Divide line 8 by the number of pay periods remaining in 2006. For example, divide by 26 if you are paid every two weeks and you complete this form in December 2005. Enter the result here and on Form W-4, line 6, page 1. This is the additional amount to be withheld from each paycheck . . . .   **9** $ _____

Table 1: Two-Earner/Two-Job Worksheet

Married Filing Jointly						All Others	
If wages from **HIGHEST** paying job are—	AND, wages from **LOWEST** paying job are—	Enter on line 2 above	If wages from **HIGHEST** paying job are—	AND, wages from **LOWEST** paying job are—	Enter on line 2 above	If wages from **LOWEST** paying job are—	Enter on line 2 above
$0 - $42,000	$0 - $4,500	0	$42,001 and over	32,001 - 38,000	6	$0 - $6,000	0
	4,501 - 9,000	1		38,001 - 46,000	7	6,001 - 12,000	1
	9,001 - 18,000	2		46,001 - 55,000	8	12,001 - 19,000	2
	18,001 and over	3		55,001 - 60,000	9	19,001 - 26,000	3
$42,001 and over	$0 - $4,500	0		60,001 - 65,000	10	26,001 - 35,000	4
	4,501 - 9,000	1		65,001 - 75,000	11	35,001 - 50,000	5
	9,001 - 18,000	2		75,001 - 95,000	12	50,001 - 65,000	6
	18,001 - 22,000	3		95,001 - 105,000	13	65,001 - 80,000	7
	22,001 - 26,000	4		105,001 - 120,000	14	80,001 - 90,000	8
	26,001 - 32,000	5		120,001 and over	15	90,001 - 120,000	9
						120,001 and over	10

Table 2: Two-Earner/Two-Job Worksheet

Married Filing Jointly		All Others	
If wages from **HIGHEST** paying job are—	Enter on line 7 above	If wages from **HIGHEST** paying job are—	Enter on line 7 above
$0 - $60,000	$500	$0 - $30,000	$500
60,001 - 115,000	830	30,001 - 75,000	830
115,001 - 165,000	920	75,001 - 145,000	920
165,001 - 290,000	1,090	145,001 - 330,000	1,090
290,001 and over	1,160	330,001 and over	1,160

 Printed on recycled paper

ATTENDANCE RECORD OF HOUSEHOLD EMPLOYEE

Employee: Date hired:
Vacation due:
Sick/personal leave due:

For the month of: _____ 20___

Date	Day of the Week	Present (Hours)	Vacation (Hours)	Sick (Hours)	Comments
1					
2					
3					
4					
5					
6					
7					
8					
9					
10					
11					
12					
13					
14					
15					
16					
17					
18					
19					
20					
21					
22					
23					
24					
25					
26					
27					
28					
29					
30					
31					

TIME OFF REQUEST FORM

Household Employee: _____

PERSONAL TIME OFF REQUESTS

<u>Paid Time Off:</u> Begins to accrue after 90 days of employment. Requests for PTO of two or more days must be submitted at least two weeks in advance.

<u>Bereavement Leave:</u> Up to three days of paid leave is available for a death in the immediate family.

	Start date	End date	Hours
Personal time off			
Bereavement			
Jury duty/witness			
Military service			
		Total paid time off	

VACATION REQUESTS

<u>Vacation Instructions:</u> Please submit your vacation request at least four weeks in advance of START DATE.

	Start date	End date	Hours	Employer approval
1st choice				
2nd choice				
3rd choice				
		Total paid time off		

Household Employee Name: _____ **Date:** _____

Employer Name: _____ **Date:** _____

PERFORMANCE EVALUATION FORM
(To be used quarterly during a one-on-one performance review meeting)

Household Employee Name: _____ Date: _____

Projects, issues, etc.	Date Addressed	Estimated Date of Completion	Assistance Needed, Issues to Resolve, etc.
Current Items			
1			
2			
3			
Items Completed			
A			
B			
C			
Areas where I can help you improve your skill set or improve your job performance			
A			
B			
Personal Job centered growth items completed last month, and future plans for personal job related growth			
A			
B			

TUITION REIMBURSEMENT REQUEST FORM

Current position held: _____

Employee name: _____

Household employer: _____

Title of course #1: _____

Course description: _____

Dates of course: _____

Name of school/entity: _____

Reason for taking course: _____

Required Coursework: It is defined as necessary for degrees, certificates or an individual course that a household employer required an employee to complete in order to meet performance standards or to keep pace with new development in the current job. Tuition will be paid at ____% (tuition or tuition and books), upon receipt of fee statements and course transcript. For reimbursement, employees must achieve a passing grade as defined by the educational organization and as approved by the household employer.

Job-Related Coursework: It is the responsibility of the employee to document the relationship of the reimbursed coursework to the household's employment needs and to obtain approval from the household employer. Tuition will be paid at ____% (tuition or tuition and books), upon receipt of fee statements and course transcript. For reimbursement, employees must achieve a passing grade as defined by the educational organization and as approved by the household employer.

NOTE: *You are required to submit the course description, proof of successful course completion along with receipts for tuition, and grades to the household employer before reimbursement will be made.*

Household employee _____ Date _____

Household employee _____ Date _____

INCIDENT REPORT

Household employee name _____

Employee position/title _____

Today's date _____

Incident time_____

Incident date _____

Incident location_____

Description of the incident that occurred

_____

_____

Witnesses to the incident (if applicable)

_____

Corrective or disciplinary action to be taken

[ ] Verbal [ ] Written [ ] Probation [ ] Suspension

[ ] Other (explain below)

_____

(If on probation, period begins _____ and ends _____.)

Corrective action(s)/improvement(s) to be achieved

_____

Consequences for failure to improve future performance or correct behavior

_____

Household Employee Statement

I acknowledge that I have read and understand the above information and consequences.

_____   _____

Household employee   Date

_____   _____

Household employer   Date

_____   _____

Witness   Date

Date_____

Index

About the Author

Guy Maddalone is founder and CEO of GTM Household Employment Experts™, which offers household payroll, human resources, and employee benefits services. Recognized in the United States household employment industry as the national expert, Maddalone has been operating businesses that attend to household employment for twenty-two years.

Maddalone founded GTM in 1991 to specialize in household employment—beginning with eldercare providers, nannies, and private-service professionals. He evolved the business to include all household employment professions and more than three hundred referral partners throughout the United States. *A New England Nanny*, a faction of GTM, is a nanny agency that Maddalone has operated for fifteen years, placing thousands of child care providers and nannies throughout upstate New York. GTM is also the nation's premier household payroll and tax service, managing more than $250 million in payroll each year.

Maddalone conducts educational seminars throughout the country on the household employment industry, household human resources, household payroll taxes, IRS audits, tax compliance, and dependent care services for corporate employers. He is also a work/life dependent care consultant to the General Electric Company, a licensed health and life insurance agent in New York, and a member of the *Society of Human Resource Management* (SHRM).

Involved with several prominent business organizations, including the executive training programs for Massachusetts Institute of Technology's (MIT) and *Inc. Magazine, Birthing of Giants,* and as president of the Albany Chapter of the *Young Entrepreneur's Organization,* Maddalone also contributes greatly to the community in which he lives—from coaching youth sports teams, mentoring local college entrepreneurs, and giving to the Make-A-Wish Foundation. Maddalone is also heavily involved with industry associations, such as *Alliance of Professional Nanny Agencies, International Nanny Association,* and serves on many committees. The eldest son of thirteen children, the importance of family is integral to Maddalone. He and his wife, Diane, reside in upstate New York with their three children.